FIFTH EDITION

Case Studies on Educational Administration

Theodore J. Kowalski

University of Dayton

Boston   New York   San Francisco
Mexico City   Montreal   Toronto   London   Madrid   Munich   Paris
Hong Kong   Singapore   Tokyo   Cape Town   Sydney

Senior Series Editor: Arnis Burvikovs
Series Editorial Assistant: Erin Reilly
Production Editor: Joe Sweeney
Editorial Production Service: Publishers' Design and Production Services, Inc.
Composition Buyer: Linda Cox
Manufacturing Buyer: Linda Morris
Electronic Composition: Publishers' Design and Production Services, Inc.
Cover Administrator: Linda Knowles

For related titles and support materials, visit our online catalog at www.ablongman.com.

Between the time website information is gathered and then published, it is not unusual for some sites to have closed. Also, the transcription of URLs can result in typographical errors. The publisher would appreciate notification where these errors occur so that they may be corrected in subsequent editions.

ISBN-10: 0-205-50907-X
ISBN-13: 978-0-205-50907-2

Printed in the United States of America

10 9 8 7 6 5 4 3 2 1   RRD-VA   11 10 09 08 07

CONTENTS

Preface   v
Matrix   vii

Introduction   1

1 Who Needs Lesson Plans?   13

2 Alternatives for an Alternative School   21

3 A Bully's Threat   29

4 Lounge Talk   39

5 Get Rid of the Sloppy Assistant Principal   47

6 Let the Committee Decide   55

7 Old School Culture and a New Principal   63

8 Feliz Navidad? Not in This School District   71

9 Sally's Socialization   77

10 A Matter of Honor   85

11 The Absent Superintendent   97

12 Break the Rules and Pay the Price   107

13 An Ambitious Assistant Principal   117

14 A One-Trick Principal   125

15 Even on Saturdays   135

16 Appropriate Punishment versus Political Expediency   141

17 The Passive Principal   149

18 A Disillusioned Assistant Principal   157

19 Who Needs Career-Technical Education?   165

20 Illegal Drugs, In-School Suspension, and the Novice
Principal   173

21 Let's Not Rap   183

22 Is the Devil Teaching Spelling?   193

23 The Dark Side of Decentralization   203

24 Who Should Create the School's Vision?   215

25 The Maverick School Board Member   223

PREFACE

Since the early 1980s, experiments with various governance and change strategies have taken place in an effort to achieve needed school improvement. In this context of dynamic practice, superintendents, principals, and other administrators have had to adjust to a series of new expectations embedded in concepts such as state deregulation, district decentralization, school restructuring, democratic leadership, and school culture change. These strategies have increased the complexity of an already demanding profession and resulted in broader parameters for effective practice. As examples, the contemporary administrator is expected to be a visionary leader as well as a competent manager; he or she is expected to be a knowledgeable professional as well as a dedicated public servant; and he or she is expected to be a moral and ethical role model as well as a cunning political strategist. Across and above all these seemingly contradictory expectations, practitioners must be problem solvers, a responsibility that requires them to build relationships, communicate openly and continuously, make difficult decisions, and take risks.

Case Studies in Educational Administration, fifth edition, is intended to help prospective and practicing administrators develop problem-solving and decision-making skills. Open-ended case studies provide an excellent venue for achieving this objective for at least two reasons. First, they inject contemporary issues into the classroom, making instruction more relevant. Second, they provide a nexus between the theoretical component of the profession's knowledge base and the realities of a changing society. Working with the cases, you are expected to engage in problem framing, critical thinking, decision making, and reflective practice. The overall goals are to have you learn how to (a) use information to identify and solve problems, (b) develop and evaluate alternative solutions, and (c) continuously refine your professional knowledge through critical analysis prior to, during, and after decision making.

The twenty-five cases cover a range of problems encountered by contemporary practitioners in districts and schools. The matrix at the front of the book and the key areas for reflection prior to the cases identify key topics; however, you are expected to define the problems integral to the situations. The cases are taken to conclusion so that you can assume the role of problem solver. A myriad of changes have been made for this edition. These are the most notable:

- The number of cases has been increased from twenty-four to twenty-five.
- The introductions to and the content for every case have been updated.
- A problem framing assignment has been added after each case.
- Case questions, suggested activities, and suggested readings have been updated.
- Additional information about problem solving and decision making has been added to the book's introduction.
- Three totally new cases have been added. Case 1 involves data-based decision making; Case 8 is about the in-migration of Mexican families into a small Mid-

western community; Case 15 describes the arrest of high school females during a weekend and off-campus initiation.

"Instructor Insights," which include instructional strategies and suggested classroom actitivities for the course, and Student Worksheets, which provide a homework assignment of five short-answer questions for every case, are available on the Education Leadership SuperSite (www.ablongman.com/edleadership). ELCC standards correlations are also available at the site.

Appreciation is expressed to those who helped me complete this edition. They include (a) district and school administrators from across the country who provided information for and comments about the cases, (b) professors and graduate students from many universities who voluntarily suggested content and format changes after they had worked with the cases, and (c) Elizabeth Pearn (my office assistant) and Lucianne Lilienthal (a doctoral student and my graduate assistant) from the University of Dayton.

I also am grateful to the following colleagues who reviewed the manuscript and provided constructive criticisms and insightful recommendations: Michael Pregot, Iona College; Virginia Roach, George Washington University; and Terry Stirling, Northeastern Illinois University.

Matrix of Topics by Case Number

Topics Case Number

Topics	1	2	3	4	5	6	7	8	9	10	11	12	13	14	15	16	17	18	19	20	21	22	23	24	25
Administrator-Teacher Relationships	*	*	*	*	*	*	*	*	*		*	*	*	*			*	*	*	*	*	*	*	*	
Alterative Schools/Programs		*													*			*	*	*	*				
Assistant Principals			*		*						*	*	*			*	*	*		*					
Assistant Superintendents/Central Office		*			*				*						*			*		*	*	*	*		
Budgeting, Fiscal Issues					*				*		*					*		*			*	*			
Business Manager						*				*															
Career Development							*										*	*							
Change Process			*	*	*	*	*			*		*	*			*		*	*			*	*		
Communication Problems			*	*	*	*	*	*	*	*	*	*	*	*	*	*	*	*	*	*	*	*	*	*	*
Community-Based Conflict			*		*		*	*	*		*	*	*	*	*	*	*							*	*
Curriculum and Instruction	*						*	*	*	*	*	*	*	*	*	*	*	*	*	*	*	*	*	*	
Decision-Making Procedures	*	*		*	*	*	*	*	*	*	*	*	*	*	*	*	*	*	*	*	*	*	*		
Educational Outcomes	*						*		*	*			*		*	*	*	*			*	*			
Elementary Schools	*						*	*	*							*	*				*	*			
Employment Practices				*	*		*						*	*					*			*		*	
Employment Security/Stress					*		*		*		*	*	*				*		*				*		*
Ethical/Moral Issues			*	*	*	*	*	*	*	*	*	*	*	*	*	*	*	*	*	*	*	*	*	*	*
Evaluation	*			*	*		*		*			*				*	*	*				*	*		
Federal Programs	*							*																	
High Schools		*	*	*	*								*			*			*	*	*			*	
Leadership Style/Theory		*	*	*	*	*			*	*	*	*	*	*	*	*	*	*	*	*	*	*	*	*	*
Legal Issues			*	*	*	*			*		*	*	*	*	*	*	*	*	*	*	*	*	*	*	
Middle Schools				*							*						*						*		
Multicultural Issues	*	*	*				*		*	*				*		*		*	*	*		*	*		

Topics Case Number (*Cont.*)

Topics	1	2	3	4	5	6	7	8	9	10	11	12	13	14	15	16	17	18	19	20	21	22	23	24	25
Organizational Theory						*	*				*			*				*					*	*	
Philosophical Issues	*	*	*	*	*	*	*	*	*	*	*	*	*	*	*	*	*	*	*	*	*	*	*	*	*
Policy Development/Analysis	*	*	*	*	*	*	*	*	*	*	*	*	*	*		*		*	*	*	*	*			
Political Behavior			*	*	*	*	*	*	*	*	*	*	*	*	*	*	*	*	*				*	*	*
Power, Use by Administrators	*		*	*	*	*	*	*	*		*	*	*	*	*	*	*	*	*				*	*	
Principals	*	*	*	*	*	*	*	*	*	*	*	*	*	*	*	*	*	*	*	*	*	*	*	*	*
Public Relations (Community Relations)	*	*	*		*		*	*	*	*	*		*	*	*	*				*	*	*		*	
Rural, Small-Town Schools								*					*						*						
School Boards			*					*		*	*				*	*					*		*	*	*
School Reform	*	*																					*		
Site-Based Management																*							*		
Student Discipline (Student Services)	*	*			*	*	*	*		*	*		*	*	*	*		*	*	*				*	*
Suburban Schools				*							*				*						*				
Superintendents	*		*	*	*	*	*	*		*	*	*	*	*	*	*		*	*			*	*	*	*
Teacher Professionalization	*			*			*		*					*			*			*		*		*	
Teacher Unions (Collective Bargaining)										*						*					*				
Urban/Larger City Schools	*		*		*	*		*		*		*		*	*	*		*	*			*	*	*	
Violence		*													*	*									
Visioning/Planning							*												*				*	*	
Vocational Schools (Career Centers)																		*							
Women Administrators				*	*	*	*	*	*	*	*	*	*	*	*	*		*	*	*		*	*	*	*

INTRODUCTION

In the varied topography of professional practice, there is a high hard ground overlooking the swamp. On the high ground, manageable problems lend themselves to solutions through the application of research-based theory and technique. In the swampy lowland, messy, confusing problems defy technical solution.

(Donald Schön, 1990, p. 3)

Most students enrolled in university-based courses in school administration are either preparing to be practitioners or they already are practitioners. They are adult learners, many in the middle stage of their careers. They appropriately expect classroom learning experiences, even those involving abstract theories, to be relevant to the real world of elementary and secondary education. Consequently, the most effective preparation programs focus on three objectives:

1. Students are expected to master theoretical knowledge that can by deployed to guide practice. Such knowledge describes, explains, or predicts behavior in schools.
2. Students are expected to master the process of reflection and to demonstrate their ability to engage in reflective practice.
3. Students are expected to develop, analyze, and critique tacit knowledge by interfacing theory and experience, especially personal experiences in school settings (Björk, Kowalski, & Ferrigno-Brown, 2005).

Donald Schön (1983) observed that practitioners in all professions are baffled when the theory and technical skills they acquired during academic preparation prove to be ineffective when they are applied to real problems. Their lack of understanding often is due to a failure to address problem solving and decision making as context-specific tasks. Context typically is a complicated mix of people, resources, societal expectations, and organizational conditions. For example, the context of disciplining a student in one middle school may be considerably different from disciplining a student in another school—even if the two middle schools are in the same community and part of the same school district. Contextual dissimilarities largely explain why administrators and students preparing to be administrators perceive a problem in different ways, even when given identical information (Kowalski, 1998).

Too often, students are divided between those who believe that theory should guide practice and those who believe that intuition and experience should guide practice. At their extremes, neither conviction is valid. The most effective practitioners rely on both theoretical knowledge and craft knowledge (also referred to as artistry). The latter is a form of tacit knowledge developed by applying theory and learning from experience. Consider motivation theories and their use in teaching and school administration. Theoretically, praising a teacher is supposed to motivate him or her; however, principals almost always encounter employees who do not respond as expected. The challenge for the principal is to determine why the application of theory is not consistently accurate; more precisely, the principal reflects on contextual variables that may explain behavior inconsistencies. Therefore, the most effective principals are those who learn to adjust the application of theory based on what they have learned from pertinent experiences. If an administrator learns from previous experiences, he or she is better prepared to deal with the situation.

Problem Solving and Decision Making

Problem solving is often characterized as a five-stage, six-step process as depicted in Figure I.1. Kowalski, Lasley, and Mahoney (2008) summarized the elements of this paradigm.

Stage 1: Understanding.

The first level of problem solving requires you understand what you are trying do. There are two steps in this stage: *framing the problem* and *analyzing the problem*.

Cognitive psychologists generally agree that a problem has three features: (a) a current state, (b) a desired state, and (c) the lack of a direct obvious way to eliminate the gap between the current state and the desired state (Mayer, 1983). Assume you are principal in a school in which 62 percent of the students have met the state's proficiency standard on achievement tests. Also assume, the state benchmark is 85 percent of the students meeting the proficiency standard. There are four possible combinations of knowledge related to framing this problem (Reitman, 1965) and they are identified here using the example of student performance on achievement tests.

1. *A well-defined current state and a well-defined desired state*. This knowledge level exists when the current level of student performance is known and specific and the state benchmark is known and specific.
2. *A well-defined current state and a poorly defined desired state*. This knowledge level exists when the current level of student performance is known and specific but the state benchmark is unknown or ambiguous.
3. *A poorly defined current state and a well-defined goal*. This knowledge level exists when the current level of student performance is unknown or ambiguous but the benchmark is known and specific.
4. *A poorly defined current state and a poorly defined goal*. This knowledge level exists when the current level of student performance is unknown or ambiguous and the state benchmark is unknown or too broad.

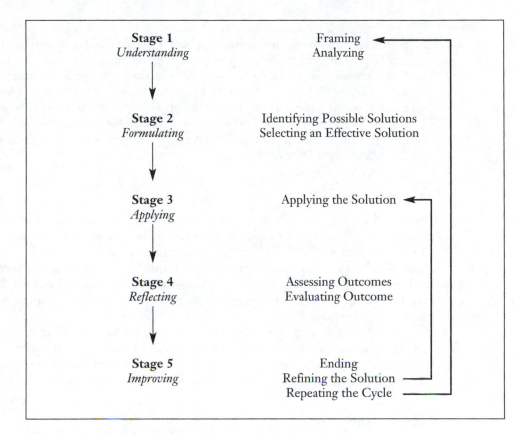

FIGURE I.1   Problem Solving as a Five-Stage Process

In the example cited, you have precise information about both student performance and the state benchmark; therefore, you are ready to frame the problem—that is, to describe the difficulty associated with moving from where you are to where you need to be. If either or both pieces of information were missing, you would need to acquire additional knowledge to frame the problem correctly. In very simple terms, a problem exists when something is needed or wanted but the decision maker is unsure what to do in order to attain it (Reys, Lindquist, Lambdin, Smith, & Suydam, 2003).

Once a problem has been correctly identified, the leader must analyze it. This step entails asking and answering pertinent questions such as these:

- *How serious is the problem?* The attention an administrator gives to a problem often depends on perceived consequences. Serious problems receive more and immediate attention.
- *What causes the problem?* Students often confuse causes and problems. Problems are products and causes are the variables responsible for the product. Not knowing how to eradicate the gap between current achievement scores and the state

benchmark may be caused by factors such as a negative school culture, incompetent leadership, ineffective teaching, a lack of employee learning opportunities (staff development), or inappropriate instructional materials.

■ *Can the problem be divided into manageable components?* By dividing a problem into parts, the search for a solution may be more efficient. For example, improving the percentage of students scoring at the proficiency level from 62 percent to 85 percent is a daunting task. If the problem is addressed over a five-year period, however, the principal can establish yearly benchmarks that incrementally move the school toward reaching the state benchmark.

Stage 2: Formulating.

This stage also has two elements: identifying possible solutions and selecting a preferred solution. Because information and time are common constraints, administrators and teachers usually identify only the most obvious solutions rather than all possible solutions and they pursue a satisfactory solution rather than conducting a protracted search for the ideal solution. This behavior is known as "satisficing," and is a defining characteristic of a concept called bounded rationality (Hanson, 2003). This topic is discussed in detail in Case 3.

Consider an example of a superintendent faced with insufficient instructional space. He may opt to place an addition onto a school building, a solution that alleviates overcrowding temporarily but does not provide sufficient space to accommodate future growth. In this vein, the addition is an acceptable but not ideal solution.

Stage 3: Applying.

At this stage, the preferred solution is applied in an effort to solve the problem. A solution's effectiveness is determined by a mix of its potentiality, the quality of application, and the context in which it is applied. Even the best solutions fail when they are applied incorrectly and inappropriately. As an example, placing an addition onto a school would alleviate the problem of insufficient instructional space only if it is large enough, designed properly, and acceptable to the public and school staff. In evaluating our choices, we must be careful to separate a solution's potential and application.

Stage 4: Reflecting.

The effects of the preferred solution should be assessed objectively and then evaluated. Assessment involves measuring; for example, determining the percentage of students who meet the state proficiency. Evaluation entails judgment; for example, determining if the amount measured is acceptable. Evaluation should be summative (i.e., determining the extent to which the solution actually resolved the problem) and formative (i.e., determining what could be done to improve the solution if the problem has not been resolved sufficiently). In some instances, both evaluations influence the administrator's decisions about moving forward. For example, the superintendent's assessment is that the addition provided 5 percent more instructional space. His summative evaluation indicates that this is insufficient because a 10 percent increase was needed. His formative evaluation indicates that continuing growth in the school district may require a solution other than facility additions (e.g., building a totally new school).

Stage 5: Improving.

At the improvement stage, one of three decisions is made: (a) the problem is deemed to be resolved so no further improvement is warranted; (b) the preferred solution is adjusted and the application stage is repeated; (c) the solution is deemed to be ineffective and the problem cycle is repeated by returning to the understanding stage.

Problem solving actually entails a series of decisions and the effectiveness of a decision is often determined by its value to problem solving. Basically, a decision has three components: *a goal, options for attaining the goal,* and *the selection of the preferred option* (Welch, 2002). In making decisions, school administrators have two important challenges. First, they must separate consequential from inconsequential decisions. Consequential decisions are those that influence serious problems. Second, they must approach consequential decisions differently than they do inconsequential decisions. For example, deciding whether to invest in a staff development program that has the potential to improve student achievement test scores is far more consequential than determining what to have for lunch. Inconsequential decisions require little forethought and analysis because they are relatively unimportant.

Basically, decisions can be guided by several forces. The most evident include:

- Rationality—a dependence on evidence and objective analysis of facts
- Emotion—feelings and sentiments
- Philosophy—values and beliefs
- Politics—self-interests or the interests of powerful groups
- School culture—basic assumptions shared by individuals and used to guide behavior

Often, these forces interact so that any given decision may reflect a combination of two or more of them.

The passage of the No Child Left Behind Act in 2001 heightened expectations that educators make data-based decisions, especially in relation to problems that affect students, schools, and society. Advocacy for rational decision making also has been affected by the realities of an information-based society. That is, the quantity and quality of information available to educators is much greater now than it was just twenty-five years ago (Popham, 2006). At the same time that educators are prompted to make fact-based decisions, they are encouraged to engage in collegiality and shared decision making. Therefore, administrators and teachers not only need to become more proficient in accessing, categorizing, storing, and using data, they must also learn to make decisions and solve problems collectively—an expectation that has not been normative to either teaching or administration in the past (Kowalski, 2003).

Reflection

Schön (1990) differentiated between "knowing-in-action" and "reflection-in-action." The former is embedded in the socially and institutionally structured context shared by members of a given profession. In school administration, for example, graduate students preparing to be principals are expected to possess basic knowledge related to their practice (e.g., curriculum theory and school law). The latter represents a form of artistry that is critical when conditions are less than rational. As an example, effective school administrators have developed skills and techniques that help them deal with problems that defy textbook solutions. If human behavior was entirely predictable, knowing-in-action would suffice. But in districts and schools, people are not always rational and they occasionally do unexpected things. When such behavior occurs, the ability to engage in reflection-in-action separates highly effective and other administrators.

Reflection does not occur naturally. The process must be learned and students should acquire the requisite skills during professional preparation. Consequently, most education professors are expected to connect theory and practice so that students learn to reflect on their actions.

Reflection actually is a form of research in which you test ideas or possible decisions by applying evidence and subjective criteria such as emotion and bias. As previously noted, the process produces tacit knowledge. Critiquing experience from multiple perspectives is a key element of true reflection. In your courses, traditional lectures and demonstrations can be effective; but even if done extremely well, they are insufficient. Learning how to gather information, observe behavior, and analyze relationships between theory and the context in which it is applied requires more active forms of instruction (Clark, 1986). *Case Studies on Educational Administration*, fifth edition, uses a proven method for studying the applications of theoretical knowledge: the case study.

Defining Case Studies

A case is a description of a situation, commonly involving a decision or problem (Erskine, Leenders, & Mauffette-Leenders, 1981). The terms *case study* and *case method* have different definitions. A case study is the general description of a situation. These narratives have several purposes. They can be deployed as (a) a method of research, (b) a method of evaluation, (c) a method of policy studies, and (d) a method of teaching. Case method, on the other hand, refers to a teaching paradigm in which case studies are the central aspect of the curriculum.

Several other terms relate to case studies. One is *case work*, a term is commonly used in psychology, sociology, social work, and medicine. It connotes the development, adjustment, remedial, or corrective procedures that appropriately follow diagnosis of the causes of maladjustment. Another term is *case history*, which refers to tracing a person, group, or organization's past (Merriam, 1998).

Unfortunately, there is no universal definition of or style for a case study; some case studies may be only a few paragraphs, while others are hundreds of pages (Immegart, 1971). As Lincoln and Guba (1985) wrote, "while the literature is replete with references to case studies and with examples of case study reports, there seems to be little agreement about what a case is" (p. 360). Variance in case length and style is often related to their intended purpose.

With respect to the manner in which they are written, cases commonly are divided into three categories:

1. *True cases.* These are factual case studies and names, dates, or other information have not been altered.
2. *Disguised cases.* These are factual case studies but names, dates, or other information have been altered.
3. *Fictitious cases.* These are hypothetical case studies written to illustrate a principle, concept, or specific set of conditions (Matejka & Cosse, 1981).

The Case Method

The case method first gained acceptance in professional preparation programs for business administration, law, and medicine. The best-known successes belong to Harvard University's Business School, where instructors use case studies to sharpen student skills with regard to problem solving, formulating and weighing alternative decisions, and assessing leadership behaviors (Christensen, 1987).

Some instructors use the case method to teach new information, concepts, and theories. For example, a professor may use a case study of a grievance in a high school to teach students the meaning of organizational conflict. When cases are used to teach new knowledge, the student learns inductively. That is, the case study is used to demonstrate associations between variables that reveal the nature of the concept being taught. When the associations found in the case recur (e.g., in other cases or in personal observations), the student is engaging in inductive learning. Cases used to teach new knowledge are usually fact-driven and complete (i.e., they include a description of outcomes) (Herreid, 1997).

Cases also can be deployed for skill development. For example, a professor may use cases to encourage moral reasoning, critical thinking, decision making, and problem solving. Cases used to develop and improve skills are typically open-ended cases; that is, they purposely are not taken to their conclusion so that learners can become actively involved as a decision maker (Kowalski, 1998). Open-ended cases are often called Type B cases.

There are two universal characteristics of teaching with cases. One is the Socratic method. This is a dialectical approach in which the instructor asks questions and encourages the critical analysis of multiple propositions. The other is the presentation of *situational knowledge*. This knowledge includes information about contextual variables such as individuals, school culture, or the local community.

As you undoubtedly will discover, students in your class will read open-ended case studies and then define problems differently. Why? We process information in different ways. This processing is called *abstraction*. Thus, each student in your class filters situational knowledge through his or her own values, beliefs, experiences, biases, and acquired knowledge. Students not only have unique filters, they also differ in their ability to process information. Consequently, differences in abstraction result in dissimilarities in problem framing, decision making, and behavior. Output variability is a critical aspect of the case method. Outputs (problem framing, decisions, and behavior) are referred to as *specific knowledge*.

Studying teacher decision making, Shavelson and Stern (1981) observed:

> . . . people selectively perceive and interpret portions of available information with respect to their goals, and construct a simplified model of reality. Using certain heuristics, attributions and other psychological mechanisms, people then make judgments and decisions that carry them out on the basis of their psychological model of reality (p. 461).

Advocacy for using case studies in school administration dates back more than sixty years. Several texts were published as early as the mid-1950s (e.g., Hamburg, 1955; Sargent & Belisle, 1955) and by the early 1960s, several leading scholars (e.g., Culbertson & Coffield, 1960; Griffiths, 1963) were promoting the use of cases to prepare practitioners. Nevertheless, the case method was largely ignored by school administration professors until the late 1980s (Kowalski, 1998).

Simulation and Case Studies

Simulations provide vicarious experiences for students—an approximation of the practitioner's challenges, problems, opportunities, and so forth. They are used at all stages of professional preparation. There are two general approaches to using this technique. In the first, students are provided complete data about a given situation and then asked to solve a problem. This approach is commonly called an *in-basket simulation* and requires students to spend considerable time studying data. As an example, a student may be given complete financial records for a school district and then asked to determine where an accounting error occurred.

In the second approach, students are provided only essential information. It is far less time consuming and is employed when general problem-solving skills are the instructional objective. Cunningham (1971) referred to this alternative as a *nonmaterial-based approach*. After studying the use of this approach with graduate students in school administration at the University of Chicago in the mid-1960s, he concluded that the technique was more efficient than and equally successful as the in-basket approach. The research caused Cunningham to change his own views about the necessity of providing students with detailed information for simulations.

Using open-ended cases, such as those in this book, to conduct simulations is a powerful teaching tool. This is especially true if the instructional objectives relate to critical thinking, moral reasoning, problem solving, and decision making.

Using Theory to Guide Practice

Some students incorrectly define theory as a dream representing the wishes of an individual or group. Others perceive it to be a supposition or speculation or a philosophy (Owens, 1998). In reality theories synthesize, organize, and classify facts that emerge from observations and data collections in varying situations (e.g., research studies). Hoy and Miskel (2005) characterize theories in educational administration as interrelated concepts, assumptions, and generalizations that systematically describe and explain regularities in behavior.

When confronted with circumstances demanding action, superintendents, principals, and other administrators may choose one of several behaviors (Kowalski, 2006):

1. They can ignore the situation, hoping that the problem will disappear or solve itself.
2. They act instinctively or intuitively, relying on "common sense."
3. They can relegate the decision to a subordinate, hoping that such action frees them of responsibility and risk.
4. They can look for a precedent; that is, they identify an administrator who faced the same problem and then duplicate that person's decision.
5. They can use their professional knowledge to formulate decisions based on the contextual variables surrounding a given problem.

Any of the first four alternatives may be effective in isolated situations, but more commonly they are ineffective.

Among the numerous decision-making models used in administration, the best known and most widely used is probably the *rational-analytical model.* This paradigm consists of four steps:

1. Defining the problem
2. Diagnosing the problem
3. Searching for alternative solutions
4. Evaluating alternative solutions (Romm & Mahler, 1986)

The paradigm captures the early stages of the problem-solving model discussed earlier. This model also is congruent with mandates for data-based decision making in NCLB.

Each case in this book includes contextual variables that should affect the choices you make. The community, the school district, the challenge, and the individual personalities are examples. When you employ theoretical constructs and technical skills to analyze these conditions in relation to the challenge presented, you are using a scientific approach to decision making. Accordingly, you should become increasingly skillful in applying general problem-solving abilities to specific situations. When using cases, however, you should recognize that emotion and bias almost always temper rationality. That is, decision makers often reject, modify, or selectively accept evidence based on their dispositions toward a problem or challenge.

The evolution of literature on decision making exhibits that the study of school administration has evolved from training to education. In training, a person learns to apply predetermined solutions to a situation; in education, a person learns to treat each situation as a unique challenge requiring diagnostics and prescriptive measures. In concluding that accumulated information about decision processes was eradicating the comfort of simple solutions, Estler (1988) wrote:

> . . . we might replace recipes with skills in analysis of organizational dynamics and contexts. Though the ambiguities of educational decision making cannot be eliminated, they can be made more understandable and less threatening. By understanding a variety of approaches to decision making and the range of organizational conditions under which they may be applicable, the administrator can be better prepared to respond to, and even enjoy, organizational ambiguity and complexity (p. 316).

More than any other element of graduate study in educational administration, it is the knowledge base relative to decision making that illuminates the value of infusing case studies into graduate education. Those who still contend that there are universally effective administrative decisions are either misguided or uninformed.

Effectively Participating in the Case Method

The objective in working with open-ended cases is not to arrive at "one right answer." Romm and Mahler (1986) noted that this is particularly true if a rational-analytical model is applied to address the perceived problem:

> Basing the analysis of the case on the rational-analytical decision-making model, implicitly carries the message that there are no "right" or "wrong" solutions to the case. By applying the model to cases, students realize that a case always has many problems, and the definition of one of these problems as the "main" problem is often subjective and arbitrary. They also realize that once a problem has been defined, it can have different reasons and be solved in different ways, depending on whose interests are being served or being given priority (p. 695).

Cases provide an open invitation to generalize (Biddle & Anderson, 1986), and consequently, you are apt to observe a range of behaviors as your peers react to them.

Remember, behavior is more or less rational but rarely completely rational. Bias, beliefs, emotions, and political considerations usually affect our judgment and decisions. This reality makes the case method even more challenging and exciting.

One other dimension of the case method is commonly undervalued. Your work with cases occurs in a social context (the classroom, chat rooms, or other discussion formats). The presence of others approximates the real world of practice because superintendents and principals rarely make decisions in isolation. Their behavior is continuously influenced and evaluated by others.

Content of This Book

This edition contains twenty-five cases selected to exemplify the diversity of challenges in contemporary school administration. The narrative formats are not uniform. Some cases are divided into sections with information about the community, school district, school, and the incident presented under subheadings. Other cases contain a great deal of dialogue. Information in the real world of practice is neither predictable nor uniform. Variance in the way information is presented in the cases reflects the unevenness of communication that exists in districts and schools. Though the narratives vary, other components are uniform. Each case includes an introduction that identifies key concepts and areas for reflection. Following each case are three components:

1. Problem framing. This component directs you to identify a primary problem that you will address.
2. Questions and suggested activities. This list can be used for class assignments, group discussions, or individual study.
3. Suggested readings. The readings provide resources for studying the concepts and issues embedded in the case.

Final Words of Advice

Engaging in case studies requires several caveats. First, the process is active and dialetical and in this vein, the case method is usually a form of cooperative learning. To achieve maximum benefits, you need to participate. Second, you should be candid and learn to take risks. The case method allows you to learn how others will respond to your leadership style and decisions. Third, you should respect and seek to understand competing viewpoints. Focus on how professional (constructs and skills) and personal (needs and motivations) variables influence administrative decisions.

REFERENCES

Biddle, B., & Anderson, D. (1986). Theory, methods, knowledge, and research on teaching. In M. Wittrock (Ed.), *Handbook of research on teaching* (3rd ed., pp. 230–252). New York: Macmillan.

Björk, L. G., Kowalski, T. J., & Ferrigno-Brown, T. (2005). Learning theory and research: A framework for changing superintendent preparation and development. In L. G. Björk & T. J. Kowalski (Eds.), *The contemporary superintendent: Preparation, practice, and development*, (pp. 71–106). Thousand Oaks, CA: Sage.

Christensen, C. (1987). *Teaching and the case method.* Boston: Harvard Business School Press.

Clark, V. (1986). The effectiveness of case studies in training principals: Using the deliberative orientation. *Peabody Journal of Education, 63*(1), 187–195.

Culbertson, J., & Coffield, W. (Eds.). (1960). *Simulation in administration training.* Columbus, OH: University Council for Educational Administration.

Cunningham, L. (1971). A powerful but underdeveloped educational tool. In D. Bolton (Ed.), *The use of simulation in educational administration* (pp. 1–29). Columbus, OH: Charles E. Merrill.

Erskine, J., Leenders, M., & Mauffette-Leenders, L. (1981). *Teaching with cases.* London, Ontario:

School of Business Administration, University of Western Ontario.

Estler, S. (1988). Decision making. In N. Boyan (Ed.), *Handbook of research on educational administration* (pp. 305–350). New York: Longman.

Griffiths, D. (1963). The case method of teaching educational administration. *Journal of Educational Administration, 2,* 81–82.

Hamburg, M. (1955). *Case studies in elementary school administration.* New York: Bureau of Publications, Teachers College, Columbia University.

Hanson, E. M. (2003). *Educational administration and organizational behavior* (5th ed.). Boston: Allyn and Bacon.

Herreid, C. F. (1997). What is a case? *Journal of College Science Teaching, 27*(2), 92–94.

Hoy, W., & Miskel, C. (2005). *Educational administration: Theory, research and practice* (7th ed.). New York: McGraw-Hill.

Immegart, G. (1971). The use of cases. In D. Bolton (Ed.), *The use of simulation in educational administration* (pp. 30–64). Columbus, OH: Charles E. Merrill.

Kowalski, T. J. (1998). Using case studies in school administration. In M. Sudzina (Ed.), *Case study applications for teacher education* (pp. 201–217). Boston: Allyn and Bacon.

Kowalski, T. J. (2003). *Contemporary school administration: An introduction* (2nd ed.). Boston: Allyn and Bacon.

Kowalski, T. J. (2006). *The school superintendent: Theory, practice, and cases* (2nd ed.). Thousand Oaks, CA: Sage.

Kowalski, T. J., Lasley, T. J., & Mahoney, J. (2008). *Data-driven decisions and school leadership: Best practices for school improvement.* Boston: Allyn and Bacon.

Lincoln, Y., & Guba, E. (1985). *Naturalistic inquiry.* Newbury Park, CA: Sage.

Matejka, J., & Cosse, T. (1981). *The business case method: An introduction.* Richmond, VA: Robert F. Dame.

Mayer, R. E. (1983). *Thinking, problem solving, cognition.* New York: W. H. Freeman and Company.

Merriam, S. B. (1998) *Qualitative research and case study applications in education.* San Francisco: Jossey-Bass.

Owens, R. (1998). *Organizational behavior in education* (6th ed.). Boston: Allyn and Bacon.

Popham, W. J. (2006). *Assessment for educational leaders.* Boston: Allyn and Bacon.

Reitman, W. R. (1965). *Cognition and thought: An information processing approach.* New York: Wiley.

Reys, R., Lindquist, M., Lambdin, D., Smith, N., & Suydam, M. (2003). *Helping children learn mathematics* (6th ed.). New York: John Wiley and Sons.

Romm, T., & Mahler, S. (1986). A three-dimensional model for using case studies in the academic classroom. *Higher Education, 15*(6), 677–696.

Sargent, C., & Belisle, E. (1955). *Educational administration: Cases and concepts.* Boston: Houghton Mifflin.

Schön, D. (1990). *Educating the reflective practitioner.* San Francisco: Jossey-Bass.

Schön, D. (1983). *The reflective practitioner.* New York: Basic Books.

Shavelson, R., & Stern, P. (1981). Research on teachers' pedagogical thoughts, judgments, decisions, and behavior. *Review of Educational Research, 51*(4), 455–498.

Welch, D. A. (2002). *Decisions, decisions: The art of effective decision making.* Amherst, NY: Prometheus Books.

1 Who Needs Lesson Plans?

Background Information

Federal interventions in public elementary and secondary education are often viewed negatively by local school officials who believe that such actions attenuate local control. The No Child Left Behind Act (NCLB), signed into law on January 8, 2002, constitutes another in a series of federal interventions that has generated criticism from both administrators and teachers.

The NCLB is a reauthorization of the Elementary and Secondary Education Act of 1965, and according to its proponents, it emphasizes local control, flexibility for local officials, and parental involvement. The law's intent is to raise the educational performance of all students by setting higher standards, requiring annual testing, using test data analysis to ensure progress, and imposing rewards and penalties for outcomes (Kowalski, Lasley, & Mahoney, 2008). Students in grades 3 through 8 must be tested each year in reading, mathematics, and science. Schools must demonstrate adequate yearly progress. All special student groups (e.g., by ethnicity, socioeconomic status) must report progress separately. At least 95 percent of each of these groups must be tested, and if one subgroup fails to make yearly progress, the school as a whole fails. In addition, NCLB requires administrators and teachers to (a) collect assessment data, (b) disaggregate those data by student groups, and (c) develop explicit plans for meeting the needs of students, especially those exhibiting low achievement (Protheroe, Shellard, & Turner, 2003).

This case is about a principal who assumes the leadership role in a troubled school. She quickly discovers that teachers have little interest in pursuing change, and they are bitter because the previous principal was dismissed. As you read this case, pay particular attention to evidence that reveals the nature of the school's culture.

Culture constitutes the organization's symbolic dimension of a school's overall climate. Culture consists of shared values and beliefs; it provides an invisible framework of norms that direct employee behavior. The guiding standards are called norms, and they are nested in assumptions about what people in the organization hold to be true, sensible, and possible (Hoy & Miskel, 2005). School cultures are neither static nor easily changed; however, scholars (e.g., Fullan, 2005; Sarason, 1996) have concluded that meaningful reform in education cannot occur without a substantial change in the shared values and beliefs of educators.

One reason why culture is so difficult to change is that underlying beliefs are often subconscious. Even so, they get translated into routine behaviors. When these assumptions (and thus the behavior they induce) are incongruent with the profession's knowledge base or with a community's prevailing philosophy, educators are usually unwilling to discuss them (Kowalski, 2003). When all or most teachers share the same assumptions, the culture is said to be "strong." When all or most of the shared assumptions are supported by the profession's knowledge base, the culture is said to be "positive" (Kowalski, 2006).

Key Areas for Reflection

1. Federal involvement in public elementary and secondary education in general, and NCLB specifically
2. School culture
3. Lesson planning
4. Change in school leadership
5. Changing unproductive values and beliefs about students

The Case

After she became principal of Buchanan Elementary School two years ago, Maureen Hulbert knew she was assuming a difficult assignment. The school is located in the most economically depressed area of an economically depressed school district, the Harper City Community Schools. As she sat in the silence in her office on a cold rainy November day, she reflected on her brief tenure in the troubled school.

Harper City

The population in Harper City has declined by more than 20 percent over the last 25 years. The largest outmigration of residents occurred in the early 1980s after a steel company closed its plant there. At its peak level of operation in 1972, the plant had slightly over 1,800 employees. After it closed, many who lost their jobs left the community. Today, Harper City is a collage of ethnic neighborhoods. The only newer homes are located near the hospital in a small neighborhood. In all other sections of the city, the homes are more than forty-five years old. Most of the single-family dwellings are prefabricated, low-cost structures that were built between 1952 and 1960. There are also four government housing projects located in the city. The unemployment rate in Harper City is 210 percent higher than the national average.

The School District

The Harper City School District serves 6,885 students. In addition to a high school, the district operates two middle schools and six elementary schools. Last year, 18 percent of the graduating seniors from Harper City High School enrolled in a four-year or two-year college and the dropout rate was 28 percent.

Nearly 70 percent of the students in the school system qualify for free and reduced lunches. Approximately two-thirds of them are identified as racial or ethnic minorities; 38 percent are African American and 22 percent are Hispanic.

Since the enactment of No Child Left Behind (NCLB), both the composition of the school board and the district's administrative staff have changed substantially. The five-member school board continues to represent the community's diversity; however, only one member who was in office when NCLB took effect is still on the board. The superintendent, Dr. Mark Simon, has been in his position for five years. Previously, he had been superintendent in two other school districts. After reaching age 55, he exercised his option to receive early retirement benefits and then applied for jobs in other states. He is an energetic leader committed to improving the school district's academic performance. He is supported by the school board and Harper City's mayor.

Since Dr. Simon's arrival in Harper City, over two-thirds of the administrative staff, including school principals, has changed. Turnover in these positions resulted from a combination of retirements, dismissals, and reassignments. Three years ago, Superintendent Simon began constructing an infrastructure to facilitate data-based decision making. He employed a new director of technology and research, increased investments in computer networking, and initiated a staff development program to assist teachers in using data in their practice.

Buchanan Elementary School

Buchanan Elementary School is located just one block from the main street that runs through the business district. The two-story brick structure was built in 1947. Originally constructed as a junior high school, the facility was renovated and converted to be used as an elementary school in 1983. Two of the government housing projects in the district are within a half mile of the school, and children living in both attend this school.

Buchanan has an enrollment of 390 students; approximately 90 percent are children of color (58 percent are African American and 31 percent are Hispanic). Last year's records indicate that 82 percent of the students qualified for free and reduced lunches. The school has the highest percentage of students in the district failing to score at or above the state proficiency level on achievement tests.

The average age of teachers at Buchanan is 53, and only six of seventeen teachers had ever been employed in a school other than Buchanan. The previous principal, Walter Sampson, was popular with the staff but had been put on probation by Superintendent Simon two years ago. Performance goals were set as a condition for removing the probation and, in the judgment of the superintendent and assistant superintendent for instruction, they were not met. Principal Sampson was informed that he would not be reemployed as Buchanan's principal and reluctantly resigned. Angered by the superintendent's decision to remove the principal, the Buchanan employees all signed a letter expressing their displeasure and sent it to the school board.

In the aftermath of NCLB, the number of student retentions in first grade increased significantly. Both the previous principal and the first-grade teachers said publicly that they were pushed to retain more students as a result of pressures to raise standards.

Principal Hulbert Arrives

Why did Maureen Hulbert accept the daunting challenge of being the principal at Buchanan Elementary School? When asked that question by a friend, her response was quick and direct: "Because the school district has a dynamic superintendent, Dr. Mark Simon, who is committed to helping students improve their learning."

Before accepting the position, Principal Hulbert had not met a single staff member in the school. Only the superintendent and two other district-level administrators were involved in the selection process. Superintendent Simon was explicit in telling Maureen that she would be assuming a difficult assignment, one in which an increase in student achievement test scores was essential. He also told her that the teachers would probably resist improvement efforts, at least initially.

After beginning her assignment at Buchanan, Principal Hulbert tried to develop personal relationships with the teachers and other staff members. She met with them individually, pledging to be their partner in improving the school's performance. Their demeanor toward her, however, was cool and their disposition toward school reform cynical. Many of them were still irritated by the dismissal of Mr. Sampson; several even implied that Superintendent Simon was a dictatorial politician who had sacrificed their principal to cover his incompetence. Moreover, their attitudes about the need for and probability of school improvement were at best unenthusiastic.

A fourth-grade teacher summarized their collective attitude: "Over the past few years, we have been unfairly criticized and threatened. Conditions changed after NCLB because principals thought that they were going to be fired and taxpayers were told that some schools might be forced to close. Morale, which wasn't very good in the first place, just got worse. The bureaucrats responsible for NCLB intend to destroy local public schools by setting goals that can't be met."

Principal Hulbert also inquired if changes, other than retaining more students in first grade, had occurred at the school since NCLB. For example, she asked if teachers had attended staff development programs and if those programs had been relevant to problems at Buchanan. She learned that the teachers were required to attend and most did not speak positively about the experience. Answers to her second question were typically evasive, but she concluded that any changes that had occurred were at best a product of "spiteful obedience."

Two years ago, at the insistence of the assistant superintendent for instruction, Mr. Sampson issued a directive requiring teachers to develop and follow unit lesson plans. The plans were to be evaluated by the principal both before and during classroom observations. Via the school "grapevine," however, Principal Sampson explained that he had been forced to issue the directive and was not personally in favor of the requirement. The plans were completed and submitted over the next several months. They had not been altered since their initial development and were on file in the principal's office. Principal Hulbert decided to read them.

Lessoned Learned from the Lesson Plans

Principal Hulbert did not expect the lesson plans to be exemplary but after reading them, she was astonished how poorly developed they were. Instead of the teachers devising their own plans, they developed grade-level plans. That is, one set of unit plans were written for each grade level. The following lesson plan for a unit on teaching fractions to second-grade students was typical.

Grade: 2

Subject: Math

Unit: Introducing fractions

Teacher Objectives: Introduce students to fractions by using several "hands-on" activities.

Activities:

1. Students cut paper circles into pie-shape pieces, color them, and then reassemble them.

2. Students are divided into four groups; each group is given an orange and told to peel and separate the sections. The students then count the number of sections and divide them into two parts, then three parts, and finally four parts.

3. The teacher uses five pennies, two nickels, and a dime to demonstrate fractions.

4. Students are divided first into two groups, then into three groups, and finally into four groups to demonstrate differences.

Evaluation: The second-grade teachers will meet and discuss outcomes after the unit is completed.

Principal Hulbert immediately noticed that both the activities and the evaluation focused on teaching and not on student learning. In other words, the lesson plans did not include learning expectations. In addition, the plans made no mention of teachers recording and using data during or following the instructional activities. Last, she noted that there was no mention of alignment between the lesson plan and standards.

At the opening faculty meeting, the principal discussed her review of the existing lesson plans. She emphasized that the documents focused largely if not exclusively on what the teachers were to do rather than on what the students were to learn. She said that the plans would have to be revised so that they were more explicit about learning expectations, evaluation, and alignment with standards. She also was emphatic that lesson plans had to include guidelines for recording information about student learning so that information would be available for future instructional decisions.

The teachers were visibly upset. Several pointed out that the previous principal thought the lesson plans were quite good, and he had never criticized them. Principal Hulbert noticed that many of the teachers were looking at Bill Osborne as the comments were being made. A fifth-grade teacher, he was one of Buchanan's most experienced teachers. He also was the most politically influential teacher in the room. For example, he had written the letter protesting Mr. Sampson's dismissal and then got every employee in the school to sign it. Noting that his colleagues wanted him to speak, he obliged.

"Ms. Hulbert," he began, "we might as well put all the cards on the table even though we haven't gotten to know each other very well. It's no secret why the superintendent put you in this job—and it's no secret that we're not happy about losing Mr. Sampson. If you force us to rewrite the lesson plans, you better find time and money, because we are not going to do the work on our own time again. We already have homework to correct and other duties. Every teacher in this room has been here for at least five years. We know these kids, we know their problems, and we know how to teach. Federal mandates, administrative dictates, and lesson plans aren't going to change reality. Many of our students aren't going to meet the state proficiency standard, and there is nothing you or we can do about that. The government can set lofty expectations and require us to use statistics, but the fact is these kids don't have much of a chance of doing well in school. Here's another fact. Motivated students learn and unmotivated students rarely learn. Poor teaching is not the reason why many Buchanan students do not do well on the state achievement tests. The real reasons are outside these four walls. Look at the effects of poverty, abuse, and emotional instability. You're the boss and you can force us to play the game. Just tell us what you want in the lesson plans, we'll copy it, and we can deal with more important issues. After we go through all of your hoops, ask yourself how much difference these plans will make when we close the classroom doors."

PROBLEM FRAMING

1. Assume you are Principal Hulbert. Describe what you would want to accomplish in dealing with the situation described in this case.

2. Based on the evidence of contextual variables, describe the difficulty associated with achieving your objective.

QUESTIONS AND SUGGESTED ACTIVITIES

1. Describe the nature of the school culture at Buchanan Elementary School.

2. To what extent does the school's culture affect teacher behavior?

3. Why do Mr. Osborne and presumably the other Buchanan teachers have such a negative attitude about NCLB?

4. Evaluate Principal Hulbert's decision to have the teachers rewrite the lesson plans.

5. Mr. Osborne implies that experienced teachers do not need lesson plans. Do you agree? Why or why not?

6. Mr. Osborne believes that many of the Buchanan students will not succeed academically because of the negative social and economic conditions they face outside of school. Do you agree? Why or why not?

7. Buchanan employees indicate that they supported the previous principal, Mr. Sampson, and they criticized the decision to remove him from the school. Is this fact relevant to shaping a plan to improve student learning? Why or why not?

8. How have teachers and principals across all districts and school responded to NCLB? What evidence do you have to support your response?

9. No Child Left Behind requires administrators and teachers to collect assessment data, disaggregate those data by student groups, and develop explicit plans for meeting the

needs of students, especially those exhibiting low achievement. Is this a realistic expectation for an elementary school teacher who has 20 or more pupils in her class? Is it a realistic expectation for a secondary school teacher who has over 100 pupils in his or her classes?

10. What actions could Principal Hulbert take to improve employee morale at Buchanan?

SUGGESTED READINGS

Calabrese, R. L. (2003). The ethical imperative to lead change: Overcoming the resistance to change. *International Journal of Educational Management, 17*(1), 7–13.

DuFour, R. (2002). The learning-centered principal. *Educational Leadership, 59*(8), 12–15.

Garcia, J. (Ed.). (2002). No Child Left Behind: Meeting challenges, seizing opportunities, improving achievement. *Achieve Policy Brief, 5.*

Hardy, L. (2002). Half full or half empty? Scrutinizing the effects of NCLB. *American School Board Journal, 193*(5), 4–6.

Hoy, W. K., Gage, C. Q., & Tarter, C. J. (2006). School mindfulness and faculty trust: Necessary conditions for each other? *Educational Administration Quarterly, 42*(2) 236–255.

Kowalski, T. J., Lasley, T. J., & Mahoney, J. (2008). *Data-driven decisions and school leadership: Best practices for school improvement.* Boston: Allyn and Bacon (Chapters 9 and 11).

Lewis, A. C. (2002). A horse called NCLB. *Phi Delta Kappan, 84*(3), 179–180.

Lewis, A. C. (2006). A muddle of NCLB. *Education Digest, 71*(9), 44–46.

Lewis, A. C. (2006). NCLB's murky mess. *Education Digest, 71*(5), 67–68.

McBride, B. (2004). Data-driven instructional methods: "One strategy fits all" doesn't work in real classrooms. *T.H.E. Journal, 31*(11), 38–39.

McCaslin, M. (2006). Student motivational dynamics in the era of school reform. *Elementary School Journal, 106*(5), 479–490.

Neill, M. (2003). High stakes, high risk: The dangerous consequences of high-stakes testing. *American School Board Journal, 190*(2), 18–21.

Paige, R., & Ferrandino, V. (2003). No principal left behind. *Principal, 82*(4), 52–55.

Porter-Magee, K. (2004). Teacher quality, controversy, and NCLB. *Clearing House, 78*(1), 26–29.

Rose, L. C. (2003). No child left behind: Promise or rhetoric? *Phi Delta Kappan, 84*(5), 338.

Thomas, M. D., & Bainbridge, W. L. (2002). No Child Left Behind: Facts and fallacies. *Phi Delta Kappan, 83*(10), 781–782.

Thompson, S. (2006, March 1). The importance of "reculturing." *Education Week, 25*(25), 44, 30–31.

Torff, B., & Sessions, D. N. (2005). Principals' perceptions of the causes of teacher ineffectiveness. *Journal of Educational Psychology, 97*(4), 530–537.

REFERENCES

Fullan, M., (2005). *Leadership and sustainability: System thinkers in action.* Thousand Oaks, CA: Corwin Press.

Hoy, W. K., & Miskel, C. G. (2005). *Educational administration: Theory, research, and practice* (7th ed.). New York: McGraw Hill.

Kowalski, T. J. (2003). *Contemporary school administration: An introduction* (2nd ed.). Boston: Allyn and Bacon.

Kowalski, T. J. (2006). *The school superintendent: Theory, practice, and cases* (2nd ed.). Thousand Oaks, CA: Sage.

Kowalski, T. J., Lasley, T. J., & Mahoney, J. (2008). *Data-driven decisions and school leadership: Best practices for school improvement.* Boston: Allyn and Bacon.

Protheroe, N., Shellard, E., & Turner, J. (2003). *A practical guide to school improvement: Meeting the challenges of NCLB.* Arlington, VA: Educational Research Service.

Sarason, S. B. (1996). *Revisiting the culture of the school and the problem of change.* New York: Teachers College Press.

Alternatives for an Alternative School

Background Information

Prior to the mid-1960s, the only distinctive options to traditional public elementary and secondary education were provided in private schools (Deal & Nolan, 1978). Largely because of the passage of the Civil Rights Act and subsequent federal interventions (e.g., Title I), alternative programs began to be established in public schools. Such programs were most directly related to the value of equity—that is, the belief that all students are entitled to reasonably equal educational opportunities. Alternative schools were established as institutions that would serve students who either did not function effectively in or were excluded from traditional schools.

During the 1970s, however, national concerns about elementary and secondary education shifted from equity to excellence. Thereafter, school boards and administrators placed considerable emphasis on basic academic programming in an effort to raise student achievement; the "back-to-basics" movement exemplifies such efforts. As a result, the development rate of alternative public schools declined. By the late 1980s, though, public alternative schools had regained popularity, largely due to a commitment among policymakers and other reformers to pursue equity and excellence concurrently (Kowalski, 2003). From 1996–1997 to 1997–1998, for example, the number of alternative schools in this country operated separately from traditional schools increased from 2,606 to 3,850, a 47 percent increase (Kleiner, Porch, & Farris, 2002). Nevertheless, outcomes of a recent study in Illinois (Foley & Pang, 2006) question the extent to which alternative schools actually enhance equity. Findings reveal that students in alternative programs are often denied resources that allow them to achieve state learner standards.

Alternative school advocates continue to argue that traditional public schools do not effectively reduce the number of students at risk of educational failure. Consequently, by 2000, policymakers in over half the states enacted provisions requiring alternative public schools; in addition, some states began providing incentives for establishing these programs (Barr & Parrett, 2001). The No Child Left Behind Act subsequently intensified pressures for local districts to provide some form of alternative education. The revitalization of alternative education is unquestionable; during the 2002–2003 school year, there were more alternative schools and alternative school principals than at any time in the past (Kowalski & Reynolds, 2003).

All too often, alternative education has been defined narrowly as a process designed to ameliorate behavioral problems and to a lesser extent, learning problems. In fact, three distinctive types of alternative schools exist, each with some capacity to enhance the probability of achieving their goal of reducing the number of at-risk students. They are described as follows:

- *Type I schools.* These are institutions of choice that any student may attend until high school graduation. They are innovative and are nontraditional in both organizational and administrative structure.
- *Type II schools.* These are placement institutions enrolling disruptive students temporarily. They provide an option to expulsion, and their primary purpose is behavior modification intended to eliminate or at least reduce unacceptable conduct that is not tolerated in traditional schools.
- *Type III schools.* These are referral institutions enrolling students with academic, social, or emotional difficulties. They focus on rehabilitating students so that they can return to and succeed in a traditional school (Raywid, 1994).

Both Type II and Type III alternative schools attempt to change the student. Type II schools focus exclusively on behavioral problems; Type III schools focus on behavioral and learning problems. Type I schools, however, are nested in the conviction that the educational environment and not the student needs to change. Consequently, they are intended to provide students at risk of failing in traditional school settings that are more accommodating with respect to their learning styles and educational needs (Raywid, 1994).

Type II alternative schools have been and remain the most common iteration of alternative education. This fact arguably has limited the adoption of alternative education as a reform initiative because research (e.g., Frazer & Baenen, 1988; McCann & Landi, 1986) indicates that Type II alternative schools are unlikely to improve overall student performance in a school district. The reason is twofold. First, some students fail to change their behavior while attending a Type II school; second, behavior changes exhibited by students in Type II schools are often temporary (i.e., students revert to negative behavior after returning to a traditional school). Leading alternative school scholars (e.g., Conrath, 2001; Gregory, 2001; Raywid, 1995) contend that most students who encounter difficulty in traditional schools do so because their learning styles and intellectual talents do not conform to traditional school norms. Consequently, their behavior in traditional schools is often deemed unacceptable. For many of them, placement in a Type I is the most effective option (Wehlage, Rutter, Smith, Lesko, & Fernandez, 1989).

This case is about conflict over establishing an alternative high school in a city school district. Administrators first disagree over the need for an alternative high school, and after a decision is made to provide such a program, they disagree regarding the type of alternative school that should be created. Both the nature of alternative schools and the manner in which the administrators deal with conflict are relevant to this situation.

Key Areas for Reflection

1. At-risk students
2. Instructional leadership
3. Competing values and beliefs
4. Alternative education
5. School culture

The Case

Sharon Gonzalez sat in her car staring at South Preston High School. The building's exterior brought back fond memories of her days as a student. Now 21 years after she had graduated from the school, she was returning as its new principal. Though the school looked pretty much as it did when she was student, the surrounding neighborhoods had changed considerably. Many of the homes, originally constructed prior to World War II, had deteriorated and most local businesses were gone.

Returning to South Preston was a difficult decision for Sharon. She no longer had relatives living in the community, and the once thriving industrial city was now a mere shell of its former existence. The steel mill and oil refinery, the primary sources of employment and tax revenue for schools, had closed during the 1980s. Enrollment in the school district had declined continuously for two decades, and the once proud school system was now recognized as one of the state's most troubled districts. But Superintendent Jackson Jones was a tremendous salesman, and he convinced Sharon that she could play a pivotal role in improving South Preston High School. At the time he began recruiting her, she was principal of an urban high school in New Jersey, where she had developed a positive reputation for working with at-risk students.

During her first weeks as principal of South Preston High School, Sharon studied statistical reports detailing student performance. Despite her extensive experience working with at-risk students, she found the following figures to be more negative than she anticipated:

- Over the past three years, 31 percent of the students who took the state's required proficiency exam for high school graduation failed.
- Over the past three years, 48 percent of the students who entered the school as freshman did not graduate within four years.
- Only 13 percent of last spring's graduating class enrolled in either a two-year or four-year college.
- Females were just as likely to drop out of school as were males; about two-thirds of the females who left school did so primarily because they were pregnant.
- Nearly 70 percent of the district's students qualified for free or reduced lunch programs.

Sharon's next surprise was discovering that no form of alternative programming was available for the district's students. Though pregnant students had the option of remaining in school, few did so. Moreover, the school district made no accommodations for female students with babies (e.g., a day-care center in the district or in the high school specifically).

Though the community and the high school now had minority majorities (i.e., a majority of the population was composed of individuals identified as racial or ethnic minorities), over half of the administrators in the school district were white males. Almost all of them had worked in the school district for more than ten years.

Sharon raised the topic of alternative education at the first principals' meeting she attended in early August. Her suggestion was not warmly received. Joe Buskovich, the assistant superintendent for secondary education and Sharon's immediate supervisor, was to first to respond to Sharon's suggestion.

"We have discussed starting an alternative school on several occasions and each time we do, there is little or no support for doing this. In my opinion, alternative schools send the wrong message to students—and parents. That is, students learn that they can break the rules and stay in school. They serve some time in an alternative school and then they're back in the regular school. It's just like sending drug dealers to jail for a year. When they get out, most of them start selling drugs again. Kids have to learn to obey rules. If they don't, they end up breaking laws. I'm definitely opposed to having an alternative school."

Sharon noted that her experience with alternative schools had been positive. She indicated that the purposes and nature of alternative education were often misinterpreted. She described different types of alternative schools and argued that those providing a real option to traditional schooling often reduced dropout rates.

As the discussion continued, Dr. Jones recognized that there was little support among the administrators for alternative education. Therefore, he brought an end to the discussion by saying, "We're not going to resolve anything today. We'll revisit this topic at a future administrative meeting."

After the meeting, Superintendent Jones told Principal Gonzalez that he agreed with her position—a point he failed to make during the meeting. He told her that he too had proposed an alternative school shortly after becoming superintendent two years ago. Over the next two months, the superintendent and high school principal met three times to discuss the feasibility of creating an alternative school. The two administrators decided that the most feasible option was to propose a Type I program that would operate as a "school-within-a-school" at the high school. Room was available due to declining enrollments, and the program could be housed in a wing of the facility. The two administrators believed that this approach would attenuate the argument that an alternative school would drain significant resources from regular programs.

Dr. Jones revisited the issue of alternative education at the November administrators' meeting. This time, however, he asked Principal Gonzalez to detail a plan to create a "school-within-a-school." After she finished speaking, opponents of alternative education reaffirmed that they did not favor an alternative school, regardless of the form it might take. This time, however, Dr. Jones did not stop the discussion. Instead he told the group, "I've thought about starting an alternative school ever since becoming superintendent. I put the idea on the back burner hoping that support for the idea would evolve. Apparently, only a few of you are supportive of the initiative, and I appreciate your candor and respect your position. Nevertheless, I have decided to pursue the possibility of implementing Principal Gonzalez's idea. I will appoint an ad hoc committee to formally evaluate the plan and render a recommendation to me regarding implementation."

The administrators were surprised by the superintendent's decision. Though they knew Dr. Jones supported alternative education, he rarely opposed a position taken by a majority of the administrators, especially when Mr. Buskovich was part of the majority. The assistant superintendent for secondary education was the most politically influential employee in the school district, an elected member of the city council and the brother of a school board member.

The five-member ad hoc committee appointed by Dr. Jones included both Joe Buskovich and Sharon Gonzalez. The remaining three members were two middle school principals and the director of federal programs. At the group's first meeting, Superintendent Jones said, "Please don't spend your time arguing over the merits of alternative education. I've already decided that we need such a program. Your assignment is to determine the merits of the plan proposed by Principal Gonzalez. I suggest you visit at least two high schools that already have a 'school-within-a-school' program."

Anticipating that opponents to alternative education would attempt to influence school board members on this matter, Superintendent Jones sent a detailed position paper to the board members indicating that an ad hoc committee had been appointed to evaluate the high school principal's proposal. Only two of the seven board members, one Mr. Buskovich's brother, informed the superintendent that they were unlikely to support any form of alternative education.

Principal Gonzalez's experience with the ad hoc committee was not pleasant. Instead of carrying out the superintendent's charge of evaluating the proposal, Mr. Buskovich and one of the middle school principals attempted rewrite the proposal. Their proposed amendments were as follows:

- Instead of being a Type I program, the program would be based on Type III alternative schools. Therefore, enrollment in the program would be temporary and students would be expected to return to the traditional program in no less than two semesters.
- An enrollment ceiling of twenty-five should be established (the original proposal did not have an enrollment ceiling).
- Middle school students would not be eligible for the program nor would another program be established in a middle school.
- If established, the program would be evaluated after one year of operation to determine if it should be continued.

Principal Gonzalez opposed all these proposals except the last one. She told the other committee members, "The type of program you are proposing is least likely to improve student retention. I don't believe the program I'm proposing is sufficient, but it is a starting point. If it is highly effective, why would we not want a similar program at the middle school level or a larger program at the high school?"

After only three meetings, Principal Gonzalez assumed that the committee would not complete its mission, at least not objectively. She informed Superintendent Jones that at least two of the committee members were attempting to reconstruct rather than evaluate her proposal for an alternative program at the high school. The other members said little during the meetings and she had no idea whether they preferred to pursue the committee's assigned mission (evaluating the proposal) or to revamp the proposal.

After listening to her assessment, the superintendent said, "Two board members are unlikely to vote for any proposal not endorsed by Joe Buskovich. One of course is his brother. I'm not sure where the others stand, although most seem to be open-minded. Given the circumstances, we need to decide if compromise is in the best interests of the school district. That is, should we refuse to alter the proposal or are we willing to begin with the type of program Joe is saying he can accept? I support your plan but a majority of the board may not do so—especially if you are outvoted and the evaluation committee recommends a different approach."

PROBLEM FRAMING

1. Assume you are Principal Gonzalez. Describe what you would want to accomplish in dealing with the situation described in this case.

2. Based on the evidence of contextual variables, describe the difficulty associated with achieving your objective.

QUESTIONS AND SUGGESTED ACTIVITIES

1. Evaluate the approach Principal Gonzalez used to pursue an alternative school.

2. Why do Mr. Buskovich and many of the principals in this case oppose alternative schools? Are their reasons valid? Why or why not?

3. Did Principal Gonzalez act too quickly in proposing an alternative school? Why or why not?

4. Discuss the three types of alternative schools. Identify the advantages and disadvantages of each type.

5. The superintendent has suggested that a compromise may be better than a political defeat because the board's rejection of the "school-within-a-school" proposal would result in the district's having no alternative education. Do you agree with his suggestion? Why or why not?

6. What factors have increased interest in alternative education?

7. What other approaches could have been taken by the superintendent and Principal Gonzalez to promote the idea of alternative education?

8. Identify alternative schools in your local area. Determine if they are Type I, II, or III schools.

9. Assume Superintendent Jones sends a memorandum to the ad hoc committee members insisting that they evaluate the plan they were given rather than trying to develop a different plan. Would such an intervention be advantageous or disadvantageous?

10. How might the conflict over the middle school affect Principal Gonzalez's ability to be an effective high school principal?

SUGGESTED READINGS

Clark, C. (2000). Coming of age at Hippie High. *Phi Delta Kappan, 81*(9), 696–700.

Duke, D. L., & Griesdorn, J. (1999). Considerations in the design of alternative schools. *Clearing House, 73*(2), 89–92.

Gold, M. (1995). Charting a course: Promise and prospects for alternative schools. *Journal of Emotional and Behavioral Problems, 3*(4), 8–11.

Gregory, T. (2001). Fear of success? Ten ways alternative schools pull their punches. *Phi Delta Kappan, 82*(8), 577–581.

Griffin, B. L (1993). Administrators can use alternative schools to meet student needs. *Journal of School Leadership, 3*(4), 416–420.

Lehr, C. A., & Lange, C. M. (2003). Alternative schools serving students with and without disabilities: What are the current issues and challenges? *Preventing School Failure, 47*(2), 59–63.

McGee, J. (2001). Reflections of an alternative school administrator. *Phi Delta Kappan, 82*(8), 588–591.

Poetter, T. S., & Knight-Abowitz, K. (2001). Possibilities and problems of school choice. *Kappa Delta Pi Record, 37*(2), 58–62.

Powell, D. E. (2003). Demystifying alternative education: Considering what really works. *Reclaiming Children and Youth, 12*(2), 68–70.

Raywid, M. A. (1994). Alternative schools: The state of the art. *Educational Leadership, 52*(1), 26–31.

Raywid, M. A. (1995). The struggles and joys of trailblazing: A tale of two charter schools. *Phi Delta Kappan, 76*(7), 555–560.

Vaughn, D. D., Slicker, E. K., & Van Hein, J. (2000). Adolescent problems and coping strategies: Alternative school versus non-alternative school students. *Research in the Schools, 7*(2), 41–47.

REFERENCES

Barr, R. D., & Parrett, W. H. (2001). *Hope fulfilled for at-risk and violent youth* (2nd ed.). Boston: Allyn and Bacon.

Conrath, J. (2001). Changing the odds for young people: Next steps for alternative education. *Phi Delta Kappa, 82* (8), 585–587.

Deal, T. E., & Nolan, R. R. (1978). An overview of alternative schools. In T. Deal & R. Nolan (Eds.), *Alternative schools: Ideologies, realities, guidelines* (pp. 1–17). Chicago: Nelson-Hall.

Foley, R. M., & Pang, L. (2006). Alternative education programs: Program and student characteristics. *The High School Journal, 89*(3), 10–21.

Frazer, L., & Baenen, N. (1988). *An alternative for high-risk students.* (ERIC Document Reproduction Service No. ED 301 333)

Gregory, T. (2001). Fear of success? Ten ways alternative schools pull their punches. *Phi Delta Kappan, 82* (8), 577–581.

Kleiner, B., Porch, R., & Farris, E. (2002). *Public alternative schools and programs for students at risk of education failure: 2000–01.* Washington, DC: U.S. Department of Education, National Center for Education Statistics.

Kowalski, T. J. (2003). *Contemporary school administration: An introduction* (2nd ed.). Boston: Allyn and Bacon.

Kowalski, T. J., & Reynolds, S. (2003). Knowledge, dispositions, and career orientations of alternative school principals. *Connections: Journal of Principal Preparation and Development, 5*, 22–31.

McCann, T., & Landi, H. (1986). Researchers cite program value. *Changing Schools, 14* (2), 2–5.

Raywid, M. (1994). Alternative schools: The state of the art. *Educational Leadership, 52*(1), 26–31.

Raywid, M. (1995). Alternative and marginal students. In M. C. Wang & M. C. Reynolds (Eds.), *Making a difference for students at risk* (pp. 119–155). Thousand Oaks, CA: Corwin Press.

Wehlage, G., Rutter, R., Smith, G., Lesko, N., & Fernandez, R. (1989). *Reducing the risk: Schools as communities of support.* Philadelphia: Falmer.

CASE
3

A Bully's Threat

Background Information

Not all administrators recognize the difference between *safety* and *security*. The former addresses issues such as accident prevention, air quality, and fire or storm damage. Security, on the other hand, is concerned with preventing and responding to criminal acts and severe misbehavior (Trump, 1998). Highly publicized criminal acts committed in schools provide clear evidence that educational environments are not immune from society's ills. The potential for violence generates three critical questions for school administrators:

1. How can behaviors that threaten a school's security be prevented?
2. What measures should be taken when threats of violence are made?
3. What measures should be taken when violence occurs?

Experts who have examined crime-related crises have concluded that many schools remain especially vulnerable to violence for the following reasons:

- Administrators are often unprepared to deal with violence, either because they have not been sufficiently educated or because they lack experiences in these situations. Kenneth Trump, one of the leading authorities on school crisis management, notes that many school officials remain unprepared to deal with most types of potential crises (Kowalski, 2002, 2005).
- School or district crisis plans are often perfunctory documents that receive little or no attention. Administrators may fear that such plans will be interpreted by parents and other taxpayers as an admission that serious security problems already exist (Moriarity, Maeyama, & Fitzgerald, 1993).
- Chaos often occurs during a crisis situation because implementation of the district's or school's plan has not been coordinated with community agencies (e.g., police and fire departments) (Kowalski, 2007).
- The content of crisis plans may have been influenced by political conditions, a factor that may dissuade administrators from adopting best practices (Trump, 1998). For example, pressures to reduce expulsions may influence the types of punishment given to students who exhibit violent behavior.

This case occurs in an urban high school. A student who has a reputation as a bully threatens the life of another student. The threat is brought to the attention of the principal, and he must decide how to deal with the situation. He enlists the counsel of three of the high school's staff members. As you read the case, try to identify conditions that may have influenced the student's behavior and principal's reaction to that behavior.

Key Areas for Reflection

1. Dealing with threats of violent behavior
2. Political influences on crisis management
3. Racial tensions in schools
4. Principal leadership style
5. Multicultural school environments

The Case

Community

Like most urban areas in the United States, Central City has experienced considerable change in the past thirty years. The total population has declined from 325,000 in 1960 to its current level of 258,000. The property tax base has been eroded by the flight of businesses and middle-class families to the suburbs. The current mayor, now serving a second four-year term, has been slightly more successful than his predecessors in curbing the erosion of population and taxable property. Two of his initiatives, inner-city renewal and a vigorous campaign to attract new businesses, have been responsible.

Central City's crime and violence rates, however, have not been reduced. Nor have poverty statistics improved. Nearly 40 percent of the school-age children live in poverty-level families, and many of them are being reared in dysfunctional families. It is estimated that as many as 15 percent of school-age children in Central City have been victims of physical or emotional abuse.

The following demographic profile extracted from the most recent national census reveals the level of racial diversity among the district's residents:

- 48 percent identified themselves as African American.
- 18 percent identified themselves as Hispanic.
- 5 percent identified themselves as Asian American.
- 28 percent identified themselves as white (non-Hispanic).
- 1 percent identified themselves as "other."
- White residents are heavily concentrated in two sections of city: Memorial Park (where virtually all of the Asian American families also reside) and Kensington.

The School District

The Central City School District (CCSD) remains the state's largest district; however, its enrollment has declined about 25 percent in the past three decades. Two high schools, two middle schools, and six elementary schools have been closed during that period. Most of the remaining school buildings are more than fifty years old and should be completely renovated or replaced.

The district is governed by a school board consisting of seven members. Five of them are elected by voters in designated geographic regions in the school district; the remaining two are elected at-large. The following data profile the present board:

Member	Board position	District	Occupation	Race
Venus Bronson	President	3	Lawyer	African American
Walter Sully	Vice President	At-large	Plumber	Caucasian
Emily Drovak	Secretary	5	Housewife	Caucasian
Alexander Adams	Member	1	Minister	African American
James Chin	Member	4	Engineer	Asian American
Rose Hildago	Member	2	Social worker	Caucasian
Maynard Truax	Member	At-large	Dentist	African American

Districts 1, 2, and 3 are in the city's core area; each has high concentrations of African American residents, with District 2 being almost evenly divided between African American and Hispanic populations. District 4, known as the Memorial Park area, is located at the southern perimeter of the city. Nearly all of the district's residents are either white or Asian American. District 5, known as Kensington, is located in the northern perimeter of the city; the population here is about 60 percent white with the remainder being predominately African American.

Dr. Ruth Perkett is the district's first female and first African American superintendent. A longtime employee of CCSD, she has been the school system's top administrator for only two years. Prior to assuming this position, she was an elementary school principal, director of federal programs, and associate superintendent for elementary education in the district. Over her long tenure in the CCSD, she has established close ties with many government officials, including Central City's current mayor.

Memorial Park High School

Forty years ago, Memorial Park High School was considered one of the state's finest academic schools. Although that is no longer true, the school remains the most academic-oriented high school in the CCSD. Memorial Park enrolls approximately 1,350 students in grades 9 to 12. Only one-third of these students, however, reside in the Memorial Park area of the city; the others are bused to the high school from other parts of the district in compliance with the district's desegregation plan, a document that was developed internally thirteen years ago.

Joseph Milhoviak has been the principal at Memorial Park High School for fourteen years. He grew up in an adjacent neighborhood and graduated from the school. After college, he returned as a teacher and coach. During his entire twenty-eight-year career as an educator, he has never worked in another school.

Prior to the adoption of the district's desegregation, Memorial Park High School enrolled just a handful of African American and Hispanic students. The present student profile reveals how much conditions have changed in little more than a decade:

- African American: 40 percent
- Hispanic: 10 percent
- Asian American: 16 percent
- Caucasian: 34 percent

Despite the student body's diversity, approximately two-thirds of the teachers and administrators identify themselves as Caucasians.

Principal Milhoviak continues to live in the Memorial Park area. He is involved in civic activities and the area's residents view him as both an educational and a community leader. Several years ago, for example, members of the Memorial Park Neighborhood Association encouraged him to become a candidate for the mayor's position in Central City. He declined.

Mr. Milhoviak maintains a reputation as a "tough" principal—a disciplinarian not afraid to act decisively and harshly when punishing disruptive students. Though his approach to managing student behavior is applauded by most parents and other taxpayers residing in Memorial Park, not everyone supports his leadership style. Most notably, Superintendent Perkett believes he has been inconsistent in disciplining students and stated this fact on his most recent performance evaluation. Her assessment of his performance has been influenced by the fact that the rate of expulsions and suspensions for minority students is approximately 200 percent higher than it is for nonminority students. Moreover, minority students who reside outside of the Memorial Park area are twice as likely to be expelled or suspended than are minority students residing in the area. Since becoming superintendent, Dr. Perkett has strongly recommended that Mr. Milhoviak deploy "more constructive" alternatives for disciplining students, options such as in-school suspension and group counseling. To date, he has not heeded her advice.

The Incident

His faced flushed and breathing heavily, Brian Isaacs entered the principal's office between the third and fourth periods. He told the receptionist, "I need to see Mr. Milhoviak right now. It's an emergency!"

"What's wrong?" the receptionist inquired.

He answered, "I need to talk with the principal. I don't think I should discuss the problem with any other person."

Convinced the student was experiencing a crisis, the receptionist asked the student to identify himself and then she interrupted Mr. Milhoviak, who was in his office meeting with a parent. The principal knew the student. A sophomore, Brian was an above-average student academically and generally well behaved. Mr. Milhoviak quickly concluded the meeting with the parent and brought Brian into his office.

The principal immediately concluded that Brian was visibly shaken. He asked the student to sit down and to try to calm himself. Brian took a deep breath and then said, "Carl Turner told me that he is going to blow my brains out. Mr. Milhoviak, he is crazy. He'll do it."

"Why is Carl threatening you?" the principal asked.

"This whole thing really isn't about me. Carl had a couple of dates with my sister, Angie, and now she doesn't want to see him any more. He's blaming my parents and me. He said we are forcing her to not see him any more. He told me he is in love with Angie. He called my parents and me racists."

Mr. Milhoviak was very familiar with Carl Turner. His family did not reside in the Memorial Park area. Though he had been a starting linebacker on the school's football team for two years, he had been dismissed from the team shortly after beginning his senior year. His dismissal was based on a series of problems that culminated in Carl's pushing one of the assistant coaches during a locker room argument. After being dismissed from the football team, he was suspended twice for fighting. The faculty and students generally regarded Carl as a bully.

Brian's sister, Angie, was a senior. Somewhat introverted, she was a good student but not very involved in extracurricular activities. Mr. Milhoviak was surprised to learn that Angie had dated Carl, primarily because the two students were so different.

Refocusing his attention on the student in his office, the principal asked, "What exactly did Carl say to you?"

"He told me that he loved Angie, and he wasn't going to let me or the rest of my family stand in the way of their relationship. He said he had a gun and would use it if he had to do so. He said unless we stopped pressuring Angie not to see him, he would get even with me and my parents."

The principal then inquired, "And what does Angie have to say about this relationship?"

"Nothing. I didn't even know that she had a date with him. I don't think my parents knew about the dates either."

"Brian, I am going to alert the security officer about this threat. The officer will keep an eye on Carl. If he threatens you again, even if it is away from school, you let me know immediately. In the meantime, I'll figure out how I'm going to handle this. Stay away from Carl. Don't speak to him, and if he tries to engage you in a conversation, just walk away."

Talking with the principal reduced Brian's anxiety. Before leaving the office, he added, "Carl said he was tired of being treated like dirt. Do you think he's crazy enough to shoot someone?"

Mr. Milhoviak responded that he did not think Carl would shoot anyone. He then convinced Brian to return to class. As soon as Brian departed, the principal asked the receptionist to get Angie Isaacs and bring her to his office. When she arrived, Mr. Milhoviak told her about the conversation he had with Brian minutes earlier. She was visibly stunned.

"I went out with Carl twice, and no one in my family knew about it. He had asked me to go out with him at least six times before I said yes. On the first date, we went to a movie. I met him in front of the theater. The second time, we went to a rock concert. My parents thought I was at a girlfriend's house both times. After the second date, I just decided that I didn't want to go out with him again. He was nice to me, but I didn't think we had a future. Two days ago, he again asked me to go out with him, and I decided to be honest with him. I told him he was a nice guy, but I didn't think we should date any more. He got really mad and said I would change my mind after I got to know him better."

"Did he threaten you in any way?" asked the principal.

"No. But he scares me. He seems nice but he gets angry very easily. For example, he almost got in a fight with a guy sitting in front of us at the rock concert just because this guy wouldn't stay in his seat. Carl threatened to punch him and the guy got a security person, who told Carl to cool it."

Mr. Milhoviak instructed Angie to return to class and to avoid contact with Carl. He also advised her to inform her parents about the situation when she got home from school that day. After she left, Mr. Milhoviak tried unsuccessfully to reach Angie's parents via telephone. He wanted to brief them on the matter and inform them that Angie was supposed to talk to them about the problem later that afternoon, but he was unable to reach either her mother or her father.

The principal then asked the school's security officer, Carl Turner's counselor, and the assistant principal in charge of student discipline to meet with him. He briefed them on the matter, including his instructions to Brian and Angie Isaacs. The four school officials agreed that Carl should be brought to the office immediately. They wanted to hear his side of the story. The principal contacted the teacher in Carl's fourth-period class via the intercom and was told that Carl was not in class. Checking the attendance records, the principal learned that Carl had attended class during the first three periods.

Carl's counselor, Mildred Breslin, urged Mr. Milhoviak to call the police and report the incident. Though she did not think Carl would use a gun, she believed he would physically attack Brian if his anger persisted. Riley Grimes, the assistant principal, wanted to delay contacting the police until they could determine whether Carl was still at the school.

"What if we call the police and then find out Brian is not telling the truth or exaggerating? If we mess this up, Dr. Perkett may be all over us for jumping to conclusions. We should try to find Carl first. If he is not in the school building, then we can call the police."

Jamel Atkins, the school's security guard and a retired deputy sheriff, offered a third opinion. He urged the principal to locate Mr. and Mrs. Isaacs before doing anything else. "If they are informed about this matter, they may elect to file a complaint with the police. That way, we are not put in a position of determining whether Brian is telling the truth. In the interim, I'll take responsibility for protecting Brian and Angie for the remainder of the school day."

Each school in the CCSD was required to have a crisis plan. The one for Memorial Park provided suggestions for handling threatened violence, but it did not require a specific course of action. Among the suggested actions were:

- Notifying the police if the incident was considered sufficiently serious
- Notifying the parents of all students involved
- Notifying the teachers of all students involved
- Suspending the student from school pending a full investigation if the incident was considered sufficiently serious

After considering the suggestions made by the three staff members and after reviewing the crisis plan, the principal decided to delay calling the police. The administrators and the security guard started searching the building for Carl, and staff in the principal's office began trying to reach Mr. and Mrs. Isaacs. The four educators were to reconvene in the principal's office in one hour if Carl was not located. The school officials did not find him, nor were staff in the principal's office able to contact Mr. or Mrs. Isaacs. Moreover, the police had not been notified of the threat. When the school officials met again in the principal's office, Principal Milhoviak again asked the three staff members for advice.

PROBLEM FRAMING

1. Assume you are the principal. Describe what you would want to accomplish in dealing with the situation described in this case.

2. Based on the evidence of contextual variables, describe the difficulty associated with achieving your objective.

QUESTIONS AND SUGGESTED ACTIVITIES

1. Share and critique the problem statements prepared by students in your class.

2. What racial, social, and economic characteristics of the community and school district are relevant to the problem presented in the case?

3. Identify and discuss factors that appear to affect the course of action being pursued by the principal and his support personnel.

4. If you were the principal, would you consider Carl Turner's record of fighting relevant to reaching a decision on this matter? Why or why not?

5. If you were the principal, would you have reported the threat to the police immediately after being told about it? Why or why not?

6. Determine if state law or school policy would have provided clearer directions for a principal in your school district in relation to this threat.

7. Identify elements of the crisis plan in your school that are pertinent to the situation described in this case.

8. List and then evaluate alternatives the principal could have considered in dealing with the situation.

9. What actions should the principal have taken to protect both the student who reported the threat and his sister?

10. Should principals have discretion in dealing with threats or should district policy disallow discretion in such situations?

SUGGESTED READINGS

Baker, J. A. (1998). Are we missing the forest for the trees? Considering the social context of school violence. *Journal of School Psychology, 36*(1), 29–44.

Black, S. (2003). Angry at the world. *American School Board Journal, 190*(6), 43–45.

Canter, A. S. (2005). Bullying at school: Strategies for intervention. *Principal, 85*(2), 42–45.

Christie, K. (2005). Chasing the bullies away. *Phi Delta Kappan, 86*(10), 725–726.

Crothers, L. M., & Levinson, E. M. (2004). Assessment of bullying: A review of methods and instruments. *Journal of Counseling and Development, 82*(4), 496–503.

Edmonson, H. M., & Bullock, L. M. (1998). Youth with aggressive and violent behaviors: Pieces of a puzzle. *Preventing School Failure, 42*(3), 135–141.

Elinoff, M., Chafouleas, S. M., & Sassu, K. A. (2004). Bullying: Considerations for defining and intervening in school settings. *Psychology in the Schools, 41*(8), 887–897.

Furlong, M. J., Felix, E. D., & Sharkey, J. D. (2005). Preventing school violence: A plan for safe and engaging schools. *Principal Leadership (High School Ed.), 6*(1), 11–15.

Halbig, W. W. (2000). Breaking the code of silence. *American School Board Journal, 187*(3), 34–36.

Haynes, R. M., & Chalker, D. M. (1999). A nation of violence. *American School Board Journal, 186*(3), 22–25.

Johns, B. H. (1998). What the new Individuals with Disabilities Act (IDEA) means for students who exhibit aggressive or violent behavior. *Preventing School Failure, 42*(3), 102–105.

Jones, R. (1997). Absolute zero. *American School Board Journal, 184*(10), 29–31.

Levin, J. (1998). Violence goes to school. *Mid-Western Educational Researcher, 11*(1), 2–7.

Lodge, J., & Frydenberg, E. (2005). The role of peer bystanders in school bullying: Positive steps toward promoting peaceful schools. *Theory into Practice, 44*(4), 329–336.

Myles, B. S., & Simpson, R. L. (1998). Aggression and violence by school-age children and youth: Understanding the aggression cycle and prevention/intervention strategies. *Intervention in School and Clinic, 33*(5), 259–264.

Orpinas, P., Horne, A. M., & Staniszewski, D. (2003). School bullying: Changing the problem by changing the school. *School Psychology Review, 32*(3), 431–444.

Page, R. M., & Hammermeister, J. (1997). Weapon-carrying youth and violence. *Adolescence, 32*(127), 505–513.

Rasicot, J. (1999). The threat of harm. *American School Board Journal, 186*(3), 14–18.

Ruder, R. (2005). A customized campaign against bullying. *Principal Leadership (Middle School Ed.), 6*(1), 36–38.

Smokowski, P. R., & Kopasz, K. H. (2005). Bullying in school: An overview of types, effects, family characteristics, and intervention strategies. *Children & Schools, 27*(2), 101–110.

Stephens, R. D. (1998). Ten steps to safer schools. *American School Board Journal, 185*(3), 30–33.

Trump, K. S. (2001). Assessing and managing student threats. *School Administrator, 58*(9), 50.

Valois, R. F., & McKewon, R. E. (1998). Frequency and correlates of fighting and carrying weapons among public school adolscents. *American Journal of Health Behavior, 22*(1), 8–17.

Will, J., & Neufeld, P. J. (2002). Taking appropriate action. *Principal Leadership, 3*(4), 51–54.

Will, J. D., & Neufeld, P. J. (2003). Keep bullying from growing into greater violence. *Education Digest, 68*(6), 32–36.

Zirkel, P. A. (2002). Written and verbal threats of violence. *Principal, 81*(5), 63–65.

REFERENCES

Kowalski, T. J. (2002). Working with the media during a crisis situation: Perspectives for school administrators. *Journal of School Public Relations, 23*(3), 178–196.

Kowalski, T. J. (2005). Revisiting communication during a crisis: Insights from Kenneth Trump. *Journal of School Public Relations, 26*(1), 47–55.

Kowalski, T. J. (2007). *School public relations* (4th ed.).

Upper Saddle River, NJ: Merrill, Prentice Hall.

Moriarity, A., Maeyama, R. G., & Fitzgerald, P. J. (1993). A clear plan for school crisis management. *NASSP Bulletin, 77*(552), 17–22.

Trump, K. S. (1998). *Practical school safety: Basic guidelines for safe and secure schools.* Thousand Oaks, CA: Corwin Press.

CASE
4

Lounge Talk

Background Information

Role conflict is a product of incompatible job expectations, and it is very common in schools. This is especially true in relation to principals. Some teachers, students, and parents expect them to be relationship oriented (i.e., friendly and caring); others expect them to be task oriented (i.e., firm and decisive managers); and still others want them to be skillful politicians (i.e., cunning and capable negotiators). School reform in general and school restructuring specifically have elevated the relevance of administrative role conflict primarily because the process illuminates inherent tensions between democracy and professionalism. Educators, and especially administrators, face conflicting expectations that their practice is guided both by a professional knowledge base and by the will of the people (Wirt & Kirst, 2001). Therefore, consequential policy is rarely established by one individual. Instead, it is promulgated in political arenas in which groups seek to advance or protect their interests. And in the context of school improvement, this usually means that some segment of a school's primary publics, including teachers, will oppose virtually any change proposed by administrators (Kowalski, 2006).

Studies of role conflict and leadership styles have contributed to theory building in the areas of *transformational* and *charismatic* leadership. As Yukl noted (1989), these two terms:

> . . . refer to the process of influencing major changes in the attitudes and assumptions of organization members and building commitment for the organization's mission and objectives. Transformational leadership is usually defined more broadly than charismatic leadership, but there is considerable overlap between the two conceptions (p. 204).

The seminal work of Burns (1978) described two contrasting administrative styles: *transactional* and *transformational leadership*. Transactional leaders tend to believe that people are primarily motivated by self-interests, and accordingly, they attempt to control behavior in others by offering rewards or threatening punishments (Yukl, 2006). Transformational leaders, by comparison, make others more aware of their responsibilities, induce them to transcend their self-interests, and emphasize higher-order needs (e.g., self-esteem, self-actualization) (Bass, 1985). In other words, they focus on intrinsic and moral motives and seek to integrate higher-order individual motives with organizational or professional goals (Kowalski, 2003). Bass concluded that though these two styles are distinct, they are not mutually exclusive because effective administrators used both depending on problems, issues, and contextual variables. Bennis and Nanus (1985) noted, however, that the transactional style has been more widely used across all types of organizations.

In the context of school reform, considerable interest has been given to promoting transformational leadership in schools (Kowalski, Petersen, & Fusarelli, 2007) because this style is nested in the conviction that leaders must believe in and trust people around them—a condition clearly enhancing the prospects of achieving organizational change (Bennis, 1984). For example, such convictions prompt principals to develop shared visions rather than foisting a personal vision on others. Other characteristics of a transformational principal are likely to include:

- Being concerned that teachers and other school employees grow professionally and achieve self-efficacy.
- Viewing and treating teachers as peer professionals rather than as subordinates.
- Viewing the school as a learning community in which many decisions are made democratically and individuals care about and help each other.

In this case, four high school teachers discuss their perceptions of the school's new principal. Three of them oppose her leadership style. In subtle ways, they question whether gender, age, and a lack of administrative experience cause her to behave in a manner that they view as unacceptable. As you read this case, apply the concepts of transactional and transformational leadership. Try to analyze the reactions of the disgruntled teachers in relations to leadership style. Also, imagine that you are a teacher in the school so that you can develop a personal perspective as to whether you would support this type of principal.

Key Areas for Reflection

1. Transformational and transactional leadership styles
2. Principal succession
3. Role conflict
4. Teacher expectations of principal behavior
5. Leadership style and change in schools

The Case

As Peter Weller entered the teachers' lounge, the room fell silent. Three colleagues—Debra Lowler, Linda Mays, and Jake Brumwell—were seated at one of the four small round tables scattered randomly across the room. No one else was present. Having a common preparation period, the four teachers often spent 10 to 15 minutes a day enjoying a cup of coffee and discussing a variety of issues. As usual, Peter was the last one to arrive at the lounge.

Peter nodded as he sat down in the remaining chair at the table, but the silence continued. After a few seconds he asked, "Okay, why are you all so quiet? You look like my students after I catch them doing something wrong."

"Peter," Linda answered, "We were just discussing your favorite principal. It's kind of eerie. Maybe she has a hidden listening device in this room and, after hearing our comments, sent you here to defend her! After a brief pause, she added, "Just a joke, Peter, so don't get hostile."

Peter smiled, "Don't you have better things to discuss? Now I realize that you are experts when it comes to critiquing principals, but your obsession with Dr. Werner is not healthy. Ease up."

Colleen Werner had been appointed principal of Drewerton South High School less than a year before. She was only the second principal in the school's fourteen-year history; the school was established as the district's second high school to accommodate a growing population. Now with an enrollment of just over 1,000 students, South High School serves the most affluent neighborhoods in Drewerton, an upscale suburban community.

George Calbo, South High School's first and only other principal, retired at the end of the previous year. He was popular and well liked, especially among teachers. He had taught social studies, coached basketball, and served as an assistant principal in the school district for twenty-one years before being named South's inaugural principal. His appointment, made a full year before the school opened, allowed him to personally select faculty and staff. As a result, most of the school's employees were former colleagues and friends. Faculty at South High School viewed Principal Calbo as their advocate and protector.

The announcement that Dr. Colleen Werner had been selected to be South's second principal surprised both the faculty and the community. More than fifty educators had applied for the position, and after an initial round of interviews, the applicant pool was reduced to five. They included four internal candidates (all males and current principals or assistant principals in the Drewerton School District) and Dr. Werner. Most observers viewed her as a "token female candidate." She was considerably younger (only 32 years old at the time of her appointment), less experienced than the men, and lacking political connections in the community. Moreover, no female had previously served as a principal or assistant principal in a secondary school in this district.

Everyone recognized that Dr. Werner and her predecessor were very different types of administrators. Mr. Calbo had devoted much of his time to managing people and material resources; Dr. Werner openly admitted that she preferred to relegate these responsibilities to her two assistants so that she could spend much of her time visiting classrooms and working on curriculum projects. Mr. Calbo spent nearly two hours every day in the teachers' lounge, listening to concerns and complaints, discussing politics, and getting updated on the latest gossip. Dr. Werner, on the other hand, rarely went to the teachers' lounge, and when she did, she usually stayed only long enough to pour a cup of coffee.

Peter Weller was one of only five or six South High School teachers who believed that Dr. Werner was a more effective principal than her predecessor. More notably, he often stated this conviction to other teachers, especially when they were criticizing the new principal or questioning her competence. Peter's disposition toward the new principal surprised his colleagues because he also had been supportive of Mr. Calbo. Peter explained the apparent contradiction by pointing out that there were different reasons why he viewed the two administrators positively. Mr. Calbo cared about teachers and students and dedicated his career to helping them; though Peter admired his good intentions, he did not agree with his political methods. With respect to Dr. Werner, Peter believed that she too cared deeply about students and school employees, and he found her professional approach to be gratifying.

After a minute of silence, Peter spoke again. "Oh, I know what's happening. You are skewering Dr. Werner again. What did she do to make you angry this time?"

Jake responded, "We have to talk about somebody, and it might as well be Colleen-the-Great."

"Unfortunately, she's the only one you talk about. You seem to be obsessed with her," Peter noted.

Debra Lowler, usually a quiet member of the group, spoke next. "I'll tell you what bothers me about Colleen. It's her repeated comments about how we should behave professionally. She uses 'professional' as a code word that means 'do extra work without additional compensation.' Instead of looking out for our interests, she promotes the idea that we should volunteer to do more without additional compensation. George [Calbo], on the other hand, fought for us. He knows what it is like to be a teacher. If the superintendent or the school board want us to do extra jobs, they should pay us accordingly."

"Agreed," Linda chimed in, "George defended his teachers. He even advised us, privately of course, not to do more work if we didn't get additional compensation. He knew how to take care of the superintendent and school board. He never let them walk all over us."

"Don't you think that Colleen also cares about us?" Peter asked. "She was and still is a teacher. She knows what the public expects. Did you ever consider that she wants everyone, including students, to be treated fairly? Just because she doesn't praise you every minute of the day and just because she isn't dangling 'carrots' in front of you constantly doesn't mean she's indifferent toward teachers."

Jake Brumwell, a mathematics teacher and track coach, was Mr. Calbo's closest friend and biggest defender among the group. He spoke next.

"Peter, Colleen was not ready for this job. She still has a lot to learn, especially about working with teachers. Just last week, for example, she asked if I would chaperone a weekend camping trip with a group of students in June. The trip is part of a dropout prevention program, so you know the type of kids who will be involved. Two other teachers already have agreed to chaperone the trip, but she wants me to go because she thinks I can connect with several of the students. When I asked her how much I would get paid for playing nursemaid in the woods, she looked at me like I was an extortionist. That condescending look made me mad. I told her I was too busy to go camping. Now, I presume, she has categorized me as one of the unprofessional teachers in this school. I resent being put in this kind of position. George would have either gotten money to pay the chaperones or he would have called off the trip."

Peter then said, "Well, Jake, I'm one of the chaperones, and I volunteered. Did you know that Colleen also is a chaperone? And I know for a fact that she asked you to go on the trip because several of the students think highly of you."

Debra came to Jake's defense. "Sure, Colleen is going. But she has a twelve-month contract. So technically she's being paid for going on the trip."

"Wrong again," Peter shot back. "To my knowledge, she does not get any additional compensation for going on a camping trip that starts on Friday afternoon and ends Saturday evening."

Linda entered the conversation again. "Look, it's more than just asking us to give up our time. Colleen's whole approach toward being a principal is different. She doesn't do things George's way. You say Colleen cares about us. I disagree. She only cares about students—and she cares most about the students with serious problems. Maybe this empathy is self-serving. Maybe she thinks the school board will reward her for these actions. Since you're her apologist, you ought to let her know that teachers, and not students, are going to determine if she is a successful principal."

"I agree totally with Linda. Colleen needs to know that principals don't do well in this district after they lose teacher support," Jake noted. "Personally, I think she would be better off paying more attention to our best students. Maybe the high achievers should be the ones who get camping trips and other favors from the principal. If you ask me, Colleen sends the wrong message to students—and she certainly has not sent any positive messages to us."

Peter was frustrated. "Do you realize that I'm not the only one in the school who supports Colleen?" he asked rhetorically. "Why don't you give her credit for some of the things she's accomplished in the short time she's been here? What about the way she helped Deloris Hutchins? Prior to Dr. Werner's working with her, she was an ineffective teacher. Colleen worked with her to improve her planning skills and classroom management. George never helped her become a better teacher; instead he covered up her deficiencies and protected her. Deloris has been transformed, and she openly attributes her improvement in the classroom to Colleen. Now you tell me, who is the better principal—the one who made excuses for poor teaching or the one who did something about it? I'll tell you how Deloris answers that question. She thinks Dr. Werner is the best administrator she has ever known. To casually charge that Colleen doesn't care about teachers is irresponsible."

Jake responded, "See, that's what I was trying to say a minute ago. No matter if she is dealing with teachers or students, she cares a lot more about low performers than she does about high performers. Where is the recognition for those of us who always have done a good job? Instead of praise and rewards, I get invited to spend a weekend with at-risk students in the woods! And because I said no, she has probably labeled me as being insensitive and unprofessional. Listen, Peter, I don't like the way Werner operates. She's never going to be effective in this school unless she wises up and develops political savvy."

Peter just shook his head in disbelief. He knew he would not convert his colleagues, not at least on this day. There had been at least a dozen previous conversations similar to this one and each had ended with all four teachers refusing to yield their convictions. Yet the discussions never affected relationships in the group and recurring critiques of Principal Werner provided an opportunity for everyone to release some steam.

"Well, colleagues," Peter said as he stood up, "time to get back to work. But before I leave, I must tell you again that you are wrong about Colleen. I hope you're teaching your students to be more objective. Our principal is a bright, energetic leader. She's not perfect, but we can help her get there."

"Wipe that smile off your face," Linda said. "Don't you recognize that you have lost another argument? Just to show you that I'm open-minded, I'll concede that Colleen has good intentions. Regrettably, she is terribly misguided."

Jake added sarcastically, "Yeah, I'll give her a 'B' for effort and a 'D' for achievement!"

The group always had a way of ending their discussions with a little humor to ease the tension. The four teachers scattered down different hallways to their next classes and their thoughts quickly shifted to other matters.

PROBLEM FRAMING

1. Assume you are the principal. Describe what you would want to accomplish in dealing with the situation described in this case.

2. Based on the evidence of contextual variables, describe the difficulty associated with achieving your objective.

QUESTIONS AND SUGGESTED ACTIVITIES

1. Share and critique the problem statements prepared by students in your class.

2. In the case, a charge is made that Dr. Werner basically ignores high-achieving teachers and students. Discuss the merits of this accusation.

3. As principal, would you be concerned if teachers had vastly different expectations of your leadership style? Why or why not?

4. Do you think that Dr. Werner should spend more time in the teachers' lounge? Why or why not?

5. Describe and then compare the leadership styles of the previous principal, Mr. Calbo, and the current principal, Dr. Werner. Discuss the strengths and weaknesses of each style.

6. The principal's critics believe they should be paid for "extra" assignments, such as chaperoning student events. Do you agree with them? Provide a brief rationale for your position.

7. Develop a list of criteria that could be used to determine if a principal is competent, then compare your criteria with those developed by other students in your class.

8. Should Peter Weller tell Dr. Werner that many of the teachers are displeased with her leadership style? Why or why not?

9. Based on the information in the case, is Principal Werner a transformational leader? Explain your response.

10. Identify actions Dr. Werner could take to reduce teacher criticism.

SUGGESTED READINGS

Bogler, R. (2001). The influence of leadership style on teacher job satisfaction. *Educational Administration Quarterly, 37*(5), 662–683.

Duncan, P. K., & Seguin, C. A. (2002). The perfect match: A case study of a first-year woman principal. *Journal of School Leadership, 12*(6), 608–639.

Eden, D. (1998). The paradox of school leadership. *Journal of Educational Administration, 36*(3–4), 249–261.

Erickson, H. (1985). Conflict and the female principal. *Phi Delta Kappan, 67,* 288–291.

Hallinger, P. (1992). The evolving role of the American principals: From managerial to instructional to transformational leaders. *Journal of Educational Administration, 3*(3), 35–48.

Hart, A. (1991). Leader succession and socialization: A synthesis. *Review of Educational Research, 61,* 451–474.

Hart, A. (1993). *Principal succession: Establishing leadership in schools.* Albany: State University of New York Press.

Kochan, F. K., Spencer, W. A., & Mathews, J. G. (2000). Gender-based perceptions of the challenges, changes, and essential skills of the principalship. *Journal of School Leadership, 10*(4), 290–310.

Kowalski, T. J. (2003). *Contemporary school administration: An introduction* (2nd ed.). Boston: Allyn and Bacon (see Chapters 9 and 15).

Krug, S. (1993). Leadership craft and the crafting of school leaders. *Phi Delta Kappan, 75*(3), 240–244.

Leithwood, K. (1992). The move toward transformational leadership. *Educational Leadership, 49*(5), 8–12.

Marks, H. M, & Printy, S. M. (2003). Principal leadership and school performance: An integration of transformational and instructional leadership. *Educational Administration Quarterly, 39*(3), 370–397.

Meadows, B. (1992). Nurturing cooperation and responsibility in a school environment. *Phi Delta Kappan, 73*(6), 480–481.

Ogawa, R. (1991). Enchantment, disenchantment, and accommodation: How a faculty made sense of the succession of its principal. *Educational Administration Quarterly, 27*(1), 30–60.

Pepper, K., & Thomas, L. H. (2002). Making a change: The effects of the leadership role on school *Learning Environments Research, 5*(2), 155–166.

Peterson, K., & Kelley, C. (2001). Transforming school leadership. *Leadership, 30*(3), 8–11.

Roesner, C. (1987). Principals' leadership behavior: Do you see yourself as your subordinates see you? *NASSP Bulletin, 71*(502), 68–71.

Rossmiller, R. (1992). The secondary school principal and teachers' quality of work life. *Educational Management and Administration, 20*(3), 132–146.

Valentine, J., & Bowman, M. (1991). Effective principal, effective school: Does research support the assumption? *NASSP Bulletin, 75*(539), 1–7.

Wallace, D. D., & Colbert, E. (2002). Not just idle talk. *Principal Leadership (High School Ed.), 2*(7), 42–44.

Wells, D. (1985). The perfect principal: A teacher's fantasy. *Principal, 65*(1), 27.

REFERENCES

Bass, B. M. (1985). *Leadership and performance beyond expectations.* New York: Free Press.

Bennis, W. B. (1984). The four competencies of leadership. *Training and Development Journal, 38*(8), 14–19.

Bennis, W. B., & Nannus, B. (1985). *Leaders: The strategies for taking charge*. New York: Harper & Row.

Burns, J. (1978). *Leadership*. New York: Harper and Row.

Kowalski, T. J. (2003). *Contemporary school administration: An introduction* (2nd ed.). Boston: Allyn and Bacon.

Kowalski, T. J. (2006). *The school superintendent: Theory, practice, and cases* (2nd ed.). Thousand Oaks, CA: Sage.

Kowalski, T. J., Petersen, G. J., & Fusarelli, L. D. (2007). *Effective communication for school administrators: An imperative in an information age*. Lanham, MD: Rowman and Littlefield Education.

Wirt, F., & Kirst, M. (2001).*The political dynamics of American education*. Berkeley, CA: McCutchan.

Yukl, G. (1989). *Leadership in organizations* (2nd ed.). Englewood Cliffs, NJ: Prentice-Hall.

Yukl, G. (2006). *Leadership in organizations* (6th ed.). Upper Saddle River, NJ: Pearson, Prentice Hall.

Get Rid of the Sloppy Assistant Principal

Background Information

Teachers quickly realize that administrators differ with respect to leadership style. Some principals and assistant principals, for instance, are controlling while others are passive. Some prefer to devote as much time as possible to management (e.g., controlling fiscal resources, applying discipline policy), while others prefer to be engaged in leadership responsibilities (e.g., visioning, planning). Behavior differences are primarily explained by two factors. First, each administrator is a unique individual who brings his or her personality, needs, and interests to the position (Hanson, 2003). Second, organizational expectations, expressed explicitly in job descriptions and implicitly in school culture, are not constant (Kowalski, 2006). Equally important, the degree to which school district officials tolerate behavior that is incongruent with established norms is inconstant.

Some school boards and superintendents may be very intolerant when it comes to dealing with behaviors they find to be unacceptable. Typically, they promulgate and then enforce policies, rules, and regulations intended to ensure that individual proclivities do not trump organizational standards (Kowalski, 2006). Many, but not all, administrators respond by being compliant, even if the behavioral norms imposed on them make them feel uncomfortable or restricted. Those who elect to ignore or combat organizational expectations are almost certain to experience *role conflict*.

Role conflict is created when an administrator encounters opposing or competing job performance expectations (Owens, 2004). Forces that are responsible for this discord may be categorized as follows:

- *Conflict between or among administrators.* Even though role expectations may be formalized in job descriptions, administrators working together may not interpret or accept them uniformly. As an example, a principal and assistant principal may disagree over the role responsibilities of an assistant principal.
- *Conflict between an administrator and a group.* Despite the presence of job descriptions, administrators often discover that teachers, other employees, students, and parents often ignore or do not accept these standards. As an example, the superintendent may expect all administrators to be loyal to the administrative team while teachers expect principals and assistant principals to be their advocates.
- *Conflict between role and personality.* One of the most frequent types of role conflict involves discord between an individual's personal dispositions and the formal

expectations established by the organization. As an example, an assistant principal may have a high need to be liked and accepted by everyone, while the organization expects him to be a stern manager and disciplinarian.

Role conflict is fueled by uncertainty and confusion. For example, the school board and superintendent may encourage a principal to take risks in pursuing school improvement; however, the prevailing performance evaluation and merit compensation programs actually reward failure avoidance. The principal receives mixed messages. The negative effects of role conflict on an administrator can range from excessive stress (e.g., Gmelch & Torelli, 1994) to reduced job satisfaction (e.g., Eckman, 2002).

Role conflict is prevalent in school administration because most principals and assistant principals are required to assume multiple and often seemingly contradictory functions. As examples, they are instructional leaders, effective managers, caring facilitators, empathetic counselors, rational planners, skillful organizers, objective evaluators, and congenial representatives of their schools (Kowalski, 2003). The knowledge, skills, and dispositions required for these assignments are not the same. Consequently, the degree of comfort associated with performing these duties varies depending on the individual. For example, an assistant principal may be comfortable conducting classroom observations but uncomfortable dealing with parents. The complexity of assignments is one reason why school administrators are often vulnerable to criticism; that is, their critics can often identify an area of responsibility in which their performance is not excellent.

This case is about role conflict encountered by a high school assistant principal employed in an affluent suburban community. The superintendent and his associate surprise the high school principal by recommending that the assistant principal be reassigned to a teaching position because of his personal appearance. In addition to role conflict, the case presents a myriad of ethical and legal questions and demonstrates how poor communication can produce or fuel conflict.

Key Areas for Reflection

1. Relationship between organizational role and individual personality
2. Behavioral transitions between teaching and administration
3. Ethical and legal dimensions of performance evaluation
4. Community environment and influence on school culture
5. Communication and organizational conflict

The Case

Community

Thomas Creek is located approximately twelve miles from a major city in the western part of New York State. With quiet, tree-lined streets and attractive homes, it is an upper-middle-class suburb. Nearly two-thirds of the adult residents are college graduates, with about 15 percent being self-employed professionals (e.g., lawyers, physicians, architects). In the latest official census, 76 percent of the population identified their race as Caucasian. The overall population, however, has declined slightly, primarily for two reasons: There is no available land for residential development, and the average age of community residents keeps increasing.

Thomas Creek School District

A brochure distributed by the local Chamber of Commerce describes Thomas Creek as "a diverse community that values education." The Thomas Creek School District (TCSD) has been recognized consistently as a top-performing system. The district includes three elementary schools (grades K–5), a middle school (grades 6–8), and a high school (grades 9–12). The overall enrollment is 2,287 students, a figure well below the peak enrollment of 3,143 that occurred 30 years ago.

Administrative and teacher salaries rank in the top 15 percent in the state and in the top 7 percent nationally. The school board has five members, each elected to a three-year term. The district's administrative staff (excluding building-level administrators) includes the superintendent, an associate superintendent, a business manager, and a director of special services.

Thomas Creek High School

The Thomas Creek High School (TCHS) is clearly the "centerpiece" of the community's commitment to education. Though more than 45 years old, the interior was recently renovated and the facility is in excellent condition. With its ivy-covered brick exterior and spacious parklike setting, the building would be an asset to the aesthetic quality of any college campus.

The school enrolls approximately 700 students in grades 9–12. Staff turnover, other than for retirements, is rare. Consequently, the average age of the faculty is 53. In the past five years, for example, only three new teachers have joined the faculty. The curriculum reflects the fact that more than 90 percent of the graduates enroll in colleges and universities.

The Principal

Allen Miller, age 38, became the principal of TCHS three years ago. Prior to this assignment, he spent three years as the principal of a larger suburban high school in a suburb of Cleveland, Ohio. He is regarded as a dedicated administrator and a friendly, outgoing person. Always attired in a coat and tie, he is highly visible in the school as he moves through the hallways and frequently visits classrooms.

Principal Miller also devotes a good bit of time to community relations. As an example, every other week, he invites 10 parents randomly to meet with him to discuss education issues. He is an active member of the local Rotary Club, a member of the board for the local United Way, and often speaks to community groups.

In order to meet his commitments to instructional leadership and to community involvement, Allen has relegated most managerial responsibilities to his assistant principal. During the two years he served as assistant principal, Allen found tasks such as supervising custodians and overseeing student discipline to be demanding but unexciting responsibilities.

The Assistant Principal

George Hopkins has been employed at TCHS for twenty-seven years. For twenty-two of those years, he coached football and taught physical education. Many of the students still address him as "Coach" but recently he acquired a nickname—"The Enforcer." His new moniker reflects his role as the administrator who handles student discipline.

Unlike Principal Miller, George prefers to spend his time with managerial duties. Though a friendly person, he is reserved and somewhat introverted. During faculty meetings, for example, he rarely speaks unless required to make a report. He maintains a close relationship with the athletic staff and rarely misses a varsity-level athletic event.

On a typical school day, George wears neither a tie nor a coat. With his hair cropped in a short crew cut, he often wears a sweater or polo shirt displaying the school logo. The contrast between George and Allen is so obvious that faculty often refer to the two administrators as the "odd couple."

George never intended to be an administrator. He was persuaded to become the assistant principal by Allen's predecessor and his close friend, John Sturby. Mr. Sturby had been principal at TCHS for twelve years and knew that he would be retiring shortly. When Allen was named the new principal, George submitted his resignation, asking that he be allowed to return to teaching. After speaking with many of the faculty, however, Allen requested George to remain as assistant principal. Allen has never regretted that decision and during each of the three years the two worked together, Allen recommended George for the maximum merit salary increase.

The Superintendent and Associate Superintendent

The superintendent, Ronald O'Brien, and the associate superintendent, Valerie Daniels, were essentially employed as a "team" two years ago. They had worked together in the same capacities for four years in another state. Dr. O'Brien, now age 57, has been a superintendent in four schools systems for a total of twenty-four years. Unlike his predecessor, Dr. Matthew Zachary, he is not a "hands-on" administrator. That is, he spends a considerable amount of his time out of the office and even out of the school district. Day-to-day operations are handled by his associate, Dr. Daniels. In fact, the district's principals and other central office administrators report directly to her and she is the only employee reporting directly to the superintendent.

After just two years in his current position, Dr. O'Brien has been appointed to the board for the local Chamber of Commerce and to the governor's task force on school improvement. In addition, he was recently elected president of the alumni association of his alma mater.

Perhaps Superintendent O'Brien's greatest strength is his ability to develop positive relationships with school board members. He invites them to his home for dinner twice a year and has lunch with each member separately at least twice each year. He already has become close personal friends with two of the board members.

Relationship between the High School Principal and the Superintendent

When he first arrived in Thomas Creek, Dr. O'Brien was disappointed to discover that Principal Miller did not have a doctoral degree. In the district where he previously served as superintendent, all but one principal had the degree. Shortly after taking the helm in the TCSD, he informed Mr. Miller that he was expected to pursue the degree, especially since the opportunity to do so on a part-time basis was available at the state university located just 15 minutes from Thomas Creek. Allen heeded the directive and applied for admission to that program.

Dr. O'Brien quickly gained confidence in the high school principal, especially after he was formally admitted to the doctoral program. After working with him for just one year, he nominated Allen for the state's principal-of-the-year award. In his letter of nomination, he wrote, "Allen Miller is an outstanding leader. He is a dedicated professional who provides a positive role model for the teachers and students. He represents the values and beliefs that make Thomas Creek High School one of the best secondary schools in the nation."

Most of Principal Miller's contact with district administration was through Dr. Daniels. She visits schools weekly and conducts staff meetings with the principals on a biweekly basis. Dr. O'Brien only occasionally attends these meetings; he was present at five of them in the past year. In two years, Allen has met alone with the superintendent on just three occasions. Even so, he has a great deal of respect for Dr. O'Brien and views him as a mentor and role model.

Performance Evaluation

The associate superintendent evaluates the performance of the principals annually. The results are presented and discussed in conferences scheduled in March. The conferences take place in Dr. O'Brien's office and he is always in attendance even though Dr. Daniels conducts the session. After she completes her evaluation and the principal has had an opportunity to respond to it, the superintendent reveals his recommendation for a merit salary increase. Administrator compensation is based solely on merit.

Administrator performance evaluation follows a specific sequence. First, principals evaluate assistant principals. During a conference in which the outcomes are discussed, the principal informs the assistant of his or her recommended salary increase category (*high merit, average merit, low merit, no increase*). By policy, the principal's recommendation can be changed by the superintendent. Next, principals meet with the associate superintendent and superintendent and receive an evaluation and are then informed of their recommended salary increase category.

The Incident

Given the fact that the superintendent had nominated him for an award, Allen assumed that this year's evaluation conference with Dr. Daniels and Dr. O'Brien would be very positive. So as he was departing the high school, he told his secretary that the scheduled 9:40 A.M. would probably be over by 10:30. He said he expected to be back at the high school no later than 11:00 A.M.

After Allen entered the superintendent's office, he sat in one of the three chairs surrounding a small round table. After the three administrators exchanged pleasantries, Dr. Daniels asked Allen to present his evaluation of George Hopkins. The district's evaluation instrument contains twenty-four items; the evaluator rates the evaluatee as excellent, above average, average, or below average for each of them. Allen rated George as being excellent on nineteen criteria; four others were rated as above average; only one, personal appearance, was rated as being average.

"You know how former coaches dress," Allen commented with a smile. "They never seem to stop looking like coaches."

Allen intended his comment to be humorous but the two administrators sitting across from him did not laugh. Affected by their lack of reaction, Allen quickly retracted his grin, and then there was an awkward moment of silence. Allen now sensed that something could be wrong. He was becoming increasingly uncomfortable but not sufficiently so to break the silence.

After what seemed like 10 minutes but actually was only 1 minute, Dr. Daniels spoke. Looking directly into Allen's eyes, she said, "The high school is a source of tremendous pride in this community. We believe your leadership has enhanced that reputation. However, we want to ensure that we keep building that reputation. When the assistant principal looks more like a custodian than an assistant principal, that employee is detracting from rather than enhancing the school's climate. Rating his appearance as average is not very objective. I've never seen him wear a coat and tie at work, and quite frankly, he just isn't very well groomed."

Allen was stunned by her harsh appraisal. George's dress habits had not changed in twenty-seven years. Why was the associate superintendent now making it an issue? He asked Dr. Daniels, "If his appearance is unacceptable, why wasn't this matter discussed last year?"

Although the question was not directed to him, Dr. O'Brien elected to answer. "We did not make it an issue because we wanted to make sure our observations were accurate. Moreover, we wanted more to build your confidence. We accepted your evaluation of George and your salary recommendation for him as a courtesy to you. In retrospect, maybe we should not have done that. Now, however, we feel it is necessary to be candid with you."

Allen responded, "So what does this mean? I have recommended George for the high merit category and I'm convinced he deserves that recommendation. His overall performance has been outstanding."

"This matter goes beyond a merit salary decision," Dr. Daniels answered. "To be blunt, we believe George should not be an assistant principal. He can return to teaching. We are willing to give him the option of teaching driver education during the summer in order to minimize his salary reduction. Our discussions with school board members revealed that George never wanted to be an administrator in the first place. Apparently, our predecessor acted with his heart and not his mind in pushing him into a job he did not want."

Allen stared across the table in disbelief. Thoughts raced through his mind and he tried to retain his composure. "I had no idea you were negative about George. So allow me to be blunt in responding. I don't agree that he should be reassigned. George has been and remains an effective assistant principal. In fact, he probably has not received the level of recognition he deserves. If he is forced to return to the classroom, my opportunities to work with teachers and with parents will be reduced. George is as loyal and dedicated as any person with whom I have been associated. He doesn't deserve to be treated in this manner."

Dr. O'Brien again spoke. "Allen, please keep an open mind. We are not asking you to change your salary recommendation or your evaluation. I will explain to the board that Valerie and I decided to not accept your recommendations. We will make it clear that reassigning George is our decision. Neither George nor the faculty can blame you. The best alternative would be for George to request a reassignment but he probably won't do that unless you ask him to do so. And given your reactions, I'm assuming that is not an option. In any event, we don't want you resisting us publicly."

"He's right, Allen," Valerie Daniels interjected. "You have provided excellent leadership and if you had an assistant who projects a much more positive image, you could be even more effective. You're focusing on what you have to lose; we are focusing on what you have to gain. We have given this issue much thought. There are many administrators who can be as effective as George in handling discipline and management responsibilities." Dr. O'Brien stood and walked to where Allen was sitting. He put his hand on Allen's shoulder and said, "We need your assurance that you will act maturely and appropriately. We're not asking you to accept our decision; we're asking you not to oppose it either with the faculty or with the public."

PROBLEM FRAMING

1. Assume you are the principal. Describe what you would want to accomplish in dealing with the situation described in this case.

2. Based on the evidence of contextual variables, describe the difficulty associated with achieving your objective.

QUESTIONS AND SUGGESTED ACTIVITIES

1. Share and critique the problem statements prepared by students in your class.

2. Discuss the reasons why some school district officials establish dress standards for principals and assistant principals.

3. Is the nature and culture of the local community a factor in this case? Why or why not?

4. New assistant principals typically experience socialization to their role. What is the process of socialization? Is it relevant to this case?

5. Determine if public schools in your geographic area have a policy concerning attire for administrators and teachers and then compare the nature of those policies.

6. Why do you think the superintendent and associate superintendent have placed so much emphasis on the assistant principal's personal appearance?

7. What values and beliefs may shape norms for administrative attire?

8. Evaluate the performance evaluation process used in the case study and identify possible weaknesses that contributed to the problem facing the principal.

9. Do you believe that there is a relationship between administrative appearance and job performance? Why or why not?

10. To what extent is the principal in this case responsible for criticism directed at his assistant?

SUGGESTED READINGS

Calabrese, R., & Tucker-Ladd, P. (1991). The principal and assistant principal: A mentoring relationship. *NASSP Bulletin, 75*(533), 67–74.

Duke, D. (1992). Concepts of administrative effectiveness and the evaluation of school administrators. *Journal of Personnel Evaluation in Education, 6*(2), 103–121.

Gerke, W. (2004). More than a disciplinarian. *Principal Leadership, 5*(3), 39–41.

Goodson, C. P. (2000). Assisting the assistant principal. *Principal, 79*(4), 56–57.

Johnson, C. M. (2004). Reflections on the vice principalship. *Leadership, 34*(1), 32–34.

Johnston, D. L. (1999). The seven no-no's of performance evaluation. *School Administrator, 56*(11), 47–48.

Lang, R. (1986). The hidden dress code dilemma. *Clearing House, 59*(6), 277–279.

Manatt, R. P. (2000). Feedback at 360 degrees. *School Administrator, 57*(9), 10–11.

Marshall, C. (1992). *The assistant principal: Leadership chores and challenges.* Newbury Park, CA: Corwin.

Marshall, C., & Greenfield, W. (1985). The socialization of the assistant principal: Implications for school leadership. *Education and Urban Society, 18*(1), 3–8.

Michel, G. J. (1996). *Socialization and career orientation of the assistant principal.* (ERIC Document Reproduction Service No. ED395 381)

Norton, M. S., & Kriekard, J. (1987). Real and ideal competencies for the assistant principal. *NASSP Bulletin, 71*(501), 23–30.

Richard, A. (2000, April 12). Toughest job in education? *Education Week, 19*(31), 44–48.

Russo, A. (2004). Evaluating administrators with portfolios. *School Administrator, 61*(9), 34–38.

Weller, L. D., & Weller, S. J. (2002). *The assistant principal: Essentials for effective school leadership.* Thousand Oaks, CA: Corwin Press.

REFERENCES

Eckman, E. W. (2002). Woman high school principals: Perspectives on role conflict, role commitment, and job satisfaction. *Journal of School Leadership, 12*(1), 57–77.

Gmelch, W. H., & Torelli, J. A. (1994). The association of role conflict and ambiguity with administrator stress and burnout. *Journal of School Leadership, 4*(3), 341–56.

Hanson, E. M. (2003). *Educational administration and organizational behavior* (5th ed.). Boston: Allyn and Bacon.

Kowalski, T. J. (2003). *Contemporary school administration: An introduction* (2nd ed.). Boston: Allyn and Bacon.

Kowalski, T. J. (2006). *The school superintendent: Theory, practice, and cases* (2nd ed.). Thousand Oaks, CA: Sage.

Owens, R. C. (2004). *Organizational behavior in education: Adaptive leadership and school reform* (8th ed.). Boston: Allyn and Bacon.

Let the Committee Decide

Background Information

During the typical work day, administrators are required to make dozens of decisions. Some are simple and nonthreatening, such as deciding what to wear to work or what to eat for lunch. Others, however, involve complex and high-risk choices, such as adjudicating conflict between two teachers. Basically, a decision has three components: a goal (what the administrator wants to accomplish by making a decision), options for attaining the goal, and the selection of the preferred option (Welch, 2002).

An administrator's approach to decision making (i.e., his or her process) is determined by an intricate mix of personal and contextual factors. On a personal level behavior is shaped by the decision maker's philosophical dispositions (personal values and beliefs), personal bias, and leadership style (Kowalski, 2006). Contextually, it is affected by demands and constraints that are generated both by society and by the district or school (Sergiovanni, 2005). When making consequential decisions, administrators are urged to consider both normative and descriptive paradigms; the former prescribe an approach for decision making and the latter explain how decisions are actually made. Four decision models have been especially prevalent in the literature on school administration (Estler, 1988).

1. *Rational-bureaucratic*: A normative paradigm emphasizing problem analysis, data collection, alternative choices, and the objective selection of the ideal decision.
2. *Participatory*: A normative paradigm nested in beliefs that participation increases productivity, morale, and the quality of information.
3. *Political*: Both a normative and descriptive paradigm that relies on reaching compromises among vested interest groups.
4. *Organized anarchy*: A descriptive paradigm revealing that many decisions are made through a mix of changing participants, opportunities for change, and predetermined preferences.

Studying various models used by district and school officials, Tartar and Hoy (1998) concluded that none was universally superior. Nevertheless, these paradigms facilitate an understanding of decision-making behavior, especially in relation to answering two essential questions about process: Were essential activities completed? How were they completed?

Scholars have long recognized that personal, social, and political variables produce behavioral inconsistencies among administrators. In many organizations, these discrepancies are viewed negatively because they contribute to uncertainty. Consequently, rational and easily understood decision-making models intended to control individualism and errors were widely promoted. Drucker (1974), for instance, reduced the act of organizational decision making to five steps:

1. Defining the problem
2. Analyzing the problem
3. Developing alternative solutions
4. Selecting a best solution
5. Taking action

Rational decision making is rooted in classical theory and generally prescribes that administrators make important decisions alone. Researchers studying district and school administrators (e.g., Crowson, 1989; Walker, 1994), however, have found that rational models, such as Drucker's proposed paradigm, either have not been deployed consistently or have not been deployed as intended. Deviations reflect the fact that educational institutions are sociopolitical systems in which power and authority is distributed among formal and informal groups. Consequently, administrators who attempt to make objective choices based on evidence often yield to emotional and political pressures exerted by individuals and groups who possess power.

In the past few decades, participatory decision making has been advocated in relation to school improvement (Anderson, 1998). Involving others, and especially teachers, is deemed appropriate for at least three reasons:

1. In a democratic society, employees, parents, and others have a right to be involved in critical matters.
2. The quality of decisions is enhanced by a broader knowledge base and a variety of viewpoints.
3. Participation increases employee morale and productivity (Kowalski, 2003).

Shared decision making, however, is not problem-free. For example, the process can (a) be inefficient (Clark, Clark, & Irvin, 1997), (b) produce decisions based on social unity rather than on facts (a condition referred to as "groupthink") (Janis, 1982), and (c) increase the probability of bias and error (because of multiple participants) (Carroll & Johnson, 1990). Moreover, administrators risk being criticized for evading their responsibility when they use committees to make important decisions (Kowalski, Lasley, & Mahoney, 2008).

This case describes a new superintendent's decision to address a controversial issue by appointing a special committee having representatives of various stakeholder groups. The conflict (over whether principals should have total control of activity funds) and the superintendent's preference for a participatory approach to resolving the conflict spawn additional tensions among the administrators. When a decision is reached, some key figures are critical and raise questions about the superintendent's leadership style.

Key Areas for Reflection

1. Decision making
2. Conflict and conflict resolution
3. Use of committees
4. Subordinate expectations of a new superintendent
5. Leadership style

The Case

Fullmer, a city of 45,000 residents, is the seat of government for Oxford County (population 78,000). Located in the western part of a mid-Atlantic state, it is known for its scenic beauty. In recent years, the population has increased about 1 percent every two years. The growth is largely attributable to the development of condominiums and apartment complexes designed primarily for retirees.

Over the past twenty years, most of the counties in this part of the state developed industrial parks, enterprise zones, and tax abatement programs in an effort to attract both foreign and domestic companies. Oxford County, however, has been the exception. Many residents fear that increased industrial development would change the character of the community and harm the environment. There are a handful of small companies scattered across the county, and executives at several of them are considering relocating to other counties that have developed industrial parks and highways.

In addition to its natural beauty, Oxford County has attracted new residents for three other reasons. First, real estate costs remain comparatively low; second, property taxes are comparatively low; third, a new hospital, costing nearly $90 million and located in Fullmer, is one of the state's most modern health facilities.

The School District

The Oxford County School District (OCSD), serving the entire county, has a current enrollment of 19,700 students. There are two high schools, four middle schools, thirteen elementary schools, and a career-technical center. The district's enrollment has declined about 1 percent over the past decade, but in the last two years, kindergarten enrollments have declined by 3 percent.

The district's central office staff has remained very stable for ten years. The two assistant superintendents, Bob Andrevet (curriculum) and Pamela Davis (business) have been in their current positions for fourteen and ten years respectively. The superintendent, Dr. Rudy Quillen, is only in his first year of service in the district. He replaced Orville Cruthers, who retired after having been superintendent for eleven years.

The Incident

Dr. Quillen arrived in Oxford County in mid-July. For the previous three years, he had been superintendent in a much smaller district (enrollment 2,400) in a neighboring state. Several OCSD board members met him when they attended his presentation on goal setting at a national conference. Impressed with his performance, they had encouraged him to apply for the impending vacancy in their district. Though he was only 38 years old, Rudy Quillen had twelve years of administrative experience.

Soon after he began his new position, Dr. Quillen faced his first controversy. The schools had activity funds that were controlled entirely by principals. They had existed for as long as anyone could remember. Two years earlier, however, Dr. Davis, the assistant superintendent for business, had recommended that they be subject to district controls. The previous superintendent decided not to deal with the issue, explaining that the matter should be addressed by the new superintendent.

Dr. Davis has been the district's top financial administrator for five years. As a former principal in the district, she was well aware of how activity funds could be used and how they were managed. Fearing that the funds might be misused, she wanted to make three changes:

1. A minimum of two persons, most likely the principal and assistant superintendent for business, would have to approve expenditures.
2. The accounting procedures for the funds would move from the principals to the district business office.
3. The district business office would complete an annual audit of the funds.

After Dr. Quillen was named the new superintendent but before he officially assumed the position, Dr. Davis decided to plant a seed with the school board. At Superintendent Cruthers' last official board meeting, she publicly told the board members that she would be recommending her proposed changes for the school activity funds to the new superintendent. Superintendent Cruthers was surprised that she made this announcement, especially since he had suggested that she first discuss the matter with the new superintendent.

Just a few days after Dr. Quillen assumed his new position, Dr. Davis presented the issue of the activity funds to him. The superintendent was familiar with the topic, and he was aware that concerns often are expressed in relation to the way in which they are managed. After listening politely to his assistant, he agreed to take the matter under consideration. After that meeting, he first talked with the school system's attorney and subsequently with one of the attorneys from the state school boards' association. Both lawyers said that the current procedures used in the school district were legal, but they added that the procedures may elevate the risk of management errors and legal violations.

Dr. Quillen held monthly administrative meetings that were attended by principals and district-level administrators. At the second of these meetings, he informed the group that Dr. Davis had requested him to examine the current procedures for activity funds management. He invited members of the administrative team to comment on the matter before the next monthly administrative meeting. Responding to the invitation, several principals sent e-mail messages to the superintendent expressing their opposition to changing current procedures. No principal expressed support for making changes.

At the November meeting, Dr. Davis was asked to describe the three changes she had proposed to the superintendent. Anticipating opposition from other administrators, she also detailed a procedure assuring that approval from the district for fund expenditures would not be unduly cumbersome or time consuming.

After she finished, Dr. Quillen shared the information he had received from the two attorneys. He then invited others to comment on the matter. Nearly all the principals said they were opposed to the recommended changes. Uniformly, they argued that Dr. Davis's proposal diminished their authority.

After principals completed their comments, Dr. Quillen spoke again. "The changes Pamela is recommending actually provide a safety valve for principals. There have been numerous incidents in other districts in which principals have gotten into legal or political difficulties with activity funds. Expenditure approvals from me or another person in my office would be based solely on two criteria: the legality of the expenditure and the sufficiency of funds to cover the expenditure. Neither Pam nor I will be second-guessing your decisions."

One of the high school principals immediately responded. "Every time we turn around, things are being centralized in this district. Mistakes are often made in business offices too. We haven't had any problems, so why penalize us?"

Judging that the issue was not going to be resolved at this meeting, Dr. Quillen tabled the matter. Dr. Davis was disappointed. She concluded that he, like his predecessor, simply did not want to make difficult decisions.

"There are some serious management questions that need to be resolved about these funds," she said with emotion. "Just because I may be alone in supporting changes does not mean that I am wrong. At the very least, I request that we study this issue and do so objectively."

Sensing that tension was escalating in the room, Dr. Quillen said, "First, I want to make it clear that I'm not rejecting Pamela's recommendation. In fact, I appreciate her persistence. I'm sure you share my desire for her to be a strong and forceful business manager. Second, I agree with her suggestion that we study this matter in greater detail. I have doubts, however, that any of us will be able to look at the proposed changes rationally. When we meet next month, I hope to have a process in place so that the recommended changes can be evaluated properly. If you have recommendations regarding how we should deal with this matter, please share them."

As pledged, Dr. Quillen revisited the activity fund controversy at the December meeting. The level of interest in this conflict was heightened by the realization that this would be his first difficult decision. Consequently, the administrators believed that how he pursued and resolved this matter would be symbolically important to his tenure as superintendent. Skeptics predicted that Dr. Quillen would behave much like his predecessor; that is, he would find a way to let the matter die a natural death. Pessimists feared that he would reveal himself to be an autocrat; that is, he would rule unilaterally once he was convinced that consensus was not possible.

Everyone at the meeting listened attentively as the superintendent began to speak.

"I have heard from many of you since our last meeting, and I have weighed your comments carefully," he said. "Some of you have framed the control of activity funds in an organizational context—that is, you see it primarily as a matter of jurisdictional dispute between district and school administration. In your eyes, this matter should be decided by Bob Andrevet because he has line authority for principals and they have control of the funds. Several framed the recommended changes as a management issue. In their eyes, all financial matters should fall within the jurisdiction of Dr. Davis. Last, several of you believe this issue should be settled by reaching an acceptable compromise between Pamela's recommendations and the status quo. For example, I should approve her recommendation for the annual audits but reject the remaining recommendations. After weighing your input, I have decided to appoint an ad hoc committee to study this issue and to then forward a recommendation to me. I am appointing the following persons to the committee: Regina Steckler, an elementary school teacher; Jackson Wells, a high school teacher; Bennett Wyler, a parent and accountant; Agnes Dupree, a parent and attorney; and Ann Major, the district's director of federal programs. I have also decided to appoint Ann as the committee's chair. Bob Andrevet and Pamela Davis will be nonvoting advisors to the committee."

The room fell silent. After a brief period, one of the principals asked, "Why are no principals appointed to this committee? They are the persons most directly involved and affected."

Dr. Quillen answered. "I want the process to be as objective as possible. It is clear that most if not all of you have already made up your minds on this matter. I spoke with Ann Major, and she assures me that she does not have an opinion on the recommendations at this time."

Immediately after the meeting, Pamela Davis spoke with the superintendent in his office. She expressed disappointment with his decision to appoint this committee. She argued that decision committees were basically political groups and consequently, she would lose on this matter because she clearly was in the minority. "Doing what is right is often unpopular," she told the superintendent. "I feel that my legitimate authority is being undermined and I resent that. School activity funds are clearly a fiscal matter and I am the chief fiscal officer. By establishing this committee, you are undermining my authority. I guarantee that we will eventually have a problem with these funds and when that happens, Bob [Andrevet] and the principals will tell the school board and public that I should have prevented it."

Dr. Quillen recognized that she was upset, so he decided not to discuss the matter further. He simply asked her to be patient and to delay judgment until the committee had concluded its assignment.

Bob Andrevet also visited the superintendent after the meeting. He too expressed displeasure with the decision to appoint the committee. He feared that Pamela would bully the committee to support the proposed changes by arguing that doing so is the legally safe alternative.

PROBLEM FRAMING

1. Assume you are the superintendent. Describe what you would want to accomplish in dealing with the situation described in this case.

2. Based on the evidence of contextual variables, describe the difficulty associated with achieving your objective.

QUESTIONS AND SUGGESTED ACTIVITIES

1. Share and critique the problem statements prepared by students in your class.

2. By appointing the ad hoc committee, has the superintendent undermined the authority of the assistant superintendent for business? Why or why not?

3. The superintendent believes that the issue of placing controls on the activity funds has been viewed in three different ways: (a) as a matter of organizational jurisdiction; (b) as a management responsibility; (c) as a political controversy. What is the essence of each perspective?

4. Because the superintendent is new to the district and relatively unknown to the other administrators, they believe his decision to appoint a committee established a precedent for his leadership style. Discuss whether you agree or disagree with this conviction.

5. The superintendent did not appoint principals to the ad hoc committee. Do you agree with this decision? Why or why not?

6. Group decision making has become increasingly common in schools. Identify factors that contribute to the popularity of this process.

7. Describe and contrast autocratic and democratic leadership styles. Identify how these styles affect the manner in which decision are made in districts and schools.

8. What options were available to the superintendent for dealing with the changes recommended by the assistant superintendent for business besides appointing the ad hoc committee?

9. The superintendent could refuse to make a decision on petty cash funds believing that the controversy will subside over time. What are the advantages and disadvantages of this alternative?

SUGGESTED READINGS

Brost, P. (2000). Shared decision making for better schools. *Principal Leadership (Middle School Ed.), 1*(3), 58–63.

Conway, J. (1984). The myth, mystery and mastery of participative decision making in education. *Educational Administration Quarterly, 20*(3), 11–40.

Cuzzetto, C. E. (2000). Student activity funds: Procedures and controls. *School Business Affairs, 66*(11), 22–25.

Feld, M. (1988). The bureaucracy, the superintendent, and change. *Education and Urban Society, 47*(8), 417–444.

Jackson, J. L. (2001). Politically competent decision making. *Principal Leadership (High School Ed.), 2*(4), 25–28.

Kessler, R. (1992). Shared decision making works! *Educational Leadership, 50*(1), 36–38.

Kowalski, T. J., Lasley, T. J., & Mahoney, J. (2008). *Data-driven decisions and school leadership: Best practices for school improvement.* Boston: Allyn and Bacon (see Chapter 4).

Lakowski, G. (1987). Values and decision making in educational administration. *Educational Administration Quarterly, 23*(4), 70–82.

Meadows, B. (1990). The rewards and risks of shared leadership. *Phi Delta Kappan, 71*(7), 545–548.

Meadows, B. J., & Saltzman, M. (2002). Shared decision making: An uneasy collaboration. *Principal, 81*(4), 41–48.

Mutter, D. W., & Parker, P. J. (2004). *School money matters: A handbook for principals.* Arlington, VA: Association for Supervision and Curriculum Development.

Negroni, P. J. (1999). The right badge of courage. *School Administrator, 56*(2), 14–16.

Rieger, B. J. (1995). Boundary realignment in the eye of the storm. *School Administrator, 52*(2), 24–26.

Tarter, C. J., & Hoy, W. K. (1998). Toward a contingency theory of decision making. *Journal of Educational Administration, 36*(3-4), 212–228.

Turnbull, B. (2003). Research note: Shared decision making—rhetoric versus reality. *Journal of School Leadership, 13*(5), 569–579.

REFERENCES

Anderson, G. L. (1998). Toward authentic participation: Deconstructing the discourses of participatory reforms in education. *American Educational Research Journal, 35*(4), 571–603.

Carroll, J. S. & Johnson, E. J. (1990). *Decision research: A field guide*. Newbury Park, CA: Sage.

Clark, S. N., Clark, D. C., & Irvin, J. L (1997). Collaborative decision making. *Middle School Journal, 28*(5), 54–56.

Crowson, R. L. (1989). Managerial ethics in educational administration: The rational choice approach. *Urban Education, 23*(4), 412–435.

Drucker, P. (1974). *Management: Tasks, responsibilities, practices*. New York: Harper and Row.

Estler, S. (1988). Decision making. In N. Boyan (Ed.), *Handbook of research on educational administration* (pp. 305–320). New York: Longman.

Janis, I. L. (1982). *Groupthink* (2nd ed.). Boston: Houghton Mifflin.

Kowalski, T. J. (2003). *Contemporary school administration: An introduction* (2nd ed.). Boston: Allyn and Bacon.

Kowalski, T. J. (2006). *The school superintendent: Theory, practice, and cases* (2nd ed.). Thousand Oaks, CA: Sage.

Kowalski, T. J., Lasley, T. J., & Mahoney, J. (2008). *Data-driven decisions and school leadership: Best practices for school improvement*. Boston: Allyn and Bacon.

Sergiovanni, T. J. (2005). *The principalship: A reflective practice approach* (5th ed.). Boston: Allyn and Bacon.

Tarter, C. J., & Hoy, W. K. (1998). Toward a contingency theory of decision making. *Journal of Educational Administration, 36*(3–4), 212–228.

Walker, K. D. (1994). Notions of "ethical" among senior educational leaders. *Alberta Journal of Educational Research, 40*(1), 21–34.

Welch, D. A. (2002). *Decisions, decisions: The art of effective decision making*. Amherst, NY: Prometheus Books.

7 Old School Culture and a New Principal

Background Information

Evidence gathered from productive schools indicates that principals are influential to building and maintaining school cultures conducive to organizational learning (e.g., Kowalski, Petersen, & Fusarelli, 2007; Sergiovanni, 2004) and to implementing reforms (e.g., Datnow & Castellano, 2001). Contrary to popular belief, however, effective principals are neither saviors nor dictators. Rather, they have leadership styles that stress collaboration, facilitation, and professionalism (Foster, Loving, & Shumate, 2000). Reviewing research spanning 15 years, Hallinger and Heck (1998) concluded that principals influenced school effectiveness and student achievement in measurable but indirect ways. Their influence was often most discernible in school improvement documents, such as collaborative vision statements and specific planning goals.

Principal role expectations differ across schools, largely because no two schools are identical. Even principals who spend their entire administrative careers in the same school often encounter conflicting and changing expectations. Over time, principals usually discover that it is difficult to transition between being an instructional leader and a rational manager and even more difficult for them to meet the competing expectations of their supervisors, teachers, and community members (Langer & Boris-Schacter, 2003). Yet when restructuring became a preferred reform strategy circa 1990, scholars such as Michael Fullan (2002) were emphatic that principals had to be both instructional leaders and change agents. Otherwise, they would be unable to lead others to perform the difficult but necessary task of rebuilding teaching and learning cultures collectively.

Leadership style reflects deeply held personal or organizational values (Goldman, 1998). If a principal views teachers as lazy uninformed subordinates, for instance, then he or she is likely to be autocratic. As demonstrated in this case, value-based conflict (e.g., between an administrator and teachers) can be detrimental to school effectiveness and a major obstacle to school improvement (Kowalski, 2003). A veteran administrator volunteers to become the principal in an urban elementary school and after assuming the difficult assignment, he attempts change several existing practices. His ideas and the manner in which he pursues them do not conform with values shared by teachers and embedded in the school's culture.

Key Areas for Reflection

1. Principal as change agent
2. Values and beliefs as a determinant of leadership style
3. Social and political dimensions of schools
4. School culture and its effect on change initiatives
5. Resistance to change

The Case

Oliver Wendell Holmes Elementary School is housed in the third-oldest facility in this large California city. Located in a deteriorating neighborhood, the drab brick building with its rectangular shape exemplifies the unimaginative school design that was prevalent circa World War II. Over time, school officials failed to repair the sidewalks around the school or to remove the graffiti that was written on the playground. The area around the school became strewn with weeds and litter, and the broken swings and seesaws suggested that school officials had stopped trying to keep the area functional.

John Lattimore became principal of this troubled school three years ago. Having previously served in the same capacity at three of the district's other elementary schools, he has been an educator for thirty-one years, twenty-two of them in the role of principal. When the position at Holmes became vacant, John was the district's only sitting principal who applied for the job. At the time, he was principal of McKinley Elementary School, arguably the best elementary school in the district. John's fellow principals were baffled when he requested the reassignment. Why would he want to go to Holmes? Why would he leave a school where he was admired and respected to go to a school that has had six principals in the last fifteen years?

The superintendent, Dr. Ernest Gray, and the assistant superintendent for elementary education, Dr. Roshanda Danton, were also surprised after they received Mr. Lattimore's request to be reassigned to Holmes. Initially, Dr. Gray was dubious about moving Mr. Lattimore to Holmes. He was highly successful in his current assignment, and the superintendent feared that some parents and teachers would be displeased if he left. But this concern was weighed against the fear that it would be very difficult to find an experienced and competent person who would want the principal's job at Holmes. In addition, Mr. Lattimore convinced the superintendent that he would make a concerted effort to improve the troubled school.

During the first year at Holmes, Mr. Lattimore met with parents, got acquainted with students, and tried to develop a positive working relationship with the school's staff. He has a pleasant personality and most everyone liked him. In the second year of his tenure at Holmes, he began pursuing changes to long-standing rules and regulations. In particular, he focused on altering practices in two areas: suspending students for disciplinary reasons and retaining students in first grade. Holmes had the highest rates for both among the district's thirty-six elementary schools.

Initially, Mr. Lattimore attempted to frame these problems in a manner that would produce teacher support for change. He quickly learned, however, that most teachers strongly supported suspensions and grade-level retentions. Moreover, they were unconcerned that these actions occurred more frequently at their school than at other schools in the district. After spending nearly an entire school year trying to enlist their support, he decided to act unilaterally.

During the summer months prior to his third year at Holmes, Principal Lattimore sent a letter to teachers and other staff members (detailing changes in out-of-school suspension and retention rules. Specifically, he announced the following changes:

- Out-of-school suspensions would be restricted to violations that required such action under school district policy. Otherwise, students would be placed in a newly developed in-school suspension program.
- In order for a student to be retained in a grade level, the teacher would be required to produce evidence that he or she attempted remedial efforts and explanations of why the efforts failed. In addition, a student recommended for retention would have to be referred to a school psychologist for an examination; the psychologist's opinion would be a factor the principal would weigh in considering the recommendation for retention.

Prior to receiving this letter, many teachers had disagreed with Principal Lattimore's attempts to change conditions in the school but their opposition had been largely covert. The missive announcing that two major changes would be implemented prompted them to publicly criticize their principal. After the letter, the teachers began describing Mr. Lattimore as being both misguided and dictatorial. Even though the start of school was still several weeks away, teachers began meeting informally to discuss ways that they could prevent Principal Lattimore from imposing his will on the school. In one of these sessions attended by six teachers, a first-grade teacher summarized her feelings: "Sure he is friendly and cares about the students, but he is also naive. We've had principals with the same soft approach in the past and if you recall, they only made things at Holmes worse. I've talked to John about failing students and about suspensions, but he is not open to opposing ideas. I was hopeful after he came to Holmes because I thought we were finally getting an experienced and successful principal. Unfortunately, he's turned out to be just another disaster."

As the school year started, dissatisfaction among the teachers intensified. They began detailing their displeasure with the principal to parents in hopes of gaining political support. In early November, the teachers opposing Mr. Lattimore (70 percent of the school's faculty) decided to take decisive action: Accompanied by forty-two parents, they signed a petition requesting the principal's removal. The petition and the following cover letter were sent to Dr. Danton, the assistant superintendent for elementary education.

Dear Dr. Danton:

Over the past two and one-half years, the teachers at Oliver Wendell Holmes Elementary School have observed the leadership style of Mr. John Lattimore. While he is friendly, caring, and intelligent, his approach to student discipline and student retention simply will not work at this school. Most of the children who attend Holmes are from families living below the poverty level. Many receive little or no direction with regard to their personal behavior outside of school. Actually, most parents and guardians want the school to provide strict discipline and to set high academic expectations. Since coming to Holmes, Mr. Lattimore has weakened staff morale and provided little if any positive leadership.

To be direct, we reject Mr. Lattimore's decisions regarding student suspensions and grade-level retentions. Allowing disruptive and emotionally unstable children to remain in a classroom and promoting students to the next grade level when they are clearly unprepared diminish our ability to teach. Consequently, these actions reduce learning opportunities for other students.

Mr. Lattimore contends that he allowed us to participate in making changes. On the surface that may appear to be true, but, in reality, he ignored our input. In the end, he simply did what he always intended to do. Equally disappointing, he made these changes during the summer, anticipating that we could not respond.

We regret that we have lost confidence in our principal. Hopefully, his talents can be utilized more productively in another assignment. He is a good person and he means well. He cannot, however, effectively lead this school. We ask that he be removed as principal as soon as possible.

Respectfully,
[signed by 70 percent of the teachers and 42 parents]
cc: Dr. Gray, superintendent
School Board members
Ms. Hutchins, president of the local teachers' union

A copy of the letter, however, was not sent to Principal Lattimore; he first learned of it from Dr. Danton via a telephone conversation. He immediately went to her office and read the letter. After seeing the signatures, he became angry. Some of signers had been warm and friendly to his face; until now, he considered them to be supporters. Sensing his outrage, Dr. Danton asked him to think about the matter and they would meet again the following day. Principal Lattimore returned to school but stayed in his office with the door closed for the remainder of the day. He waited until all the teachers had left before going home.

The next morning, Mr. Lattimore and Dr. Danton met again. They had been friends and colleagues for many years. When Dr. Danton applied to be assistant superintendent for elementary education, he wrote a letter of support for her. John was still angry when he entered her office. He said he had thought about the situation and had concluded that the teachers had acted unethically, first by involving parents and then by writing the letter without informing him.

"You mean you had no idea that the teachers were this dissatisfied and that they were involving parents?" Dr. Danton asked.

"No," John answered. "I tried to do things correctly. I could have imposed change immediately after arriving at the school three years ago. The school was a mess. But I elected to give the faculty a chance to be part of the change process. I tried to get them to look at these issues. They refused to be open-minded. All they did was resist. No change was acceptable to them. The fact of the matter is that a small group of teachers has been running this school for a long time. No principal is going to succeed as long as they remain more powerful than the administrator. Quite frankly, I got to the point last year where I asked myself, Who is more important, the students or the teachers? My answer was the students. Did I know that some of teachers disagreed with the changes? Yes, I knew that. But I never thought they would stoop to involving parents and sending you this letter."

"John, did you allow them to have input before you made changes?" Dr. Danton inquired.

"The nature of the changes was discussed in faculty meetings last year. We never voted on them. A few teachers voiced opposition but most appeared indifferent. I told teachers they could see me privately if they felt uncomfortable discussing the changes in faculty meetings. Only two teachers did that and they both said they supported my ideas. Listen, I've been around these children in this school district for a long time—and so have you. Many have lives filled with grief and disappointments. Why should school be another unpleasant experience? Maybe, just maybe, by showing some love and compassion we could turn a few lives around. Maybe we could convince a few children that someone cares about them. Isn't that important? What do we accomplish when we suspend and fail children? We're punishing the parent, not the child. How will we ever teach these children to be responsible for their own behavior if we constantly rely on negative reinforcements?"

"What about social promotions? Are you really telling teachers not to fail students at any grade level?" asked the assistant superintendent.

"Failing children who are already at risk simply does not work. They prefer to say that I favor social promotions. I prefer to say that I condemn failing children when it just makes it more likely they will never succeed as students; they will never graduate from high school."

Dr. Danton looked at him and asked, "John, would you consider another assignment at this time? I can arrange for you to be in the central office. Dr. Gray and I discussed this matter last night. He already has gotten calls from two board members about the petition. We are willing to assign you as assistant director of pupil personnel services immediately. This spring, Sheila Macey is retiring, and you would then move up to become the director. You would get a salary increase, and we would have a solution to the conflict at Holmes. Dr. Gray has said he would approve if you agree to accept the reassignment. I want to be clear, however, that we are not trying to push you from the school. If you decide to stay, we will work with you to try to resolve these problems. What do you think?"

"Roshanda, you should already know my answer. I've had other opportunities to work in the central office. I like being around students. No, I'm sorry, I'm not going to cut and run. I'm right, and if you give me time, I think I can turn the parents and teachers around."

"But John, I don't know if we have time. Dr. Gray doesn't want more political problems. One of the parents who signed the petition has a brother-in-law on the school board, and he is an influential minister in Holmes area. And if the union weighs in, we could really have trouble. Dr. Gray doesn't want to go to war on this issue."

John got up from his chair and nodded that he understood. He shook Dr. Danton's hand and left her office. As soon as he departed, Dr. Danton was disappointed because she anticipated he was not going to accept her offer to change positions. Mr. Lattimore also belonged to a union, the district's principals' union. He was highly respected by other administrators, and if he convinced them to support his position, a war between the teachers' union and the principals' union could develop. She began to see the dispute as a politically explosive issue.

PROBLEM FRAMING

1. Assume you are the principal. Describe what you would want to accomplish in dealing with the situation described in this case.

2. Based on the evidence of contextual variables, describe the difficulty associated with achieving your objective.

QUESTIONS SUGGESTED ACTIVITIES

1. Share and critique the problem statements prepared by students in your class.

2. Do you consider Mr. Lattimore to be an autocratic principal? Why or why not?

3. Identify factors that contributed to the conflict between a majority of the teachers and the principals in this case.

4. Assume Principal Lattimore changes his mind and accepts the offer to be reassigned to the central office. Will his transfer result in an acceptable resolution to problems at Holmes Elementary School? Why or why not?

5. Evaluate the principal's approach to pursuing change and then identify strengths and weaknesses associated with this approach.

6. Identify evidence in the case that provide insights into the school's culture.

7. Describe the leadership style of the principal and then explain why you support or oppose his leadership style.

8. Did the teachers act ethically in criticizing the principal to parents?

9. Did the teachers act ethically in preparing and signing a petition requesting the removal of Principal Lattimore?

10. The assistant superintendent could reassign the principal or support him by endorsing the changes he made. Are there options she could pursue to resolve the conflict at Holmes Elementary School?

SUGGESTED READINGS

Bali, V. A., Anagnostopoulos, D., & Roberts, R. (2005). Toward a political explanation of grade retention. *Educational Evaluation and Policy Analysis, 27*(2), 133–155.

Bertram, V. M. (2004). Reinventing a school. *Principal Leadership (High School Ed.), 4*(6), 38–42.

Bowman, L. J. (2005). Grade retention: Is it a help or hindrance to student academic success? *Preventing School Failure, 49*(3), 42–46.

Copland, M. A. (2001). The myth of the superprincipal. *Phi Delta Kappan, 82*(7), 528–533.

Emmons, C. L., Hagopian, G., & Efimba, M. O. (1998). A school transformed: The case of Norman S. Weir. *Journal of Education for Students Placed at Risk, 3*(1), 39–51.

Fullan, M. (2002). The change leader. *Educational Leadership, 59*(8), 16–20.

Houston, W. R. (1998). Innovators as catalysts for restructuring schools. *Educational Forum, 62*(3), 204–210.

Jimerson, S. R., Graydon, K., & Pletcher, S. M. W. (2006), Beyond grade retention and social promotion: Promoting the social and academic competence of students. *Psychology in the Schools, 43*(1), 85–97.

Johnson, P. E., Holder, C., Carrick, C., & Sanford, N. (1998). A model for restructuring governance: Developing a culture of respect and teamwork. *ERS Spectrum, 16*(2), 28–36.

Mendez, L. M., &. Knoff, H. M. (2003). Who gets suspended from school and why: A demographic analysis of schools and disciplinary infractions in a large school district. *Education and Treatment of Children, 26*(1), 30–51.

Prestine, N. (1993). Shared decision making in restructuring essential schools: The role of the principal. *Planning and Changing, 22*(3-4), 160–177.

Protheroe, N. (2004). Professional learning communities. *Principal, 83*(5), 39–42.

Rosen, M. (1993). Sharing power: A blueprint for collaboration. *Principal, 72*(3), 37–39.

Sikes, P. (1992). Imposed change and the experienced teacher. In M. Fullan & A. Hargreaves (Eds.), *Teacher development and educational change* (pp. 36–55). Bristol, PA: Falmer Press.

Thomas, C., & Fitzhugh-Walker, P. (1998). The role of the urban principal in school restructuring. *International Journal of Leadership in Education, 1*(3), 297–306.

Wager, B. (1993). No more suspension: Creating a shared ethical culture. *Educational Leadership, 50*(4), 34–37.

Wilmore, E., & Thomas, C. (2001). The new century: Is it too late for transformational leadership? *Educational Horizons, 79*(3), 115–123.

REFERENCES

Datnow, A., & Castellano, M. E. (2001). Managing and guiding school reform: Leadership in success for all schools. *Educational Administration Quarterly, 37*(2), 219–249.

Foster, E. S., Loving, C. C., & Shumate, A. (2000). Effective principals, effective professional development schools. *Teaching and Change, 8*(1), 76–97.

Fullan, M. (2002). The change leader. *Educational Leadership, 59*(8), 16–20.

Goldman, E. (1998). The significance of leadership style. *Educational Leadership, 55*(7), 20–22.

Hallinger, P., & Heck, R. H. (1998). Exploring the principal's contribution to school effectiveness: 1980–1995. *School Effectiveness and School Improvement, 9*(2), 157–191.

Kowalski, T. J. (2003). *Contemporary school administration: An introduction* (2nd ed.). Boston: Allyn and Bacon.

Kowalski, T. J., Petersen, G. J., & Fusarelli, L. D. (2007). *Effective communication for school administrators: An imperative in an information age*. Lanham, MD: Rowman and Littlefield Education.

Langer, S., & Boris-Schacter, S. (2003). Challenging the image of the American principalship. *Principal, 83*(1), 14–18.

Sergiovanni, T. J. (2004). Collaborative cultures and communities of practice. *Principal Leadership (High School Ed.), 5*(1), 48–52.

8 Feliz Navidad? Not in This School District

Background Information

The influx of legal and illegal aliens from Mexico remains a major challenge for public school districts across the country. Primarily because of migrant farm workers, this issue has been as relevant for rural districts as it has for urban districts.

Scholars (e.g., Lopez, Mahitivanichcha, & Scribner, 2001) who have studied migrant families have concluded that they are among the most marginalized groups in U.S. society. When migrant parents enroll their children in public schools, they often find that their involvement is either impossible (e.g., because of language barriers) or unwelcome (e.g., because of bias or prejudice). Yet migrant students, like all other students, benefit when their parents are involved with schools.

Williams and Chavkin (1989) identified seven common characteristics in successful parental involvement programs:

1. Written policies that specifically address parental involvement
2. Sufficient resources that keep programs running
3. Ongoing training that prepares staff and parents
4. Approaches that foster partnerships between schools and families
5. Two-way interactions that allow for regular and frequent communication
6. Networking with other programs to facilitate external collaboration
7. Procedures or measures that allow for continuous evaluation.

Experiences with migrant families indicate that school officials face two primary challenges. First, they must establish mutual trust and confidence; second, they need to create meaningful opportunities for parents to involve themselves in the schools. Relational communication is at the core of both challenges. Relational communication is interpersonal and symmetrical. Interpersonal communication involves two-way exchanges in which persons influence one another's behavior over and above their organizational role, rank, and status (Cappella, 1987). Symmetrical communication benefits all interactants (Grunig, 1989), meaning that the interactants behave similarly, thus minimizing their formal authority and actual power differences (Burgoon & Hale, 1984). In essence, relational communication produces mutual understandings, mutual influence, negotiation, openness, credibility, and trust (Kowalski, Petersen, & Fusarelli, 2007).

This case is about the migration of Mexican families into a small Midwestern city. Once situated, the children enter the local public schools. Conflict emerges when the families leave for the entire month of December to return to Mexico for the holidays. Both the school board and many administrators believe that the absences should be classified as unexcused and that the students should incur punishment. One elementary principal, however, has a different perspective.

Key Areas for Reflection

1. Cultural conflict
2. Communication with minority group parents
3. Enforcement of school policy
4. Political versus ethical dimensions of decision making
5. Bilingual education

The Case

Professor Elaine Dugan teaches school administration and curriculum courses at a state university in the central part of the United States. For the past year, she has been working with two public elementary schools located about 75 miles from campus. The school district had a curriculum-improvement grant from the state department of education, and she is the evaluation consultant for that project.

On the first Tuesday of each month, Professor Dugan meets with the principals from the two schools regarding an ongoing evaluation of the project. The meetings alternate between the two schools, Jonesville East Elementary School and Jonesville Central Elementary School; however, both principals attend each meeting.

Jonesville has about 12,000 residents and the community has declined about 1 percent in population in each of the last U.S. Census reports. There is a small industrial park located about two miles west of downtown that includes four manufacturing plants. Employment across the four companies has also declined slightly in the last few years.

About eighteen months ago, an out-of-state firm, Midwestern Meats, purchased a meat-packing plant in the small town of Apple Ridge. The plant had been idle after the owner went bankrupt four years ago. Located about 26 miles from Jonesville, Apple Ridge had less than 1,500 residents. Before purchasing the plant, executives from Midwestern Meats knew they faced two challenges: They would have to import most of the labor to operate the plant because there did not appear to be a sufficient supply of local workers, and they had to find low-cost residential property to purchase or rent in order to import labor. After studying their options, the company purchased about 20 houses and two apartment buildings in Jonesville. They then recruited workers, primarily from Mexico. The workers and their families were provided housing in Jonesville and employees were transported to and from Apple Ridge daily via company-leased buses.

At first, Superintendent Joe Hankins considered the influx of new students a blessing. For the first time in eight years, the district's enrollment had increased—a

factor that resulted in additional state financial aid. By the end of last school year, however, opinions about the students from Mexico had changed. Jonesville had virtually no
minority population prior to the arrival of these families, and many of the residents did
not respond positively to their new neighbors.

By the start of the current school year, the school district enrolled over 120 students from Mexico, more than half of whom were not fluent in English. Seventy of
these students were in elementary schools, with the remainder enrolled at either the
middle school or high school. Of those in elementary school, all attended Jonesville
Central Elementary School. According to the superintendent, the decision to have all
the students from Mexico attend a single elementary school was based on four factors:

1. Central had space to accommodate the students. It was formerly the district's
   high school, and prior to the influx of Mexican students only 60 percent of the
   classrooms were being used.
2. All the housing purchased by Midwestern Meats was located within the current
   attendance boundaries for Central.
3. The students required special assistance (e.g., bilingual instruction) and providing the assistance at one site would be more economical.
4. The principal at Central spoke Spanish, at least well enough to communicate
   with students and their parents about essential aspects of schooling.

The political dimension of the decision to have all the Mexican students attend
Central, however, was not mentioned. Located in the center of the city, the elementary
school serves the lowest income and arguably least influential families in Jonesville.

Meredith Lancaster is the principal at Central. Unlike the principals at the middle school and high school, she has a positive attitude about the Mexican students. She
believes their presence is beneficial to Jonesville students who otherwise would not
have multicultural experiences—at least not until they left the community. Ever since
the Mexican families began arriving, she has reached out to them and tried to make
them feel welcome. Conversely, her colleagues at the two secondary schools did little
to accommodate the Mexican students, and they continuously complained about problems they attributed to these students.

Principal Lancaster had studied Spanish in high school and she honed her skills
in using the language while traveling in foreign countries on vacations. In addition, her
sister-in-law is from Chile and she often speaks Spanish when conversing with her.
Though all three schools enrolling students from Mexico initiated bilingual education
programs, Meredith Lancaster was the only principal who did so enthusiastically.

Professor Dugan arrived at Central Elementary School a few minutes prior to
the scheduled meeting with the two principals. Michael Bogut, the principal at East Elementary, and Principal Lancaster were waiting for her in the school's conference
room. Before they started to discuss the curriculum-improvement project, Principal
Lancaster asked the other two if they would be able to join her and Superintendent
Hankins for lunch at noon. Professor Dugan said yes but Principal Bogut declined.

After the meeting at Central Elementary School ended, Principal Lancaster and
Professor Dugan walked a few blocks to a restaurant, where they met the superintendent.

Superintendent Hankins had met Principal Lancaster on at least two previous occasions, both in conjunction with the grant. Professor Dugan had assumed that the luncheon was merely a social event—perhaps a way for the superintendent to express his appreciation for her involvement with the curriculum-improvement project. She soon learned that the two administrators had something else in mind.

Because of her work with the elementary schools, Professor Dugan knew about the Mexican students and the reason why they were in Jonesville. A bilingual program was initiated in conjunction with the curriculum-improvement project, so she also knew about the challenges the Mexican students presented to Principal Lancaster and the teachers. She did not know, however, that these students were about to initiate a major controversy for which the school officials were unprepared.

"Elaine, we want your advice on a potentially explosive matter," Superintendent Hankins began. "Last year, Midwestern Meats shut down their plant in Apple Ridge for the entire month of December. They did so because the Mexican workers wanted to return to their country for Christmas. Many of the workers indicated that they would leave on December 1 even if it meant losing their jobs. The company decided to close the plant for a month. When they did this last December, they caught us completely off guard. The Mexican students just left and we did not know why until they returned after January 1. As school started this August, we notified the families that we would not excuse the students for absences between December 1 and December 20. Meredith has a very good relationship with the Mexican families, and she has learned that most if not all are again planning to return to Mexico for the entire month of December. Christmas is a very sacred holiday for them and they want their children to be with grandparents and other members of their extended families."

"What did you do last year after the students returned in January?" Meredith inquired.

"We could have designated their absences as unexcused but we did not. The students were allowed to make up the work they missed," Meredith responded. "We concluded that punishing the students for a decision made by their parents would be wrong. We thought that alerting the parents to our policy would rectify the issue."

Anticipating that the families would return to Mexico again in December, Superintendent Hankins began discussing alternatives with the principals as early as mid-October.

"Last year," the superintendent said, "the two secondary school principals reluctantly allowed the Mexican students to make up the work they missed. That was an unpopular decision with most teachers and they have indicated that they will not do the same thing this year. Both have indicated that the students will be penalized as per district policy and school rules covering unexcused absences. For some Mexican students, this will likely mean failing one or more of their classes."

"What do you plan to do, Meredith?" the professor asked.

"At my request, Mr. Hankins has discussed the possibility of creating a special policy provision for the Mexican students with the school board members. I believe such a provision is the right thing to do."

"And the board members were adamant that they would not approve a policy exception or create a special policy for the Mexican students," the superintendent injected. "Several board members said that making such concessions for them would set a dangerous precedent. And I agree. What if other students asked to be excused so they could visit relatives for the month of December?"

"What does current policy require?" the professor asked.

"The policy states that students may be penalized for an unexcused absence, including losing points in relation to their grades," the superintendent responded.

"Elaine," Meredith said, "I was hoping you would have advice, at least regarding what we should do at Central Elementary School. If I allow the students to make up the work and the other two principals do not, we are likely to have a 'controversy after the controversy.' If I punish the students by not allowing them to make up the work, I'm going to have a hard time living with myself."

"I wish there were an easy and obvious answer, but there is not," Elaine told Meredith. "Politically, the best option is to be aligned with the other principals. Ethically, you have to decide what is best for the students you serve. I realize you were looking for a magic solution, but I don't have one."

"Meredith is correct," the superintendent said. "If the principals make different decisions on this matter, it will only make things worse. Penalizing some students and not others will add fuel to the fire. Some board members, for example, already question whether Meredith is too accommodating in relation to the Mexican families. The board members know, and continuously remind me, that the residents of Jonesville are not happy about the Mexicans being here."

As the three educators left the restaurant, Meredith still had not decided what she would do. Elaine had merely defined the tension between acting politically and acting ethically but did so in a way that emphasized the ethical dimension of this critical decision. The superintendent, while trying to appear neutral, seems to favor the position supported by the school board and the two secondary school principals. As Meredith reflected on the decision she had to make, she realized how alone principals can feel at certain times.

PROBLEM FRAMING

1. Assume you are Principal Lancaster. Describe what you would want to accomplish in dealing with the situation described in this case.

2. Based on the evidence of contextual variables, describe the difficulty associated with achieving your objective.

QUESTIONS AND SUGGESTED ACTIVITIES

1. Evaluate the school district's policy on unexcused absences.

2. What does Principal Lancaster mean when she refers to a "controversy after the controversy"?

3. After reading the case, do you believe the school officials have created a framework to involve the parents of the Mexican students in the schools? Why or why not?

4. Professor Dugan suggests that it would be politically advantageous for Principal Lancaster to join the two secondary principals in punishing the students for unexcused absences. What did she mean?

5. Professor Dugan also refers to the ethical nature of the decision that Principal Lancaster must make. What are ethics? Who determines the parameters for ethical behavior in school administration?

6. Evaluate the role of Superintendent Hankins. Do you believe he is acting responsibly? Why or why not?

7. If Principal Lancaster decides to allow the students from Central Elementary School to make up the school work they missed during December, is she likely to face negative con-

sequences? What evidence do you have to support your response?

8. If you were Principal Lancaster, what efforts would you make to establish closer ties with the Mexican families?

9. Why do some people oppose bilingual education? Do you think opposition to this program is a factor in this case? Why or why not?

10. Determine if the school district in which you work or reside has a policy or rule concerning punishment for unexcused absences from school. If so, determine if the policy provides for exceptions.

SUGGESTED READINGS

Armendariz, A. L. (2000). The impact of racial prejudice on the socialization of Mexican American students in the public schools. *Equity and Excellence in Education, 33*(3), 59–63.

Brunn, M. (1999). The absence of language policy and its effects on the education of Mexican migrant children. *Bilingual Research Journal, 23*(4), 319–344.

Fuentes, F., Cantu, V. D., & Stechuk, R. (1996). Migrant Head Start: What does it mean to involve parents in program services? *Children Today, 24*(1), 16–18.

Green, P. E. (2003). The undocumented: Educating the children of migrant workers in America. *Bilingual Research Journal, 27*(1), 51–71.

Lopez, G. R., Mahitivanichcha, K.,. & Scribner, J. D. (2001). Redefining parental involvement: Lessons

from high-performing migrant-impacted schools. *American Educational Research Journal, 38*(2), 253–288.

Oviatt, T. (1997, April). Success for Hispanic students. *Education Digest, 62*, 48–51.

Retish, P., & Kavanaugh, P. (1992, April). Myth: America's public schools are educating Mexican American students. *Journal of Multicultural Counseling and Development, 20*, 89–96.

Rolon, C. A. (2005). Succeeding with Latino students. *Principal, 85*(2), 30–34.

Romanowski, M. H. (2003). Cultural capital of migrant students: Teachers' and students' perspectives and understandings. *Rural Educator, 24*(3), 40–48.

Romanowski, M. H. (2003). Meeting the unique needs of the children of migrant farm workers. *Clearing House, 77*(1), 27–33.

REFERENCES

Burgoon, J. K., & Hale, J. L. (1984). The fundamental topoi of relational communication. *Communication Monographs, 51*, 193–214.

Cappella, J. N. (1987). Interpersonal communication: Definitions and fundamental questions. In C. R. Berger & S. H. Chaffee (Eds.), *Handbook of communication science* (pp. 184–238). Newbury Park, CA: Sage.

Grunig, J. E. (1989). Symmetrical presuppositions as a framework for public relations theory. In C. H. Botan (Ed.), *Public relations theory* (pp. 17–44). Hillsdale, NJ: Lawrence Erlbaum Associates.

Kowalski, T. J., Petersen, G. J., & Fusarelli, L. D. (2007). *Effective communication for school administrators: An imperative in an information age.* Lanham, MD: Rowman and Littlefield Education.

Lopez, G. R., Mahitivanichcha, K., & Scribner, J. D. (2001). Redefining parental involvement: Lessons from high-performing migrant-impacted schools. *American Educational Research Journal, 38*(2), 253–288.

Williams, D. L., & Chavkin, N. F. (1989). Essential elements of strong parent involvement programs. *Educational Leadership, 47*(2), 18–20.

CASE
9

Sally's Socialization

Background Information

All organizations have cultures consisting of shared values and beliefs and providing an invisible framework of norms that guide employees as they encounter confusion, ambiguity, uncertainty, and other problems (Deal & Kennedy, 1982). Often, it is difficult to accurately diagnose a school's culture because the values, beliefs, and norms are not readily apparent. Generally, school cultures can be visualized using three variables (Kowalski, 2003):

1. *Strength.* School cultures fall along a continuum from strong to weak. In strong cultures, values and beliefs are shared by all or nearly all employees; in weak cultures, they are fragmented and thus less influential.
2. *Value.* School cultures fall along a continuum from positive to negative. In positive cultures, shared values and beliefs are congruous with the professional knowledge base; in negative cultures, they are not.
3. *Alignment.* School cultures fall along a continuum from aligned to misaligned. In aligned cultures, shared values and beliefs are congruous with the values and beliefs espoused by the formal organization (e.g., by district policy and school philosophy); in misaligned cultures, they are not.

Organizational members protect culture by attempting to socialize newcomers (Van Maanen & Schein, 1979). Socialization involves routine and social pressure intended to result in conformity (Hart, 1991). These pressures are delivered through formal (e.g., faculty orientation, staff meetings) and informal (e.g., social interaction) experiences. Basically, socialization informs new teachers about how to deal with common problems of practice (Hanson, 2003). In misaligned organizations, the accepted way of doing things differs from espoused solutions found in policy manuals and philosophy statements. Consequently, protectors of the prevailing culture (e.g., experienced teachers) continuously remind newcomers, "Ignore the policy manual. This is the way we really deal with this type of problem."

Many novice teachers encounter role-related or value-related conflict during socialization. The former pertains to inconsistencies between two or more role expectations. As an example, a new teacher struggles between being an empowered professional and being an obedient member of a school's culture. The latter pertains to philosophical inconsistencies. As an example, the values and norms of a school's culture are incompatible with the accepted values and norms of the teaching profession.

Teacher empowerment has been interpreted in different ways but definitions essentially are anchored in professionalism; that is, empowerment focuses on a professional orientation to teaching (Ponticell, Olson, & Charlier, 1995). Scholars who have examined school reform (e.g., Fullan, 2001; Hall & Hord, 2001) conclude that meaningful improvement is much more likely when teachers function as professionals and change agents. Empowerment, however, often contradicts beliefs and norms entrenched in many schools (Kowalski, 1995). As examples, professionalism increases independence and reliance on professional knowledge to guide practice; conversely, strong negative cultures demand conformity and obedience—even in situations where the school's norm is not supported by established theory (Kowalski, Lasley, & Mahoney, 2008).

Many principals have been apprehensive about allowing teachers to chart their own pedagogical and classroom management agendas, largely for two reasons.

1. *Aversion to risk.* Principals may have a negative disposition toward risk taking, and consequently they view teacher empowerment as a threat to their authority and job security. If teachers make independent decisions about homework and discipline, the potential for parental dissatisfaction increases. And if problems occur as a result of independent teacher decisions, the principal may be held accountable.

2. *Protection of school culture.* Principals are often key figures in a school's culture. If the culture is strong, teachers and other employees expect a principal to protect and foster dominant beliefs and norms. Empowerment essentially redefines the parameters for acceptable teacher behavior because greater importance is placed on personal responsibility for professional practice and less importance is placed on social acceptance.

Administrator behavior is often analyzed in the context of competing leadership styles. For example, the literature suggests that principals fall somewhere on a continuum ranging from transactional to transformational leadership. A transactional style is characterized by exchanges between leader and follower for purposes of achieving personal objectives; it often entails a bargaining process focused on self-interests (Sergiovanni, 2001). In essence, a transactional leader believes that people are motivated by self-interests, and therefore their behavior can be controlled through extrinsic rewards (or threats). Conversely, transformational leadership involves attempts to influence behavior by appealing to higher ideals and moral values; the leader and followers share common goals, are guided by ethical and moral principles, and are motivated by higher-order needs (Burns, 1978). In essence, transactional leadership is a political process involving a quid pro quo, and transformational leadership is an ethical, moral, and professional process involving commitments to personal and organizational growth (Kowalski, 2003).

In this case, a novice first-grade teacher refuses to recommend the retention of two pupils. Her decision generates considerable tension as conflicting elements of school culture, teacher empowerment and principal leadership style, converge.

Key Areas for Reflection

1. School culture
2. Teacher empowerment
3. Principal leadership style
4. Ethical behavior

The Case

Sally Vasquez sat alone in her first-grade classroom in Westside Elementary School. It was 4:30 P.M. and the students had departed more than an hour ago. As she stared aimlessly out the window at the empty playground, her thoughts meandered between her recollections of her role model, Mrs. Eagan, and the difficult decision she would have to make the next day.

Sally's intention to become an educator developed after having Mrs. Eagan as her teacher in the fourth grade. At the time, Mrs. Eagan was only 27 years old. She was energetic, kind, and consistently positive with her students. Over the course of that year, Sally developed self-confidence and a positive attitude toward school and she attributed this progress to Mrs. Eagan's caring, optimistic teaching style.

Ten months ago, after graduating from college, Sally assumed her role as a first-grade teacher. Westside Elementary School is located in one of the older neighborhoods in Maplewood, a community that developed as a middle-class suburb in the early 1950s. Since 1980, however, it has changed considerably. Property values have fallen, the median family income has declined, and the population has become more ethnically and racially diverse. Hispanics, constituting less than 1 percent of the city's population 30 years ago, now account for 37 percent of the city's residents.

When Sally began teaching at Westside, she joined a group of first-grade teachers that included Martha Bigler, April Musilich, and Sharon Quigly. The other three teachers were highly experienced (their levels of teaching experience ranged from twelve to twenty-nine years) and each had been at Westside for more than eight years. Sally quickly discovered that Mrs. Quigly, the most experienced and oldest first-grade teacher, exerted considerable influence—not only among her peers assigned to teach first grade, but also among other faculty, parents, and even the principal.

The first-grade teachers at Westside Elementary School have a long tradition of meeting once a month to discuss curriculum and common concerns. Their meetings are held on the third Tuesday of each month during the school year. The meetings take place in Mrs. Quigly's classroom 15 minutes after school adjourns. The sessions last about an hour. Initially, Sally found them to be very informative. The other teachers gave her advice about classroom activities, shared instructional materials, and answered her questions.

Three years prior to Sally's arrival, the first-grade teachers developed criteria for determining if students should be retained in grade. Though not mandatory, the criteria were intended to ensure that retention decisions would be made consistently among the four first-grade teachers. Since being developed, 2 to 5 percent of the first-grade students have been retained at Westside. The criteria address both academic progress and social development.

The topic of grade retention was first raised with Sally in mid-October at the monthly first-grade teachers' meeting. The existence of the criteria and rate of retentions surprised her. As a teacher education student, she was required to read several journal articles on retaining students in first grade. This research indicated that the negatives associated with this decision outweighed the positives. Most notably, she remembered reading that any gains attributable to repeating first grade usually dissipated after just one or two years. On the other hand, the harmful effects to a student's self-efficacy and self-esteem tended to endure even through high school. She also remembered reading that retention increased the probability that the student would never graduate from high school. This conclusion was reinforced by her supervising teacher during student teaching.

Initially, Sally was intimidated by the other first-grade teachers at Westside so she did not divulge her true feelings on this topic. However, in February, she was asked to develop a list of students who might be retained. Recognizing a potential problem between the expectation of other teachers and her own convictions, she opted to discuss the issue with the principal, Carmen Pelfrey.

Mrs. Pelfrey has been principal at Westside for six years. She is well liked by the teachers and supported enthusiastically by parents. Sally also had become fond of her and judged her to be a competent leader.

During their meeting, Sally candidly expressed opposition to retaining first-grade students. She admitted that she had not yet expressed those feelings to other teachers, fearing that doing so would result in negative reactions. Mrs. Pelfrey explained that neither district policy nor school rules required or prohibited grade retentions. Then, however, she began to praise the other first-grade teachers and defended their use of the criteria. She referred to Mrs. Quigly as an ideal teacher-leader and identified her as perhaps the most powerful teacher in the school. Though her comments related to the issue of grade retention, Mrs. Pelfrey never expressed a personal position on the topic. Instead, she encouraged Sally to express her views to other first-grade teachers.

At the next first-grade teachers' meeting, Sally followed Principal Pelfrey's suggestion. She told the other teachers that she did not have a favorable view of retaining students and explained why she had developed this stance. Mrs. Quigly, appearing to be displeased, told Sally that she was not sufficiently experienced to develop such an inflexible position.

"You need to keep an open mind about retention," she told Sally. "Apparently, you have only heard one side of the argument. We have a great deal of experience retaining students and we can assure you, most students benefit from being retained."

The other two teachers immediately agreed by saying that Mrs. Quigly was absolutely correct. At that point, Mrs. Quigly thanked Sally for her candor but reiterated that she was still expected to develop a list of students who might be retained.

After the meeting, Sally walked to parking lot with Mrs. Bigler, the least experienced of the other three first-grade teachers. She told Sally that she too once had been apprehensive about failing students. She explained that experience had changed her perspective; she now was convinced that some students simply were not prepared to be promoted to second grade.

The following morning, Sally again met with Principal Pelfrey. She described the discussion that occurred the previous afternoon. She emphasized that despite Mrs. Quigly's insistence that she develop a list of potentially failing students, she did not intend to comply.

Mrs. Pelfrey acted surprised. "You realize you will appear to be inflexible. The other teachers are not asking you to identify students who will be retained; they only expect you to identify students who might fail because they meet some or all of the criteria. By refusing to even consider retention, you will appear to be stubborn and uncooperative."

Despite the principal's warning, Sally stood by her convictions. She informed the other three teachers in late February that she would not develop the list and moreover, she had no intention of retaining any students. After learning of Sally's decision, Mrs. Quigly met with Principal Pelfrey and expressed disappointment in Sally's behavior.

"She has many fine qualities, and she could become a great teacher. She loves children, and she is bright. But she is obviously not open to ideas that do not conform with her beliefs. Mrs. Bigler, Mrs. Musilich, and I have tried to help her, but she does not listen well. We would be willing to meet with you to discuss this further, but overall you need to know that we question whether she belongs at Westside."

Mrs. Quigly's veiled suggestion that Sally not be reemployed bothered Principal Pelfrey. On three occasions, she had conducted formal observations of Sally's teaching, and in each instance her assessments were positive. Moreover, comments from parents had been consistently complimentary. Not reemploying a teacher simply because she did not "fit in" would be problematic—especially if Sally resisted. On the other hand, ignoring the wishes of the three teachers could damage principal-faculty relationships.

Weighing the dilemma she faced, Principal Pelfrey again appealed to Sally to reconsider the retention question. Sally said she had given the matter considerable thought and decided not to change her position. Principal Pelfrey then told her that the other first-grade teachers would have input into her evaluation as a first-year teacher.

"I admire your conviction, but you should know that this issue could be detrimental. I'm sure you do not want to work in a school where the other first-grade teachers don't accept you as a colleague. I will have to weigh the consequences of this conflict when I complete your final evaluation."

Understandably shaken by the principal's warning, Sally made an appointment to see the district superintendent, Dr. Frank Jobe. She had met him during her employment interview and remembered his comments about teacher professionalism and empowerment. She reminded him of those comments before detailing the conflict with the other teachers and the warning she received from the principal. She also pointed out that neither district policy nor school regulations directed teachers to take a position on grade retention. Dr. Jobe listened attentively and told Sally he would respond to her concerns after discussing the matter with Mrs. Pelfrey.

Several days later, Sally received a message that Principal Pelfrey wanted to meet with her later that day. As she walked into the principal's office, Sally immediately detected tension. Carmen Pelfrey appeared angry, a demeanor that Sally had not seen previously.

The principal stared into Sally's eyes and said, "You went to see the superintendent without my permission? Maybe the other teachers are correct about you. I tried to advise you so that you could be successful at Westside. Believe it or not, we all want you to be successful. But apparently, you have your own agenda."

"You hinted that I might not be reemployed just because I refuse to identify potentially failing students. My position on retention does not violate policy. I sought your support but you simply told me to be a team player. I will not support or engage in a practice that is not supported by the professional knowledge base. If I offended you by seeing the superintendent, I'm sorry. But you did not give me an option. What would you have done if you were in my shoes?"

"I would have been more open-minded and cooperative. Look, I am not going to recommend nonrenewal for you. If you want to remain at Westside, you have to get along with other teachers. Otherwise, you're going to be an outcast. I probably cannot recommend dismissal solely on the basis of this issue, but this friction is almost certain to create other problems. You have put me in a difficult position. I don't want to choose between you and the other teachers and really don't want the superintendent getting involved. So here is what I have decided. You either develop the list for Mrs. Quigly by March 15 or I will recommend that you be transferred to another school, effective next school year. If I were you, I'd think about my options carefully."

As she sat in the silence of her classroom, Sally's eyes moved from the window to the calendar on the wall. March 15 was less than two weeks away. The next day, she again met with the superintendent and detailed her most recent discussion with Principal Pelfrey.

PROBLEM FRAMING

1. Assume you are the superintendent. Describe what you would want to accomplish in dealing with the situation described in this case.

2. Based on the evidence of contextual variables, describe the difficulty associated with achieving your objective.

QUESTIONS AND SUGGESTED ACTIVITIES

1. Share and critique the problem statements prepared by students in your class.

2. Do you believe that the principal has the primary responsibility to resolve the conflict between Sally and other first-grade teachers? Why or why not?

3. Review research on grade retention in first grade and then engage in small group discussions about personal agreements with such research findings.

4. Based on evidence presented in the case, do you believe the principal has been an

effective instructional leader? Why or why not?

5. Why are teachers and administrators pressured to conform to existing school culture?

6. What is likely to occur to Sally if she refuses to conform?

7. Determine if the school district in which you are employed (or reside if you are not currently practicing as an educator) has a policy addressing grade retention. Share the outcomes in class and identifying differences in such policies.

8. Reflecting on your own experiences as a novice teacher, identify critical incidents that

you believe were part of your socialization to a workplace. Then determine if these experiences were beneficial. Share the incidents with in class.

9. Principal Pelfrey threatens to recommend that Sally be transferred to another school because she refuses to cooperate with other first-grade teachers. Do you consider the principal's threat to be ethical? Why or why not?

10. Identify options the superintendent has in resolving this matter. Then evaluate the options and select the preferred option.

SUGGESTED READINGS

Beck-Frazier, S. (2005). To stay or not to stay: That's the dilemma. *Delta Kappa Gamma Bulletin, 71*(2), 28–33.

Bullough, R. V. (2005). Teacher vulnerability and teachability: A case study of a mentor and two interns. *Teacher Education Quarterly, 32*(2), 23–39.

Burk, D. I., & Fry, P. G. (1997). Autonomy for democracy in a primary classroom: A first year teacher's struggle. *Teaching and Teacher Education, 13,* 645–658.

Flores, M. A., & Day, C. (2006). Contexts which shape and reshape new teachers' identities: A multi-perspective study. *Teaching and Teacher Education, 22*(2), 219–232.

Johnson, P. E., & Short, P. M. (1998). Principal's leader power, teacher empowerment, teacher compliance and conflict. *Educational Management and Administration, 26*(2), 147–159.

Kowalski, T. J. (1995). Preparing teachers to be leaders: Barriers in the workplace. In M. O'Hair & S. Odell (Eds.), *Educating teachers for leadership and change: Teacher Education Yearbook III* (pp. 243–256). Thousand Oaks, CA: Corwin Press.

Mauer, E., & Zimmerman, E. (2000). Mentoring new teachers. *Principal, 79*(3), 26–28.

McCoy, A. R., & Reynolds, A. J. (1999). Grade retention and school performance: An extended investigation. *Journal of School Psychology, 37*(3), 273–298.

Normore, A. H., & Floyd, A. (2005). A roller coaster ride: The twists and turns of a novice teacher's relationship with her principal. *Phi Delta Kappan, 86*(10), 767–771.

Potter, L. (2003). Between a rock and a hard place. *Principal Leadership (Middle School Ed.), 3*(8), 46–48.

Short, P. M., & Short, R. J. (1998). Teacher empowerment and principal leadership: Understanding the influence process. *Educational Administration Quarterly, 34,* 630–649.

Weiss, E. M. (1999). Perceived workplace conditions and first-year teachers' morale, career choice commitment, and planned retention: A secondary analysis. *Teaching and Teacher Education, 15*(8), 861–879.

REFERENCES

Burns, J. M. (1978). *Leadership.* New York: Harper Torchbooks.

Deal, T. E., & Kennedy, A. A. (1982). *Corporate cultures: The rites and rituals of corporate life.* Reading, MA: Addison-Wesley.

Fullan, M. (2001). *Leading in a culture of change.* San Francisco: Jossey-Bass.

Hall, G. E., & Hord. S. M. (2001). *Implementing change: Patterns, principles, and potholes.* Allyn and Bacon.

Hanson, E. M. (2003). *Educational administration and organizational behavior* (5th ed.). Boston: Allyn and Bacon.

Hart, A. W. (1991). Leader succession and socialization: A synthesis. *Review of Educational Research, 61*(4), 451–474.

Kowalski, T. J. (1995). Preparing teachers to be leaders: Barriers in the workplace. In M. O'Hair & S. Odell (Eds.), *Educating teachers for leadership and change: Teacher education yearbook III* (pp. 243–256). Thousand Oaks, CA: Corwin.

Kowalski, T. J. (2003). *Contemporary school administration: An introduction* (2nd ed.). Boston: Allyn and Bacon.

Kowalski, T. J., Lasley, T. J., & Mahoney, J. (2008). *Data-driven decisions and school leadership: Best practices for school improvement.* Boston: Allyn and Bacon.

Ponticell, J. A., Olson G. E., & Charlier, P. S. (1995). Project MASTER: Peer coaching and collaboration as catalysts for professional growth in urban high schools. In M. J. O'Hair & S. J. Odell (Eds.), *Educating teachers for leadership and change: Teacher education yearbook III* (pp. 96–116). Thousand Oaks, CA: Corwin.

Sergiovanni, T. J. (2001). *The principalship: A reflective practice perspective* (4th ed.). Boston: Allyn and Bacon.

Van Maanen, J., & Schein, E. H. (1979). Toward a theory of organizational socialization. In B. Staw (Ed.), *Research in organizational behavior* (pp. 209–264). Greenwich, CT: JAI Press.

CASE
10

A Matter of Honor

Background Information

Authors examining the decision-making behavior of administrators (e.g., Begley, 2000; Kowalski, Lasley, & Mahoney, 2008; Willower, 1994) have commonly found that emotion, personal values, and political contexts contribute to subjectivity. Sergiovanni (1992) observed that three leadership dimensions may influence decisions. He labeled them the heart, the head, and the hand. The *heart* pertains to personal beliefs, values, dreams, and commitments; the *head* pertains to theories of practice that evolve by integrating theoretical and craft knowledge; and the *hand* has to do with the actions and behaviors used as strategies institutionalized in district policies and normative procedures. When these dimensions are discordant, administrators almost always experience personal conflict because they must make a choice between doing what is professionally and ethically correct or doing what is politically expedient (Kowalski et al., 2008).

In this case, a student is accused of plagiarizing a book report in a senior honors English class. The teacher, invoking school district policy, informs the principal that she intends to give the student a failing grade for the semester. The principal is apprehensive about following policy in this instance because the student is considered a role model. She has an unblemished academic record; she is a gifted athlete; she is the first African American student at the school to receive an appointment to a national military academy. Giving her a failing grade in English would almost certainly mean that her appointment to the military academy would be rescinded—a penalty that could have serious repercussions in the community.

As the case unfolds, the principal finds that he must choose between enforcing the district's policy, as demanded by the teacher, and forging a political compromise, as suggested by both the school district's attorney and the student's attorney. Though the principal favors compromise, he fears that the teachers' union defense of the English teacher will result in serious problems for him, the superintendent, and the community.

Decisions such as the one confronting the principal in this case have moral and ethical aspects. Hodgkinson (1991) noted that "values, morals, and ethics are the very stuff of leadership and administrative life" (p. 11). Morality focuses on "right" and "wrong" and may or may not involve illegalities (Kowalski, 2006). Ethics, however, "begin where laws and doctrines of right and wrong leave off" (Howlett, 1991, p. 19), and these standards are commonly encapsulated in codes of conduct for professions.

Student discipline is a demanding component of school administration because it almost always results in an intricate mix of political, professional, moral, and ethical issues. Ideally, district policies and school rules result in consistency but as evidenced by zero-tolerance policies, too many regulations usually spawn criticism and detract from professionalism (i.e., the authority of administrators and teachers to decide what is best for students). Eliminating discretion through mandatory policy prevents principals from applying their professional knowledge and from appropriately considering moral and ethical dimensions of a given situation (Kowalski, 2003, 2006). For example, zero-tolerance policies do not allow administrators to consider a student's total record in relation to punishment.

Key Areas for Reflection

1. Rational versus subjective decision making
2. Ethical and moral dimensions of student discipline
3. Mandatory versus discretionary policy
4. Political contexts and their effect on administrative decisions
5. Plagiarism and appropriate penalties

The Case

Community

Newton, Michigan, has fallen on hard times in recent years. The local economy was devastated by the closing of two automobile-related factories, a transmission plant and a battery plant. Union strife, lower domestic automobile sales, high labor costs, and automation contributed to their demise. The parent companies diverted much of the work from Newton to new operations in Mexico—a pattern that had become all too common and exasperating for many residents in auto-producing communities.

Newton had grown rapidly after World War II. High salaries in local factories attracted a steady stream of new residents between 1950 and 1970, and Newton quickly became a larger and much more diverse community. During that period, the vast majority of new residents were either of eastern European extraction or African extraction. The former group of new residents had migrated primarily from large midwestern cities, such as Chicago, Detroit, and Pittsburgh. The latter group had migrated primarily from southern states, such as Alabama, Mississippi, and Tennessee. Since the mid-1990s, the community has become even more diverse because of the in-migration of Hispanics.

Union Influence

When factories related to the auto industry were booming, virtually every nonmanagement employee was a loyal member of a local union. In the mid-1960s, labor unions were the most powerful political, social, and economic force in Newton. Union leaders, either by virtue of holding public office or by virtue of exercising power over those who did, essentially controlled almost everything. When a resident wanted a pothole fixed, for example, he or she was more likely to call a union official than to call the mayor or street commissioner.

Local union officials also assumed an important community social role that was especially instrumental in building racial harmony. The union halls were essentially community centers that brought residents of all colors and beliefs together—an important factor given the fact that the community was racially divided in relation to housing patterns and churches.

Economic and political conditions began to change in Newton circa 1980. Factory jobs dwindled as the companies struggled, and a loss of jobs translated into a loss of union members. In 1985, the two largest factories closed completely and union membership in Newton dropped to its lowest point since 1948. The changes affected virtually every aspect of community life. As an example, the once-a-month socials at the union halls featuring free beer and music were no longer held.

A New Mayor

The 1990s remained a difficult time for Newton residents. The city had lost more than 20 percent of its population and property values plummeted. In the midst of downturn, Newton residents desperately tried to recapture the past as evidenced by the election of Stanley Diviak, a 65-year-old retired tool-and-dye maker, to be mayor. He had been president of the largest local union from 1965 to 1978, and in the eyes of many of the older residents he was still a hero.

Stanley Diviak remains a shrewd and capable politician. As a union president, he had more power than any other Newton resident, and he had few enemies. For the older residents, he personified their values. He keeps his word, he helps his friends, he is a devoted father and grandfather, he relies on common sense, and he goes to church regularly.

When he ran for mayor, Stanley faced only token opposition from a Republican candidate, a 28-year-old lawyer. The election's outcome was never in doubt. Rather than comparing the merits of the candidates, residents who routinely gathered at Gloria's Diner and Kelsey's Bar reminisced about the good old days when Stanley Diviak "got things done." Many deluded themselves into believing that Newton's fate would had been different had there been more Stanley Diviaks to combat the auto company executives. Suggestions that a global economy or the United States becoming an information-based society were responsible for the community's downturn were dismissed as Republican propaganda.

Following his election, Stanley appointed former union associates to key administrative posts in city government. He took special care to select individuals who represented the various publics being served. He also appointed a special committee to develop a plan for attracting new industry. His most popular initiative, however, was reestablishing the annual Fourth of July parade and picnic, an event that had been cancelled twelve years earlier for financial reasons.

Newton High School

Ask a Newton resident about the local public schools and inevitably he or she will refer to athletics. The high school, located just four blocks from the center of town in a two-story building now nearly fifty years old, is adorned with dozens of trophy cases and pictures of past teams and individual athletes.

The principal, Nick Furtoski, attended Newton High School and returned to be a teacher after college and a two-year tour of duty in the military. He and his wife live in the house his parents had built prior to World War II. While a Newton High School student, he played on a state championship football team and was captain of the baseball team.

Principal Furtoski's love for Newton High School is never more apparent than when he reminisces about past athletic victories. Those who visit his office, including students and school employees, rarely leave without hearing at least one story about a former athlete, an important game, or a state championship. Despite having lost nearly one-third of its enrollment since 1975, athletics remain the most successful program at Newton High School; last year, thirteen students received full or partial athletic scholarships from colleges.

Newton School District

Overall the school district's enrollment has declined from about 8,500 in 1975 to a present level of just over 6,000 students. Superintendent Andrew Sposis has survived seven difficult years in office. During his tenure, two elementary schools have been closed, resulting in the reduction of twenty-one teaching positions, three administrative positions, and fourteen support staff positions. Superintendent Sposis has also had to manage three employee strikes, two involving the teachers' union and one involving the custodians' union.

Historically, the local school board has had an unwritten policy of promoting from within the organization. Superintendent Sposis is a product of that policy; he has never worked in another school system. Over thirty-two years in the Newton school district, he has been a teacher, elementary school principal, assistant superintendent for business, and now superintendent.

The school board has five members and they are elected to office for three-year terms. In the past ten years, the entire composition of the board has changed. Consequently, there is only one member remaining in office who was on the board when Mr. Sposis was elevated to be superintendent. The current board consists of the following members:

- Casmir Barchek, a postal worker
- Yolanda Cody, a nurse
- Matthew Miskiewicz, an auto mechanic
- Angela Sanchez, a housewife
- Darnell Turner, a physician

Mr. Miskiewicz is president of the board and Dr. Turner is the vice president. Both Mrs. Cody and Dr. Turner are African Americans; Mrs. Sanchez is a Hispanic. Matt Miskiewicz is married to Mayor Diviak's sister.

Incident

Sheila Allison is a senior at Newton High School. She is a good student (slightly better than a *B* average), an outstanding athlete, and one of the most popular students. She also is an African American. For the past two years, she was named to the all-state basketball team. Not unexpectedly, she received scholarship offers from more than 25 colleges and universities. And in the fall of her senior year, she was elected homecoming queen. However, her most notable honor came on March 1 during her senior year, when she received a congressional appointment to one of the national military academies. The news spread throughout Newton quickly after her picture appeared on the front page of the local newspaper. In a community desperate for good news, Sheila's accomplishment provided a reason for residents to feel good.

Sheila's life, however, took a dramatic turn several weeks later. On March 17, Janice Durnitz, an English teacher, entered the principal's office requesting to see Mr. Furtoski. The secretary told her that he was in the cafeteria having lunch. After learning that the matter Mrs. Durnitz wanted to discuss was important, the secretary interrupted the principal's lunch and suggested that he meet with Mrs. Durnitz immediately.

Upon returning to his office, Principal Furtoski asked, "Janice, what's the problem?"

"I've got potentially bad news," she responded.

At that point, he motioned for her to have a seat and closed the office door. As soon as the principal returned to his desk Mrs. Durnitz said, "Sheila Allison is in my honors English class and until last week, she was performing quite well."

"Well, then, what's the problem?" inquired the principal.

"Students are expected to complete a critique of a contemporary novel. The assignment is made at the beginning of the semester. The deadline for submitting the critique was two days ago, and Sheila just gave me the assignment yesterday."

"You interrupted my lunch because a student turned in her assignment late?" Mr. Furtoski inquired.

"No. I read her paper last night and discovered that she committed plagiarism. I checked her paper carefully. She copied portions of a review from a website and then submitted them without references in her critique."

"You are absolutely sure about this?" asked the principal.

"Yes. Her paper contains verbatim passages from a book review that appeared in a literary magazine about six months ago and is now accessible on the magazine's website. I had read the review when it was first published and I recognized the language. So I checked the website and that's when I discovered the review was available online. I estimate that 65 percent of Sheila's paper was copied from the book review. As you know, there is a zero-tolerance policy for cheating and plagiarizing in an honors class. Students found guilty automatically receive a failing grade and must repeat the course."

"Have you confronted Sheila with this issue?" the principal asked.

"Yes. She admits taking the material from the website but contends that she did not know doing so constituted plagiarism. She said she read the book she critiqued and agreed with the review she found on the Web. Therefore, she thought it was permissible to write the same things."

A pained look came over Mr. Furtoski's face and he stared across the room as though in deep thought. After a few seconds, his eyes turned to Mrs. Durnitz.

"What do you plan to do about this?" he asked.

"District policy gives me no choice. Sheila will fail and she must retake the course to graduate."

"Janice, we have worked together for over fifteen years. We have never had a student at Newton High School flunk a course because of plagiarism. Hell, half the people in this town don't even know what the word means. Isn't there another solution? Can't we give Sheila the benefit of the doubt? Maybe she is telling the truth and didn't know she was breaking a rule. You know that if you give her an *F*, and especially an *F* for plagiarism, her appointment to the military academy is likely to be rescinded. At the very least, she will have to go to summer school in order to graduate, and I'm not sure she can do that in time to report to the academy in late June. What if I talk to the superintendent and recommend an alternative penalty? For example, Sheila could be required to do a different assignment and receive a grade reduction."

"Nick, this policy was recommended by the teachers assigned to honors courses and you, and the superintendent endorsed the recommendation. Plagiarism is an ethical violation; it's cheating, and cheating has no place in an honors class. Not enforcing the policy because of Sheila's circumstances in essence rescinds the policy. I feel bad, but I'm not willing to let my emotions interfere with my duty. Even if Sheila is telling the truth, ignorance is no excuse. Plagiarism is defined in the student handbook. I'm here because I wanted you to know about this as soon as possible." At that point, the teacher got up from her chair and walked out of the principal's office.

Mr. Furtoski slumped in his chair and stared at the picture hanging on the wall across the room; it was a picture of the state championship football team of which he was a member many years ago. About 15 minutes later, he called Superintendent Sposis to convey the bad news. As he waited to talk to him, he was still unsure how he would approach the matter. The easiest alternative would be to hide behind the policy and support Mrs. Durnitz. But he could not bring himself to do that for at least three reasons:

1. He feared that failing Sheila would cause serious political problems in the school and community.
2. He knew and liked the Allison family and surmised that Sheila's not going to the military academy would devastate them.
3. He now believed that he had erred in supporting the zero-tolerance policy because, for some students, the penalty was excessive.

When the superintendent came on the line, Mr. Furtoski told him about the problem.

Mr. Sposis then responded, "This is just what I need, Nick! Do you know what will happen if Sheila's appointment to the academy is withdrawn? The mayor has been bragging about this every chance he gets. The Allison family was just at city hall two days ago taking pictures with the mayor and city council. We need to find a way out of this."

"Mrs. Durnitz does not appear flexible. I don't know about her personal relationship with Sheila, but I don't think it is an issue in her decision. She made it clear that she is going to follow the policy and give Sheila an *F*. Janice's influence in the teachers' union is a factor to consider. As you recall, the policy in question was endorsed by the union and us. At this point, Janice is not willing to back off."

"You're the principal. Can't you override a teacher decision about a grade?" Mr. Sposis asked.

"And you're the superintendent. Can't you do the same? I don't think either of us wants to be in that position. One other option is to circumvent the policy because Sheila did not understand the nature of plagiarism. If we can prove this point, a lesser punishment might be acceptable. Another option would be to get the school board to rescind the policy."

The conversation between the two administrators continued for another 10 minutes. It concluded when the superintendent told the principal he would inform the school board and then get to back to him. After ending his conversation with the superintendent, Mr. Furtoski spoke to both Mrs. Durnitz and Sheila Allison, asking them to keep the matter confidential until the school board had been briefed.

After learning about the situation, the school board turned to its attorney, June VanSilten, for advice. She made three recommendations to board and superintendent:

1. Following the policy literally would result in serious conflict in the community and possibly in the school. She did not specify, however, whether the nature of this conflict would be legal or political.
2. Board members were advised not to discuss the matter with the media or anyone else. If the policy was enforced and the student appealed, the due process procedure required board members to judge the merits of the appeal.
3. The superintendent and board were advised not to take any action until the teacher had submitted a formal recommendation to fail the student and the principal had either endorsed or rebutted that recommendation.

The board agreed to follow her advice.

After the meeting, Superintendent Sposis called the principal and briefed him on his meeting with the board members. He emphasized that the board was expecting him to make a formal recommendation. He added that this should not be done until Mrs. Durnitz submitted a written statement providing a rationale for enforcing the policy. The superintendent also explained that everyone needed to be careful about violating procedures since Sheila's parents could pursue legal recourse.

The next day, the principal again met with Mrs. Durnitz to examine evidence. She showed him Sheila's assignment and copies of the published review, as it appeared in the magazine and as it appeared on the Web page. Clearly, the student had extracted content from the published review without giving credit to the author. Noting that the evidence revealed plagiarism, he raised the issue of whether Sheila could have violated the policy if she, as claimed, did not understand the concept of plagiarism. The teacher responded by reiterating that plagiarism is defined in the school's student handbook and that school board policy did not allow for exceptions. She then handed the principal a letter detailing her assessment of the situation; the letter included a recommendation that Sheila be excused from the class for the remainder of the semester and receive a failing grade. As per a notation at the bottom of the letter, a copy had been sent to the teachers' union president.

The next morning, Principal Furtoski received a telephone call from the teachers' union president, Janelle Thompson. She informed him that the union's executive board had met the prior evening and voted unanimously to support Mrs. Durnitz's recommendation. She also said that the union members expected him to follow policy and support the recommendation.

After putting down the telephone, Principal Furtoski realized that keeping the matter confidential was no longer a realistic goal. He then placed a call to Sheila's parents to determine if they knew about the situation and to inform them of the position being taken by Mrs. Durnitz. The principal had known Sheila's parents for more than twenty years and he considered them to be reasonable individuals. Deloris Allison, Sheila's mother, answered the call. She indicated that Sheila had told her and Mr. Allison about the problem the prior day. She also emphasized that both she and her husband do not believe that Sheila knowingly committed plagiarism. Mr. Furtoski indicated that he was working with other school officials to investigate the matter fully and to arrive at a resolution that was in the best interests of all parties.

After completing his conversation with Mrs. Allison, the principal met with two teachers he trusted implicitly. He learned two things from that encounter. First, most teachers already knew about the incident because the building representative for the teachers' union had distributed a memorandum to members about the matter that morning. Second, the memorandum indicated that the union's executive board had voted to support Mrs. Durnitz and stated the reasons for their support.

Shortly before leaving his office that day, Principal Furtoski received a telephone call from the reporter who regularly covered school news. He informed the principal that the paper would carry a story about the Sheila Allison issue the next morning and he wanted to give the principal an opportunity to comment.

Principal Furtoski told the reporter, "There has been an accusation of plagiarism, and I and other officials are looking into the matter. In fairness to the student, I don't think you should publish this story until the charge of plagiarism has been proven. At this point, I have no further comments."

"When will you have results of the investigation?" asked the reporter.

"No comment."

The next morning, the newspaper published an article about the issue. Appearing on page 2, the headline read, "Honor Student Accused of Plagiarism." The article included the following quote from Mrs. Allison:

My husband and I believe our daughter is being treated unfairly. She did not knowingly violate the policy on plagiarism. She never tried to hide what she did because she did not think her work violated any rules. If plagiarism is such an important issue, why didn't the principal and teachers instruct students on this matter?

The article also noted that the superintendent was unavailable to comment on the matter and that the principal refused to comment.

As he arrived at school that morning, Principal Furtoski found Superintendent Sposis sitting in his office.

"Have you read the paper?" the superintendent asked.

"I have, and I tried to dissuade the reporter from writing this article. I informed him that we were investigating the matter, yet he simply indicates that I refused to comment."

The superintendent then asked the principal if he had conducted his own investigation and if he had received a formal recommendation from Mrs. Durnitz. The principal responded in the affirmative to both queries.

The superintendent then stood up, indicating he was about to depart. He stared directly at the principal and said, "This is an absolute mess. I had hoped that we could avoid this problem before it reached crisis proportions. This situation could divide the community and result in serious problems for both of us. You need to decide what you're going to recommend on this matter. My advice is to be creative."

Not waiting for a response, the superintendent walked to the office door but turned back to look at the principal before opening it. Pointing at the principal, he said, "You need to find a way for us to get out of this mess."

PROBLEM FRAMING

1. Assume you are Principal Furtoski. Describe what you would want to accomplish in dealing with the situation described in this case.

2. Based on the evidence of contextual variables, describe the difficulty associated with achieving your objective.

QUESTIONS AND SUGGESTED ACTIVITIES

1. Share and critique the problem statements prepared by students in your class.

2. Discuss the potential merits and pitfalls of zero-tolerance policies.

3. What is a zero-tolerance policy? What is the rationale for such policy? Should educators support zero-tolerance policy?

4. Evaluate Principal Furtoski's behavior in dealing with (a) Mrs. Durnitz, (b) Mrs. Alli-

son, (c) Superintendent Sposis, and (d) the newspaper reporter.

5. Did Principal Furtoski investigate the charge of plagiarism appropriately? Why or why not?

6. As noted in the introduction for this case, administrative decisions often involve a confrontation between ethics and politics. To what extent is this true in the case?

7. Determine whether principals or superintendents in your state have legal authority to change student grades. Then discuss the merits of giving administrators this authority.

8. Evaluate the behavior of Mrs. Durnitz in the case. Did she act professionally? Why or why not?

9. The teacher and the teachers' union president argue that the plagiarism policy for honors classes was recommended by teachers, the principal, and the superintendent. Moreover, they contend that ignorance is not a valid defense because of content in the student handbook. The student's parents, however, argue that school personnel did not instruct their daughter on the concept of plagiarism, and therefore they are basically responsible for the fact that she did not understand the policy. Discuss the merits of these arguments.

10. Evaluate the behavior of the superintendent in the case. Has he acted professionally? Why or why not?

SUGGESTED READINGS

Bartlett, L. (1987). Academic evaluation and student discipline don't mix: A critical review. *Journal of Law and Education, 16*(2), 155–165.

Casella, R. (2003). Zero tolerance policy in schools: Rationale, consequences, and alternatives *Teachers College Record, 105*(5), 872–892.

Corey, S. F., & Zeck, P. A. (2003). *Combating plagiarism.* Fastback #514. Bloomington, IN: Phi Delta Kappa Educational Foundation.

Dempster, N., Carter, L., Freakley, M., & Parry, L. (2004). Conflicts, confusions and contradictions in principals' ethical decision making. *Journal of Educational Administration, 42*(4), 450–461.

Dowling-Sendor, B. (2001). What did he know, and when did he know it? *American School Board Journal, 188*(3), 14–15, 51.

Fennimore, B. S. (1997). When mediation and equity are at odds: Potential lessons in democracy. *Theory-into-Practice, 36*(1), 59–64.

Fris, J. (1992). Principals' encounters with conflict: Tactics they and others use. *Alberta Journal of Educational Research, 38*(1), 65–78.

Goldman, E. (1998). The significance of leadership style. *Educational Leadership, 55*(7), 20–22.

Gorman, K., & Pauken, P. (2003). The ethics of zero tolerance. *Journal of Educational Administration, 41*(1), 24–36.

Hayes, N., & Introna, L. D. (2005). Cultural values, plagiarism, and fairness: When plagiarism gets in the way of learning. *Ethics and Behavior, 15*(3), 213–231.

Henault, C. (2001). Zero tolerance in schools. *Journal of Law and Education, 30*(3), 547–553.

Hobbs, G. J. (1992). The legality of reducing student grades as a disciplinary measure. *Clearing House, 65,* 284–285.

Holloway, J. H. (2002). The dilemma of zero tolerance. *Educational Leadership, 59*(4), 84–85.

McGregor, J. H., & Williamson, K. (2005). Appropriate use of information at the secondary school level: Understanding and avoiding plagiarism *Library and Information Science Research, 27*(4), 496–512.

Saunders, E. J. (1993). Confronting academic dishonesty. *Journal of Social Work Education, 29*(2), 224–231.

Skiba, R., & Peterson, R. (1999). The dark side of zero tolerance: Can punishment lead to safe schools? *Phi Delta Kappan, 80*(5), 372–376, 381–382.

Verdugo, R. R. (2002). Race-ethnicity, social class, and zero-tolerance policies: The cultural and structural wars. *Education and Urban Society, 35*(1), 50–75.

REFERENCES

Begley, P. T. (2000). Values and leadership: Theory development, new research, and an agenda for the future. *Alberta Journal of Educational Research, 46*(3), 233–249.

Hodgkinson, C. (1991). *Educational leadership: The moral art*. Albany: State University of New York Press.

Howlett, P. (1991). How you can stay on the straight and narrow. *Executive Educator, 13*(2), 19–21, 35.

Kowalski, T. J. (2003). *Contemporary school administration: An introduction* (2nd ed.). Boston: Allyn and Bacon.

Kowalski, T. J. (2006). *The school superintendent: Theory, practice, and cases* (2nd ed.). Thousand Oaks, CA: Sage.

Kowalski, T. J., Lasley, T. J., & Mahoney, J. (2008). *Data-driven decisions and school leadership: Best practices for school improvement*. Boston: Allyn and Bacon.

Kowalski, T. J., Peterson, G. J., & Fusarelli, L. D. (2007). *Effective communication for school administrators: An imperative in an information age*. Lanham, MD: Rowman & Littlefield Education.

Sergiovanni, T. J. (1992). *Moral leadership: Getting to the heart of school improvement*. San Francisco: Jossey-Bass.

Willower, D. J. (1994). Values, valuation and explanation in school organizations. *Journal of School Leadership, 4*(5), 466–483.

11

The Absent Superintendent

Background Information

Since approximately 1980, there has been mounting evidence that effective communication is essential to school administrators (e.g., Carter & Cunningham, 1997; Kowalski, 2005; Kowalski, Petersen, & Fusarelli, 2007). In fact, effective communicative behavior has been found to influence both school culture and productivity (e.g., Friedkin & Slater, 1994; Morgan & Petersen, 2002; Petersen & Short, 2002). Findings linking leader communication and organizational outcomes certainly are not novel to education; many authors (e.g., Toth, 2000; Vihera & Nurmela, 2001) have described a nexus between open interpersonal communication by business executives and organizational effectiveness. Yet the topic of communication has received only modest attention in the literature on school administration and has been essentially ignored in relation to school reform (Kowalski, 2001, 2005).

Early studies of administrative behavior were based on an assumption that great leaders possessed unique personal qualities. These qualities or traits were first detailed in case biographies of great leaders and subsequently examined by researchers. Trait studies grew in popularity after World War II and their primary objective was to test associations between effective administrative practice and selected psychological characteristics (e.g., personality type). By the 1960s, however, scholars recognized that an administrator's approach to work (commonly referred to as leadership style) and not personal traits determined effectiveness (Hanson, 2003).

Research demonstrates that one's leadership style goes beyond personal traits. This critical variable is actually molded by the intricate mix of at least five factors (Kowalski, 2003):

1. Personality—the visible aspects of one's character (e.g., being introverted or extraverted)
2. Personal values and beliefs—philosophical disposition developed outside of the professional knowledge base
3. Socialization—conformity to the cultures of a profession and workplace (e.g., accepting certain values and beliefs as effective solutions to problems of practice)
4. Context—the human and physical variables surrounding the administrator's work
5. Professional knowledge—theoretical knowledge acquired during formal preparation and craft knowledge (artistry) acquired during practice

Dissimilar communicative behaviors among administrators are also the product of organizational perspectives (Kowalski, Petersen, & Fusarelli, 2007). Some superintendents, for example, stress order and efficiency, and therefore they embrace many of the tenets of classical theory (or bureaucracy). Classical theory had a profound effect during much of the last century, especially in promoting one-way, top-down communication. Top-level executives were encouraged to devalue employee input, both because their ideas and comments were deemed inconsequential and because such interaction would be inefficient (e.g., employees would be sending or exchanging information with their supervisors instead of doing their assigned jobs) (Hanson, 2003). Consequently, supervisors were taught to provide information to subordinates only on an "as needed" basis (Kowalski, 2004).

Unfortunately, the communicative behavior of bureaucrats was emulated by many superintendents for one or several of the following reasons:

- Some administrators assumed that behaving like a business executive was personally and organizationally beneficial (Kowalski, 2004, 2005).
- Some administrators treated information as power; by protecting information, they assumed that they were protecting or even expanding their personal power (Hoy & Miskel, 2005).
- Some administrators assumed that subordinates had neither useful information nor special knowledge and skills. Therefore, exchanging information with them freely was unessential (Hanson, 2003).

In this case, a newly appointed superintendent in a relatively small but highly affluent school district spends considerable time away from his office. Even when he is present, he rarely interacts with employees. Even other central office administrators have difficulty arranging meetings with him. His communicative behavior becomes problematic when a director is unable to meet with him concerning a grant opportunity.

Key Areas for Reflection

1. Leadership style
2. Communicative behavior
3. Context and leader behavior
4. Community values and employee expectations
5. Delegating authority

The Case

Community

Placid Falls is a suburban community that began developing in the early 1950s. Located approximately 35 miles from New York City, it is considered a community of choice by many upper-class families. House values range from approximately $550,000 to $1,500,000. The population is approximately 7,500 and the average family income is over $340,000 per year. All of the land suitable for single-family dwellings in the community has been developed.

A five-member town council, mayor, and town manager govern the city of Placid Falls. The council members and mayor serve four-year terms. The city has never had a "full-time" mayor and currently the position is held by a retired stockbroker. The town manager, appointed by the council, is a full-time employee and is responsible for managing the town on a day-to-day basis.

School District

The Placid Falls School District consists of four schools: two elementary schools (grades K–5), a middle school (grades 6–8), and a high school (grades 9–12). The district's enrollment has declined about 1 percent per year during the past decade; the current enrollment is approximately 1,800.

The community has always been proud of its local public schools. Approximately 90 percent of the high school graduates enroll in four-year institutions of higher learning within two years of completing the twelfth grade; about one-third of them are admitted to highly selective, prestigious colleges and universities. Academic competition among students, especially at the high school, is intense. Precollegiate programs dominate the curriculum and less than 1 percent of the students enroll in vocational courses offered at an area career-technical school.

Per-pupil expenditures are high, even by suburban New York City standards. Nearly 15 percent of the teachers and 75 percent of the administrators have doctoral degrees. Teacher and administrator salaries, among the highest in the state, are a primary reason why the district receives literally dozens of applications for every vacancy.

Search for a New Superintendent

Three years ago when the Placid Falls school board searched for a new superintendent, they received 123 applications, most from highly qualified and experienced administrators. Dr. George Frieman, a well-known professor and placement consultant, was retained to assist the school board. His primary responsibilities were to develop vacancy materials, recruit promising candidates, and assist the school board in screening applicants.

The first stage of the selection process involved an evaluation of the applications. Dr. Frieman was assigned this task. He was to eliminate applicants who did not meet the basic criteria and then recommend no fewer than ten of the applicants to the school board. The administrators he recommended included some of the best-known superintendents in the United States.

After studying the written application materials, the school board members selected five candidates to be interviewed. One was Dr. Andrew Sagossi, then a superintendent of a large county school system in North Carolina. After the initial interviews, he received the highest composite ranking from the school board members. He and one other applicant were invited to return to Placid Falls for a second interview. After those interviews were conducted, the board voted unanimously to offer the position to Dr. Sagossi.

He responded to the offer by telling the board president that he would accept the position if his attorney could negotiate a contract suitable to him and the school board. Such a stipulation would probably have alienated many school board members, but in the eyes of the Placid Falls board president, it was another affirmation of Dr. Sagossi's management skills. The other board members also were impressed that Dr. Sagossi had the foresight to retain an attorney to represent him in this matter.

Within a week, the attorney and school board president agreed on a four-year contract. In the first year of the agreement, Dr. Sagossi would receive direct compensation in the amount of $185,000 and indirect compensation (fringe benefits) estimated to be about $42,000. His fringe benefits included unrestricted use of a leased automobile and a generous individual retirement account that was in addition to his state retirement account.

Dr. Sagossi's friends were surprised when they learned he was moving to Placid Falls. Prior to this decision, he had moved progressively to larger school systems. Now, he was leaving a district with over 40,000 students and going to one with fewer than 2,000 students. Even so, he actually was increasing his salary by about 15 percent. In addition, his mother resided 27 miles from Placid Falls and she was in poor health. Last, Dr. Sagossi needed five more years of service in New York to become eligible for maximum pension benefits in that state.

Instead of mentioning the real reasons why he wanted to move to Placid Falls, Dr. Sagossi had told the board members that he wanted to be in a situation where he could have more direct contact with schools and the local community. In response to specific questions about his interest in Placid Falls, he offered the following explanation:

> I have been superintendent in several large school systems and I no longer view the organizational size as an indicator of job quality. In a community such as Placid Falls, the superintendent has more opportunities to work with community and state leaders to achieve educational excellence. Quite frankly, I don't want to spend the remainder of my career defending public schools that are not performing well. I'd rather be doing positive things in a community where good administrators, good teachers, and good schools are appreciated.

Assistant Superintendents

At the time of Dr. Sagossi's appointment, there were two assistant superintendents, Dr. Al Yanko and Dr. Joan Myers. Dr. Yanko was responsible for business management and facilities; Dr. Myers was responsible for curriculum. Dr. Yanko had been employed in the district for twenty-one years, the last seven in his current position. Dr. Myers had been employed just six months before Dr. Sagossi arrived.

Joan Myers is a former teacher who became an assistant principal in suburban Philadelphia shortly after finishing her master's degree in school administration. Two years later, she resigned and became a doctoral fellow at a large state university. At about the same time that she completed her doctoral studies, her husband was transferred to suburban New York City.

After relocating, Joan applied for a myriad of vacancies. Though she had less experience than other candidates for the Placid Falls position, the search committee was impressed with her, concluding that she had the intelligence and demeanor to succeed in the school district.

Though her official title was "assistant superintendent," Dr. Myers actually was a staff administrator. That is, her responsibilities focused primarily on facilitating the work of principals and teachers. She had no line authority over principals or any other district employees. Primarily she collaborated with other administrators and teachers on curriculum projects, staff development, instructional technology, and performance evaluations.

Dr. Sagossi Arrives

During the first two to three weeks in Placid Falls, Dr. Sagossi held several administrative staff meetings and met with administrators individually. During these sessions, he outlined expectations and developed several general goals that he had for the school system. The administrative staff members judged that he was much like his predecessor—confident, articulate, and capable.

By early October, however, contact between the superintendent and other administrators lessened. Even the central office secretaries commented about how little time he spent in his office. And when he was in the office, he either had appointments or worked with his personal secretary behind a closed door. His lack of visibility distinguished Dr. Sagossi from his predecessor. The former superintendent spent a considerable amount of time at the district's administrative offices, and he frequently joined secretaries and other administrators in the lounge for coffee.

The district's four principals were also curious about the superintendent's work habits. Dr. Sagossi's predecessor typically met privately with them twice a month. Dr. Sagossi only contacted the principals when he felt it was necessary to do so, and almost always the conversations were conducted via telephone. When principals tried to contact him, the secretary would inquire about the nature of the call and refer them to Dr. Yanko.

Dr. Sagossi had relegated routine administrative responsibilities to his assistant for business—a decision that pleased Dr. Yanko. When principals asked questions about access to the superintendent, Dr. Yanko would explain that Dr. Sagossi was busy building community support for the schools. For example, he told one principal, "Dr. Sagossi is a community-oriented administrator. He is doing many positive things that do not directly involve schools, but his activities are important for the district."

This description of Dr. Sagossi was basically accurate. In less than four months, Dr. Sagossi was highly involved in the Placid Falls community. As examples, he was appointed to a local bank's board of directors and to the local United Way board. Less known to the principals and other district employees, Dr. Sagossi was also highly involved in two other activities. He was a member of the alumni council at his alma mater, and he had recently become president-elect of a national suburban superintendents' association.

The Problem

In early December, Dr. Myers attended a national conference on gifted and talented education where she met Maggie Zerich, a program officer with a private foundation. The foundation had initiated a network of highly effective gifted education programs. Currently, thirteen school districts were involved. Dr. Myers learned that the foundation was accepting applications for new members. Being admitted to the network resulted in an initial $50,000 grant. Ms. Zerich was familiar with the Placid Falls Community School District, and she encouraged Dr. Myers to submit an application.

Joan inquired about the network's objectives and was told that the primary purpose was to examine the benefits of linking students in the seventh grade with mentors for two years. The mentors were typically local government officials, business leaders, or professional practitioners, such as physicians or lawyers. The grants were provided to assist with the development of the program, to provide operating funds, and to support a required annual evaluation.

Dr. Myers returned to Placid Falls eager to pursue the application. She could hardly wait to tell Dr. Sagossi about the opportunity; she thought that getting the grant would be a significant accomplishment. The one challenge she faced was a tight timeline. The proposal had to be received by the foundation by January 20.

After to returning to her office on December 8, Dr. Myers identified four things she needed to accomplish:

1. She had to meet with the middle school principal to gain his support and cooperation since the project would be based in his school. He and the gifted-education teacher would be part of the network if they were admitted.
2. She had to develop selection procedures for students and mentors. Hopefully, the middle school principal and the gifted education teacher would assist her in this task.
3. She had to construct a list of prospective mentors.
4. She had to get Dr. Sagossi's approval and commitment to appropriate $50,000 in matching funds—a commitment that was essential to be admitted to the network.

After finishing her list, Dr. Myers walked across the hall and asked to see Dr. Sagossi. Miss Halston, his secretary, told her that the superintendent was out of town at a conference and would not return until December 13. Miss Halston suggested that she talk to Dr. Yanko, especially if the matter she wanted to discuss with the superintendent was important.

Dr. Meyers walked across the hall to Dr. Yanko's office. She explained the proposal to him and asked if he could commit the required matching funds.

"Only the superintendent and the school board can appropriate the funds," Dr. Yanko told her. "Policy requires that all proposals for outside funding must be approved by the school board before they are submitted to funding agencies. And as you know, nothing goes to the school board for consideration unless the superintendent has placed it on the agenda. When do you have to submit the proposal?"

"I'm estimating that the last possible date is January 12," Dr. Myers replied.

"Well, you still have the January board meeting. Let's see; the first Wednesday in January is the 4th. You'll be okay."

After the conversation, Dr. Myers went back to Miss Halston to make an appointment with the superintendent so she could meet with him after he returned to the district. The secretary scheduled her for 10:00 A.M. on December 13. She explained that December 12 would not be possible because the superintendent would not be available.

Dr. Myers completed the proposal and saw Superintendent Sagossi briefly on Wednesday the 12th, the day he returned to Placid Falls. The two exchanged greetings in the hallway of the administrative office and she mentioned that she had an appointment with him the next day. The following morning, there was an administrative staff meeting at 8:00 A.M. Staff meetings were scheduled by the superintendent on an "as needed" basis. This meeting focused on a review of state reports on school progress. It ended at approximately 9:30 A.M. At 9:55 A.M., Joan arrived at Dr. Sagossi's office for her 10:00 A.M. appointment.

As she entered, Miss Halston said, "I was just trying to reach you on the phone, Dr. Myers. I'm afraid I have to reschedule your appointment. Dr. Sagossi's mother is quite ill. He intends to be back in the office on Monday the 15th. He asked me to reschedule you for 9:00 A.M. that day."

After Dr. Myers arrived for her rescheduled appointment on December 15th, Miss Halston told her that the board president was meeting with the superintendent. He had arrived about 30 minutes earlier and did not have an appointment. Since Miss Halston did not know why the two men were meeting, she had no idea when the superintendent would be available to see Dr. Myers. Dr. Myers said she would be in her office and asked that she be contacted as soon as the board president left.

At about 10:30 A.M., Miss Halston called Dr. Myers and told her that a problem had surfaced. Her appointment would have to be moved to the next day. Dr. Myers looked at her calendar and told the secretary that she could not meet on Tuesday because she was attending a meeting in Albany.

"How about Wednesday?" asked Dr. Myers. "Is he available on Wednesday?"

"No," the secretary answered. "He has to be at a university alumni board meeting. He will be back on Thursday."

Dr. Myers' frustration turned to anger. She told Miss Halston, "Look, I need to see him about a grant proposal. This is not General Motors. I find it difficult to understand why I can't arrange to see the superintendent for just 30 minutes. There are thousands of dollars at stake, not to mention an excellent educational opportunity. I'm sure that if Dr. Sagossi knew why I wanted to see him, he would find time."

"Dr. Myers," replied the secretary, "I'm just doing my job. Let me talk to Dr. Sagossi to see if he can see you before the end of the week."

Fifteen minutes later the secretary called back and told Dr. Myers that she should talk to Dr. Yanko about the grant.

"I have already tried to talk to him. He referred me to the superintendent. Please tell Dr. Sagossi that I will send him something in writing and perhaps he can respond after he reads it."

After putting down the telephone, Dr. Myers realized that school would be dismissing for the holiday break in just four days. Further, she realized that the agenda for the January 4th board meeting was probably being prepared. She went to the superintendent's office to see when board materials would be distributed for the meeting. The secretary said that the packets, including the agenda, would be distributed as always one week before the meeting. Because Dr. Sagossi was going on vacation for ten days commencing December 23, he intended to complete the board packets by the afternoon of Friday the 22nd. Now Dr. Myers had even less time than she thought.

"Look, the only possible date left is Thursday, December 21. What if something else comes up and he cancels the appointment again?" Dr. Myers asked.

The secretary looked at her and said slowly, "Dr. Sagossi is a busy person. He isn't trying to avoid you. His mother is ill and he has a busy schedule."

Dejected, Dr. Myers walked back to her office.

PROBLEM FRAMING

1. Assume you are Dr. Myers. Describe what you would want to accomplish in dealing with the situation described in this case.

2. Based on the evidence of contextual variables, describe the difficulty associated with achieving your objective.

QUESTIONS AND SUGGESTED ACTIVITIES

1. What factors may have contributed to the superintendent's behavior in general and his communicative behavior with employees specifically?

2. In a moment of anger, Dr. Myers comments to the superintendent's secretary, "This is not General Motors." What was she implying?

3. Is it possible for a superintendent to spend most of his or her time away from the school district and still be highly effective? What evidence do you have to support your response?

4. What alternatives does Dr. Myers have to resolve the problem she faces?

5. Evaluate the Dr. Myers's behavior in this case. Did she contribute to the problem she faces?

6. Do you believe the superintendent is an effective administrator? Why or why not?

7. Think of the most effective superintendent you have known. Describe this person's communicative behavior and then compare it to Dr. Sagossi's communicative behavior.

8. The superintendent meets with his administrative staff only when he deems it essential to do so. Is this an effective arrangement? Why or why not?

SUGGESTED READINGS

Brunner, C. C. (1997). Exercising power. *School Administrator, 54*(6), 6–9.

Chalker, D., & Hurley, S. (1993). Beastly people. *Executive Educator, 15*(1), 24–26.

Comer, D. (1991). Organizational newcomers' acquisition of information from peers. *Management Communication Quarterly, 5*(1), 64–89.

Diggins, P. B. (1997). Reflections on leadership characteristics necessary to develop and sustain learning school communities. *School Leadership and Management, 17*(3), 413–425.

Duke, D. L. (1998). The normative context of organizational leadership. *Educational Administration Quarterly, 34*(2), 165–195.

Duttweiler, P. (1988). The dysfunctions of bureaucratic structure. *Educational Policy and Practice*, Issue 3.

Geddes, D. (1993). Empowerment through communication: Key people-to-people and organizational success. *People and Education, 1*(1), 76–104.

Goldman, E. (1998). The significance of leadership style. *Educational Leadership, 55*(7), 20–22.

Goldman, J. P. (2004). A ground's-eye style of leading. *School Administrator, 61*(10), 59.

Hoy, W., Newland, W., & Blaxovsky, R. (1977). Subordinate loyalty to superior, esprit, and aspects of bureaucratic structure. *Educational Administration Quarterly, 13*(1), 71–85.

Immegart, G. (1988). Leadership and leader behavior. In N. Boyan (Ed.), *Handbook of research on educational administration* (pp. 259–278). New York: Longman.

Kowalski, T. J. (1998). The role of communication in providing leadership for school restructuring. *Mid-Western Educational Researcher, 11*(1), 32–40.

Kowalski, T. J. (2005). Evolution of the school superintendent as communicator. *Communication Education, 54*(2), 101–117.

Loose, W., & McManus, J. (1987). Corporate management techniques in the superintendent's office. *Thrust, 16*(7), 11–13.

Osterman, K. F. (1994). Communication skills: A key to collaboration and change. *Journal of School Leadership, 4*(4), 382–398.

Rusch, E. A. (1998). Leadership in evolving democratic school communities. *Journal of School Leadership, 8*(3), 214–250.

Shelton, M. M., & Powell, T. (1997). The ethics question. *American School Board Journal, 184*(12), 36–37.

Spaulding, A., & O'Hair, M. J. (2004). Public relations in a communication context (3rd ed.). In T. J. Kowalski (Ed.), *Public relations in schools* (pp. 96–124). Upper Saddle River, NJ: Merrill, Prentice Hall.

REFERENCES

Carter, G. R., & Cunningham, W. G. (1997). *The American school superintendent.* San Francisco: Jossey-Bass.

Friedkin, N. E., & Slater, M. R. (1994). School leadership and performance: A social network approach. *Sociology of Education, 67,* 139–157.

Hanson, E. M. (2003). *Educational administration and organizational behavior* (5th ed.). Boston: Allyn and Bacon.

Hoy, W. K., & Miskel, C. G. (2005). *Educational administration: Theory, research, and practice* (8th ed.). New York: McGraw-Hill.

Kowalski, T. J. (2001). Cultural change paradigms and administrator communication. *Journal of School Public Relations, 22*(3), 4–11.

Kowalski, T. J. (2003). *Contemporary school administration: An introduction* (2nd ed.). Boston: Allyn and Bacon.

Kowalski, T. J. (2004). School public relations: A new agenda. In T. J. Kowalski (Ed.), *Public relations in schools* (pp. 3–29). Upper Saddle River, NJ: Merrill, Prentice Hall.

Kowalski, T. J. (2005). *Evolution of the school superintendent as communicator. Communication Education, 54*(2), 101–117.

Kowalski, T. J., Petersen, G. J., & Fusarelli, L. D. (2007). *Effective communication for school administrators: An imperative in an information age.* Lanham, MD: Rowman and Littlefield Education.

Morgan, C. L., & Petersen, G. J. (2002). The role of the district superintendent in leading academically successful school districts. In B. S. Cooper & L. D. Fusarelli (Eds.), *The promises and perils facing today's school superintendent* (pp. 175–196). Lanham, MD: Scarecrow Education.

Petersen, G. J., & Short, P. M. (2002). An examination of school board presidents' perceptions of their superintendent's interpersonal communication competence and board decision making. *Journal of School Leadership, 12*(4), 411–436.

Toth, E. L. (2000). From personal influence to interpersonal influence: A model for relationship management. In J. A. Ledingham & S. D. Bruning (Eds.), *Public relations as relationship management* (pp. 205–220). Mahwah, NJ: Lawrence Erlbaum Associates.

Vihera, M. L., & Nurmela, J. (2001). Communication capability as an intrinsic determinant for an information age. *Futures, 33*(3/4), 245–265.

Break the Rules and Pay the Price

Background Information

Role theory addresses variables that shape work behavior. These models provide conceptual frameworks that assist analysts to study job performance in relation to performance expectations (Gaynor, 1998). Such analysis often uncovers *role conflict*, disharmony between actual and ideal behavior. This common problem, experienced by most school principals, may be attributable to several factors. One of the most common is ambiguity. Role ambiguity results when their formal role (i.e., the one designated by their employer) is not clearly defined or when the administrator does not comprehend the employer's expectations accurately (Hanson, 2003).

Even when a principal's formal role is stated clearly, individuals and groups may have differing expectations of him or her. This variability is rooted in philosophical dispositions; that is, members of a school's broad community almost always hold different and sometimes competing values and beliefs. These philosophical differences are expressed as informal role expectations (Kowalski, 2003). During a teachers' strike, for example, teachers may expect the principal to be a peer professional (i.e., someone who is sympathetic to their cause). Conversely, the school board and superintendent may expect the principal to be an organizational administrator (i.e., someone who protects the organization's interests by enforcing its policies, rules, and directives).

Role conflict may also be intrapersonal (Owens, 2001). For example, a principal may seek to be both stern and well liked. If one goal does not consistently take precedent over the other, the principal's behavior may be unpredictable—and confusing to others.

When confronted with role conflict, a principal may behave in several different ways. Using the example in which a principal encounters competing expectations during a teachers' strike, the following are possible choices:

- *Picking one expectation over others.* In pursuing this alternative, the principal decides whether to meet the teachers' expectations or the superintendent/school board expectations.
- *Withdrawing.* In pursuing this alternative, the principal retreats; for example, he resigns and seeks another position.

- *Seeking reconciliation.* In pursuing the alternative, the principal attempts to reconcile the differing expectations; for example, he attempts to explain his dilemma to all parties in hopes that they will lessen their expectations.
- *Trying to satisfy everyone.* In pursuing this alternative, the principal attempts to be all things to all parties; for example, he wants the teachers to believe that he is on their side and he wants the superintendent and school board to believe that he is on their side.
- *Seeking protection for supervisors.* In pursuing this alternative, the principal attempts to gain relief by having the superintendent or a designee intervene; for example, the superintendent tells the teachers that the principal's first and only duty is to keep the school open during a strike.
- *Ignoring the situation.* In pursuing this alternative, the principal hopes that the situation will resolve itself; for example, the strike will end.

Contextual variables over which the principal has little or no control often determine if the various alternatives will be successful. In sum, there is no "one best way" to deal with role conflict.

This case involves a principal who often suspends middle school students for what he considers serious violations of the school's code of conduct. Suspension is a disciplinary sanction that requires the student to be excluded from the school building for a specified period of time; it is one of the most common disciplinary consequences for unacceptable behavior. Research, however, indicates that a temporary exclusion from school rarely reduces the negative behavior being punished (Christle, Nelson, & Jolivette, 2004). Many parents in this case, however, believe otherwise. Moreover, they are convinced that the principal's tough disciplinary actions have contributed to an effective learning environment and a positive school image. Several teachers at the school disagree with these convictions. They see the principal as a misguided administrator who bases his behavior on personal experiences and intuition rather than on professional knowledge. Divergent expectations surface after the principal suspends a student for criticizing a teacher.

Key Area for Reflection

1. Role expectations
2. Role conflict
3. School and community cultures
4. Student learning and discipline
5. Zero-tolerance policy

The Case

School Profile

Rogers Middle School is located in a major city in a southwestern state. The school was built nine years ago to accommodate population growth in low-cost housing areas.

The attractive and well-maintained building is a source of pride for local families. Although houses in the surrounding neighborhoods are less than twenty-five years old, many of the inexpensive prefabricated structures are already in poor condition.

Many Rogers Middle School students are bilingual. A statistical report prepared for district administration provided the following racial-ethnic profile:

Hispanic: 41 percent
African American: 15 percent
Caucasian: 24 percent
Native American: 9 percent
Asian American: 9 percent
Other: 2 percent

The profile of the school's professional staff, however, is dissimilar. Nearly 70 percent of the teachers, counselors, and administrators identify themselves as Caucasian.

Rogers Middle School contains grades 6, 7, and 8 and accommodates a total enrollment of about 1,150. Data for the last three years indicate that students at Rogers have made greater gains on the state proficiency test than the other six middle schools in the district. However, Rogers also has the highest suspension rate of any of the middle schools. Both outcomes are commonly attributed to the school's principal, Hector Sanchez.

Principal Profile

Ever since he was in the third grade, Hector Sanchez wanted to become a teacher. One of nine children reared in a lower-middle-class family, he decided to pursue his dream by working in a local factory and driving 45 miles twice a week to take night classes at the nearest state university. After six years, he had completed three-fourths of the degree requirements and saved enough money so that he could finish his last year of undergraduate studies as a full-time student. As a part-time student, Hector had maintained an A average. After becoming a full-time student, he received As in all the courses he completed.

After graduating, Hector was anxious to start teaching. He was married, and his wife was now pregnant. He accepted a position at a high school that included teaching mathematics, coaching football (as an assistant coach), and coaching boys' track (as the head coach). Two years later, he began studying for his master's degree in educational administration, a program he completed four years later.

Within months of receiving his principal's license, Hector was hired as an assistant high school principal in an urban school district. His primary responsibilities were student discipline and athletics. The principal, Carl Brown, was known as a taskmaster. He told Hector that he needed to be stern in disciplining students. This expectation was not a problem for Hector because he too believed that school personnel had to be uncompromising when it came to punishing students. The two administrators quickly developed a mentor-protégé relationship.

After having served just three years as an assistant principal, Mr. Brown nominated Hector for a middle school principal vacancy in the district. After completing his application, Hector interviewed for the vacancy. During his interview, he was questioned about his overall lack of experience and his total lack of experience in middle schools. He responded by telling the committee members that he understood the context of middle school education and that he could provide essential leadership because he related well to the types of students who would be attending this new school. He added that many students from low-income and one-parent families required high expectations, discipline, and direction and that he was adept at meeting those needs.

A member of the selection committee, the assistant superintendent for pupil services, was familiar with Mr. Sanchez's record as a disciplinarian. She asked him two questions: Did he have any evidence that suspension had a positive effect on students? And would he encourage his assistant principal to suspend students for infractions that did not require this punishment (as per school board policy)?

Hector reflected for a moment and then answered. "As a teacher, coach, and assistant principal, I have observed how students react to being disciplined. Though there are exceptions, most students do not want to be suspended, and they usually stay out of trouble after reentering school. I suspended several students who came back to see me after they graduated. They thanked me for being tough. They said that their eyes were opened after being suspended. In addition, I believe I have a responsibility to make the school a safe environment. When I suspend a student, I'm also thinking about the welfare of other students."

Hector then asked the assistant superintendent to restate her second question. After she did so, he thanked her and answered.

"Mr. Brown set expectations for me after I became his assistant. These expectations included suggestions regarding student discipline. However, Mr. Brown always has given me the latitude to do my job. Yes, I knew that he wanted to have a safe and functional school, and he has relied on me to provide student discipline in relation to that goal. I plan to do the same thing with my assistant principal."

Student discipline was a contentious topic in this 24,000-student school district. Despite efforts on the part of some principals to have the school board adopt policy that set specific requirements for all student suspensions, the superintendent refused to make such a recommendation. Certain infractions did mandate suspensions (e.g., possession or use of an illegal drug); however, principals had considerable discretion in suspending students for other offenses. Administrators across the school district were divided over this issue and as a result, suspension rates varied considerably.

All six selection committee members knew that the high school where Mr. Sanchez currently was assigned as an assistant principal had the highest suspension rate in the district. After the interview, two members said they would not support his candidacy because they disagreed with his discipline philosophy, especially if it were applied at the middle school level. However, he was supported by the remaining committee members, and he was recommended for the position.

Student Suspensions

Shortly after Rogers Middle School became operational, Principal Sanchez established a parent association. He appointed association members to various school committees, including the Student Discipline Committee (SDC). The SDC was an advisory panel composed of seven parents, three teachers, and the assistant principal. The SDC met monthly and members reviewed pertinent rules and records. The committee's main responsibility was to serve as sounding board for the principal.

During its first year of operation, the SDC did not deal with controversial issues. Midway through the second year, student suspensions became a topic of discussion. The subject was raised by a teacher on the committee. She pointed out that despite the school's being less than two years old, more students had been suspended there than at any of the district's other middle schools. She argued that nearly half the suspensions were for offenses that would not result in the same level of punishment at other middle schools. Principal Sanchez responded by first distributing a copy of the school district's policy pertaining to the issue:

- A school principal (hereafter including an assistant principal, acting principal, or a legitimate designee) may suspend a student when, in the principal's judgment, the action is required. In the exercise of this authority, the principal is subject to all provisions of law and school board policy.
- Students may be suspended from school for up to five (5) school days by the school principal without concurrence from the superintendent or his/her designee.
- Prior to imposing a suspension, the principal must inform the student of the intent to suspend and provide an explanation of charges. The student is required to sign a form indicating he or she has been informed of these matters.
- If the student denies the charges, a written explanation of facts is given to the student and to his or her parent or guardian. Students whose presence poses a continuing danger to persons or property or an ongoing threat of disruption may be removed from school immediately.
- After a decision is made to suspend a student for five (5) school days or less, the principal shall report the facts of the case in writing to the Superintendent or his or her designee, the student's parent or guardian, and the student as soon as practicable.
- Appeals of out-of-school suspensions are governed by board policy concerning suspensions and expulsions.

After reviewing the policy with the SDC members, Principal Sanchez emphasized that Rogers Middle School was and would remain a safe environment. He told the committee members that suspensions had a positive effect on most students who received them, and they certainly were in the best interests of the school. He added that student discipline needed to be evaluated in relation to student learning. All but two of the SDC members (both teachers) agreed with his comments.

Now in its third year of operation, Rogers Middle School was receiving positive publicity, largely because the percentage of students meeting the state proficiency standard on achievement tests had steadily increased. Principal Sanchez was portrayed by the media as a "no-nonsense" administrator, and his firm stand on student discipline was linked to student academic performance. A reporter who had written two stories about the school noted that students referred to Principal Sanchez as "Captain Punishment."

In mid-February, the superintendent announced that he had nominated Mr. Sanchez to receive the state's "Principal of the Year" award. A local television station did a profile of the principal and Rogers Middle School after the superintendent's announcement. The reporter assigned to do the profile discovered that not all teachers supported the principal's tough stance toward disciplining students. His most outspoken critic was Aaron Carson, a social studies instructor.

Mr. Carson had moved to the Southwest seeking relief for his chronic asthma. Previously, he had taught in a high school in suburban Washington, DC. He openly disagreed with the principal's frequent use of suspensions, arguing that removing students from school temporarily was an ineffective form of punishment that simply ensured that the students would suffer academically. Initially, several colleagues supported the views expressed by Mr. Carson, but in the aftermath of positive publicity about the school and the principal, they were reluctant to be critical.

On two occasions, Principal Sanchez and Mr. Carson discussed their differing philosophies about student discipline. The conversations were candid but not malevolent. Neither encounter resolved their differences.

Conflict Intensifies

Most everyone at Rogers Middle School either knew or knew about Jimmy Malenga. He was a good athlete with a knack for finding trouble. His father was deceased and he lived with his mother and two sisters. Unfortunately, Jimmy's performance in the classroom did not match his performance on the athletic field. However, he did do well in one subject, social studies, and his favorite teacher was Mr. Carson.

Unlike many middle schools, Rogers did not organize instruction around teacher teams, and block scheduling was not used. The daily schedule was constructed around seven periods, each 43 minutes long. Jimmy's first period class was his least favorite, language arts. His teacher, Mr. Draycroft, was also his least favorite teacher. Jimmy found diagramming sentences, studying grammar, and reading poetry to be boring and irrelevant. One day, Mr. Draycroft was giving Jimmy a tongue-lashing before the entire class for not having completed an assigned homework. When the teacher finished, Jimmy looked directly at him and said, "This stuff we do in here is all crap. Why don't you teach us something that's useful?"

Most students laughed but silence quickly fell over the room after Mr. Draycroft shook his finger at Jimmy. "Young man," he said "you are going to the principal's office. I have had it with you."

The class period ended a few minutes later and Mr. Draycroft escorted Jimmy to the principal's office. Because he had to return for his second-period class in a few minutes, he told the secretary that he had to see Mr. Sanchez immediately. Mr. Draycroft met with Principal Sanchez while Jimmy sat in the reception office. After a few minutes, Mr. Draycroft left and Jimmy was brought into Mr. Sanchez's office. Jimmy and the principal were not strangers. Jimmy had been suspended from school on two previous occasions, each time for three days.

"Jimmy," Mr. Sanchez began, "when are you going to learn? Mr. Draycroft told me what you said in front of the class." The principal then restated what the teacher had told him and asked Jimmy if the comments attributed to him were accurate.

Jimmy answered, "Yes. I said these things because they're true. He's a bad teacher."

"Jimmy, I don't think you are in a position to judge teachers. Your remarks were disrespectful, and you have to learn that there are consequences for improper behavior. I am notifying you now of my intent to suspend you for three days. You need to sign this form indicating that I've told you of my intent and then I'll notify your mother that you are entitled to have an informal hearing."

Jimmy stared at the principal and said, "This is unfair. You're just protecting a crummy teacher. I don't need this crap." He then ran out of the principal's office without signing the form.

Principal Sanchez telephoned Jimmy's mother, who was at work at the time. He informed her that he had suspended Jimmy for three days and explained the reasons. He then added that Jimmy had left school after being told that he would be suspended.

Mrs. Malenga left work immediately in hopes of finding her son. Her effort was unsuccessful, and Jimmy did not come home that night. At 11:30 P.M., she contacted the police and reported that he was missing.

Various accounts of the incident spread quickly through the school. Aaron Carson learned of the problem as he was leaving school that day. The next morning, he was still furious as he met with Principal Sanchez before first period. Unlike previous encounters, this one was not civil. Harsh words were exchanged in a conversation that lasted about five minutes. Later during his preparation period, Mr. Carson telephoned Dr. Penelope Mackee, the assistant superintendent for secondary education and Mr. Sanchez's immediate supervisor. He blamed the principal for Jimmy's disappearance and said he would pursue the matter with the school board if she did not investigate. She expressed concern for the student's welfare and said she would discuss the matter with Principal Sanchez.

Assuming that the assistant superintendent and other school officials would blindly protect Hector Sanchez, Aaron Carson wrote the following letter to the city's major newspaper that evening. The letter was printed on the editorial page two days later:

The public needs to know the story of Jimmy Malenga, a young Native American student at Rogers Middle School who apparently is now a runaway. Jimmy is one of my students and over the past few months, he has been making considerable progress in my class. He was going to be suspended from school for expressing a viewpoint about another teacher. Though his behavior was improper, so was the proposed punishment. Jimmy Malenga is now somewhere on the streets because officials at Rogers Middle School thought it was more important to punish him than to help him. What happened to Jimmy unfortunately is not atypical at our school. The principal routinely suspends students rather than providing them with counseling or constructive behavior modification. I urge the superintendent and school board to revise policy so that the indiscriminate use of suspensions is not possible. I hope others will do the same.

Sincerely,
Aaron Carson
Social studies teacher, Rogers Middle School

After the letter appeared in the newspaper, over 300 citizens called the superintendent or school board members supporting Mr. Carson's views. His letter also prompted the education editor to write a story about suspensions at Rogers Middle School. The article pointed out that the rate of suspensions at the school was higher than at other middle schools, and quotes from Principal Sanchez defending his actions were included. After that article was published, a series of letters to the editor were published, most defending Principal Sanchez but some criticizing him.

The lingering controversy disturbed school board members, and they directed the superintendent, Dr. Fred Lopson, to investigate the matter. They also wanted the superintendent to explain why principals continued to have considerable latitude with respect to suspensions. Before he could write a report, he and the board members received the following petition that was signed by more than 400 parents and teachers associated with Rogers Middle School:

We the undersigned fully support the leadership of Principal Hector Sanchez. He has made Rogers Middle School the most successful and safest middle school in this district. Obviously, the incident involving Jimmy Malenga is unfortunate. We hope that Jimmy returns home and continues his schooling. However, we believe it is unfair to blame Mr. Sanchez for the student's poor decisions. We urge the school board to join us in supporting a great principal and an outstanding school.

A large group of Mr. Sanchez's supporters attended the next school board meeting knowing that Dr. Lopson would be presenting his report on the Jimmy Malenga incident. In his verbal summary of the document, the superintendent pointed out that existing school district policy did not prohibit the prescribed penalty assigned by Principal Sanchez. The superintendent added that many parents and most teachers supported the principal's discipline procedures, as evidenced by the petition. He also reported that the SDC supported the principal's position regarding this form of punishment. The superintendent then explained why he was reluctant to change existing policy. He argued that principals were professional administrators and as such, they should have discretion in assigning punishment. He noted that creating zero-tolerance policy would reduce administrators and teachers to acting as policemen.

After Superintendent Lopson finished his report, George Manulita, a board member, asked to be recognized.

"We are all aware that Mr. Sanchez is a popular principal. In my opinion, he is also a successful principal in terms of improving student learning. But his success and popularity are not the issues. The real issue is whether he or any other principal should have the authority to suspend students for any infraction of the rules. We are all saddened that Jimmy Malenga is missing. Hopefully, he will be found and will return to school. I urge you, Dr. Lopson, to recommend policy changes that will prevent the indiscriminate use of suspensions."

Mr. Manulita's suggestion sparked shouts of "no" from the principal's supporters in the audience.

Darren Marshall, another board member, spoke next. "Remember that we're talking about one of our best schools. Do we want to get in the way of a highly successful principal? Mr. Sanchez has done a great job. Quite frankly, I'm comfortable with current policy. I agree with Dr. Lopson. Mr. Sanchez is a professional and he should be given the authority to determine appropriate punishment. Maybe we should be talking about efforts to destroy a fine principal's reputation."

The principal's supporters stood, applauded, and then chanted, "Mr. Sanchez, Mr. Sanchez."

PROBLEM FRAMING

1. Assume you are Superintendent Lopson. Describe what you would want to accomplish in dealing with the situation described in this case.

2. Based on the evidence of contextual variables, describe the difficulty associated with achieving your objective.

QUESTIONS AND SUGGESTED ACTIVITIES

1. Discuss the intended purposes and merits of student suspensions. What does research on this topic reveal?

2. Do you agree with Principal Sanchez's beliefs about using school suspensions? Why or why not?

3. To what extent are Superintendent Lopson and Assistant Superintendent Mackee responsible for the conflict described in this case?

4. What alternatives could have been used by Principal Sanchez to discipline students while protecting the safety of all students?

5. To what extent are student learning and discipline connected? What evidence do you have for your response?

6. Principal Sanchez believes that he relates well to students from low-income and one-parent families. What evidence in the case

supports this contention? What evidence in the case refutes this contention?

7. Identify policy and rules governing student suspensions in the school district in which you are employed or live. Compare results with the policy presented in this case and with policies obtained by other students in your class.

8. In your opinion, did Mr. Carson, the teacher who wrote the letter to the editor of the local newspaper, behave professionally in criticizing Principal Sanchez? Why or why not?

9. If you were a principal in this school district, would you prefer the current policy on student suspensions or a policy that would prohibit suspension except for specified offenses? Defend your response.

10. Is Principal Sanchez an effective administrator? Why or why not?

SUGGESTED READINGS

Carey, M. (1986). School discipline: Better to be loved or feared? *Momentum, 17*(2), 20–21.

Christle, C., Nelson, C. M., & Jolivette, K. (2004). School characteristics related to the use of suspension. *Education and Treatment of Children, 27*(4), 509–526.

Costenbader, V., & Markson, S. (1998). School suspension: A study with secondary students. *Journal of School Psychology, 36*(1), 59–82.

Denney, K. A., & Van Gorder, C. H. (2004). A team approach to exclusionary sanctions. *Principal Leadership (Middle School Ed.), 4*(5), 52–55.

Henley, M. (1997). Why punishment doesn't work. *Principal, 77*(2), 45–46.

Mukuria, G. (2002). Disciplinary challenges: How do principals address this dilemma? *Urban Education, 37*(3), 432–452.

Nichols, J. D. (2004). An exploration of discipline and suspension data. *Journal of Negro Education, 73*(4), 408–423.

Pantesco, V. (2005). An immediate response protocol for addressing intolerant behavior. *Principal Leadership (Middle School Ed.), 6*(3), 8–9.

Raffaele-Mendez, L. M., & Knoff, H. M. (2003). Who gets suspended from school and why: A demographic analysis of schools and disciplinary infractions in a large school district. *Education and Treatment of Children, 26*(1), 30–51.

Raffaele-Mendez, L. M., Knoff, H. M., & Ferron, J. M. (2002). School demographic variables and out-of-school suspension rates: A quantitative and qualitative analysis of a large, ethnically diverse school district. *Psychology in the Schools, 39*(3), 259–277.

Rosen, L. (1997). *School discipline: Best practices for administrators.* Thousand Oaks, CA: Corwin Press.

Scott, T. M., & Nelson, C. M. (1999). Universal school discipline strategies: Facilitating positive learning environments. *Effective School Practice, 17*(4), 54–64.

Stader, D. L. (2004). Zero tolerance as public policy: The good, the bad, and the ugly. *Clearing House, 78*(2), 62–66.

Sughrue, J. A. (2003). Zero tolerance for children: Two wrongs do not make a right. *Educational Administration Quarterly, 39*(2), 238–258.

REFERENCES

Christle, C., Nelson, C. M., & Jolivette, K. (2004). School characteristics related to the use of suspension. *Education and Treatment of Children, 27*(4), 509–526.

Gaynor, A. K. (1998). *Analyzing problems in schools and school systems: A theoretical approach.* Mahwah, NJ: L. Erlbaum Associates.

Hanson, E. M. (2003). *Educational administration and organizational behavior* (5th ed.). Boston: Allyn and Bacon.

Kowalski, T. J. (2003). *Contemporary school administration* (2nd ed.). Boston: Allyn and Bacon.

Owens, R. (2001). *Organizational behavior in education* (7th ed.). Boston: Allyn and Bacon.

13 An Ambitious Assistant Principal

Background Information

Research on administrator career patterns has focused on regularities associated with practitioners ascending from lower-level to higher-level positions. Logically, the assistant principalship has been the common entry level position, especially in secondary schools (Miklos, 1988; Weller & Weller, 2001). Because many practitioners see this assignment as a stepping-stone, turnover in the position has been relatively high. Today, however, fewer people who hold this position appear willing to relocate or change employers to become a principal.

Principal attitudes toward setting criteria for employing assistant principals are less than uniform. Whereas some principals have no qualms about hiring a person who wants to become a principal as soon as possible, others prefer to employ an assistant who vows to remain in the job for at least five years.

Remaining an assistant principal for a long period of time, even for an entire career, has become more acceptable in the profession for several reasons. First, job satisfaction research (e.g., Chen, Bledinger, & McGrath, 2000; Sutter, 1996) often finds that most assistant principals believe that their position is fulfilling. Second, some assistant principals now place more emphasis on family and quality-of-life interests and less emphasis on career advancement, a disposition that makes them unwilling to relocate to receive a promotion.

Career decisions are not entirely personal; they also involve legal and ethical issues as demonstrated by these common queries. Are administrators legally and ethically bound to fulfill the terms of an employment contract before accepting another position? Should an applicant be honest with a prospective employer about career intentions? Or should he or she provide answers that enhance employment? Upwardly mobile applicants (i.e., those viewing the assistant principalship as a stepping stone) realize that telling an employer the truth about their career aspirations could prevent them from being selected. Conversely, employers face other ethical problems. For instance, a principal may expect her assistant to remain in the position for a long period of time simply to prevent her from having to select and tutor a replacement.

As the locus of school improvement has shifted gradually to the school level, stability in both the principal and assistant principal positions has become a more cogent concern. Having revolving doors on these administrative offices makes it much more difficult to complete essential reform assignments, such as shared visioning and strategic planning (Kowalski, 2003).

This case describes a dilemma faced by an ambitious young teacher who becomes an assistant principal in a small rural secondary school. As an applicant, he makes a commitment to remain in the position for at least five years. Actually, he has no intent to remain in a rural community or in the assistant principal position for that length of time.

Key Areas for Reflection

1. Administrator career patterns
2. Ethical and legal dimensions of career decisions
3. The assistant principalship
4. Principal and assistant principal relationships

The Case

Bentonville, located in northern Iowa, is a farming community. Many of the 2,500 residents have never lived elsewhere, and the level of community pride is exceedingly high. The downtown area is just a few blocks of old stores and commercial buildings including a bank, a Sears outlet store, a restaurant, a grocery store, several taverns, and a farm equipment business. A Catholic church is located at the eastern edge of downtown, and a Lutheran church is located at the western end.

There are few secrets in Bentonville. Though families are divided religiously by their membership in the two churches, the community's social, political, and cultural structure is homogeneous. In some fashion, nearly all the families are engaged in farming or farm-related businesses.

Bentonville Junior/Senior High School

Bentonville Community School District spans two townships and operates just two schools: a combined junior and senior high school and an elementary school. The Bentonville Junior/Senior High School enrolls approximately 450 pupils in grades 7 to 12. The building, located less than one mile outside the town of Bentonville in a rural setting, was constructed about sixteen years ago. Oscar McCammick, the principal, has never been employed in another school. Having just completed his tenth year as principal, he previously served as the assistant principal for six years and as science and mathematics teacher for seven years.

Hiring a New Assistant Principal

When Mr. McCammick was promoted to be principal, he convinced the superintendent and school board to hire George Stileke, a close friend and coach at the school, to be assistant principal. The superintendent, Becky Potter, favored employing a younger person because she feared that Mr. Stileke and Mr. McCammick would retire at approximately the same time. After Mr. Stileke promised not to retire for at least seven years, she recommended and the school board approved that he be employed as assistant principal. Mr. Stileke not only kept his word, he actually remained in the position for ten years before retiring.

Initially, an internal job search was conducted in hopes that one or more of the three teachers qualified to fill the vacancy would apply. Despite encouragement from Principal McCammick, none did. In early June, Superintendent Potter began seeking applicants from outside of the school district. By the application deadline of July 15, she had received only six applications. One was eliminated from consideration because he did not qualify for the required administrative license. The remaining five files were sent to Principal McCammick for his consideration. After completing reference checks, the principal eliminated three of the five; the two survivors were invited to come to Bentonville for an interview.

Norman Emons was the first finalist to be interviewed. He was 51 years old and a middle school teacher from Des Moines. During his interview, he told the superintendent and principal that he recently obtained his principal's license and now wanted to become an administrator. When asked why he waited so long to consider a career in administration, he responded, "There are two reasons. First, shortly after I started teaching, I established a small house painting company with two other teachers. We worked primarily during the summer and our business did quite well. Two years ago, I sold my interest because of a bad back. Second, I plan to retire in about twelve to fifteen years and I want to build up my salary to improve my retirement benefits."

Raymond Tyler, the other finalist, was only 29 years old and a teacher from Davenport. He too had no previous administrative experience. Shortly after the interview began, the principal asked Raymond, "If you are selected for this job, how long do you plan remaining with us?" Raymond responded, "How long do you want a person to remain in this job?"

Mr. McCammick answered, "At least five years; hopefully, even longer."

Raymond commented immediately, "That would not be a problem. I want to work for a highly experienced principal such as you for at least five years. I'm planning to complete a doctorate and then move to a higher level position. Finishing the degree as a part-time student is probably going to take at least four years and I don't plan to start until next year."

The superintendent then asked him to express his feelings about living in a rural community.

"I love Iowa and although I've not lived in a town as small as Bentonville, I look forward to having the experience. I have been accepted into a Ph.D. program at one of the state universities located 45 miles from here. Being this close to a university is a factor that attracts me to this job. I'm also planning to get married in about a year and my fiancée will be pursuing a Ph.D. at the same university, but as a full-time student. Between going to school and working, I'll be very busy. My only real concern is finding a place to live."

After the interview, the superintendent turned to the principal and said, "This fellow is too good to be true. He's well-groomed, self-confident, and articulate." In a letter of reference, Raymond's current principal described him as the "best young teacher I have ever supervised." Despite the high praise from these two individuals, Principal McCammick was skeptical. He questioned if Mr. Tyler was a "good fit" for Bentonville. "Simply attending college in Iowa," he told the superintendent, "does not prepare you to live in a small town. Mr. Tyler was raised in an affluent Chicago suburb, and he is ambitious. I don't think he will adjust well to living and working here."

Despite his reservations, Mr. McCammick eventually concurred with the superintendent that Raymond was the best candidate. He was offered the position the next morning and accepted it immediately.

First Year

Raymond Tyler officially became assistant principal on August 10. The first two months were hectic for him. For example, he was not used to having weekend responsibilities, such as attending Friday night football games. And in addition to his job responsibilities, he was enrolled in a Wednesday evening class at the nearby university.

Initially, Mr. McCammick was very pleased with Raymond's performance, and he even began to question if his earlier reservations were valid. Raymond related well with students, and his job performance pleased the principal; teachers and parents also developed positive impressions of the new assistant principal. By Thanksgiving, Mr. McCammick told Superintendent Potter, "I think we have selected the perfect assistant principal."

The following week, Raymond informed the principal that he was moving to Lincoln, the county seat about 16 miles away. He explained that the sleeping room he was renting in Bentonville from a retired teacher was too small. Mr. McCammick was not pleased. Administrators customarily have lived in the school district, and though there was no requirement to that effect, he felt Raymond had indirectly committed to living in Bentonville. He told his assistant, "I hope your relocation does not affect your job performance."

Raymond had become friends with two Bentonville coaches. The three were approximately the same age, and in the fall, they had attended several college football games together. During casual conversations, Ray commented to his friends that he had underestimated how difficult it would be to live and work in a rural community. He predicted he might stay two or three years but then wanted to return to a larger city.

In early April, Ray had his evaluation conference with Mr. McCammick. The principal was satisfied with his overall performance but still unhappy that Ray no longer resided in the school district. All seven performance ratings were either "average" or "above average." In the comment section, Mr. McCammick noted that Ray needed to act more maturely when dealing with students—but he did not explain the intended meaning of this statement.

Ray was surprised and displeased with his evaluation. He was accustomed to receiving "excellent" ratings; all of his previous teaching evaluations were extremely positive. Moreover, Mr. McCammick had been much more positive about his performance prior to the formal evaluation. He told the principal he was not pleased with the evaluation and disagreed with the ratings.

Mr. McCammick responded, "This is a pretty good evaluation for a first-year assistant principal. And I have recommended that you be reemployed with a salary increase."

Ray decided to sign the evaluation form as required by district policy without challenging the content. He judged that being cooperative was the most prudent decisions given the likelihood that the principal could affect his career negatively.

Conflict Intensifies

As the second semester was drawing to a close in late May, one of the coaches alerted Ray to the fact that the principal was asking teachers if his assistant planned to resign. "Mr. McCammick is snooping around asking about your career plans," the coach told Ray. "I told him that I did not think you would be leaving and asked why he thought you might be doing so. He said you are a terrific guy and some superintendent or principal may try to persuade you to change jobs."

A week later, Mr. McCammick received a telephone call from Dr. Jean Carmen, a principal in a suburban Chicago school district. She was inquiring about Ray Tyler. Dr. Carmen told Mr. McCammick that Ray had just interviewed for an assistant principal's position with her. Mr. McCammick immediately asked for clarification.

"He's an applicant for a job in your school for the upcoming school year?"

"That's correct."

"Did he tell you that he has been in his current position for less than a year?"

"He did."

"Well, aren't you concerned as to why he is looking for a new job already?"

There was a pause and then Dr. Carmen said, "Frankly, I'm not concerned about that issue. Our school has 2,100 students, four assistant principals, and the salary is substantially higher than his current salary. Mr. Tyler also indicated that he had been admitted to a doctoral program in suburban Chicago, and he wants to begin the program on a part-time basis in the fall. My purpose in calling you is to seek your input about his performance as an assistant principal. Obviously, my impressions of him after the interview are positive, and this is why I am collecting additional information."

"When I hired Ray last summer," Mr. McCammick responded, "he assured the superintendent and me that he would remain in the position for at least five years. Apparently, he was not being truthful. He also agreed to reside in the school district and he reneged on that commitment after a few months. As you might detect, I'm not pleased to learn he is seeking another position; I don't look forward to another assistant principal search. Under the present circumstances, I am not willing to give you a positive assessment of his performance."

Dr. Carmen thanked Mr. McCammick for talking with her and then ended the conversation. Mr. McCammick immediately called Superintendent Potter and expressed his anger.

"Is there some way we can make him stay here? Legally, I mean. Doesn't he have a contractual obligation to remain here as he promised?"

"Even if there were a legal constraint," the superintendent responded, "would you want to force him to stay here?"

Mr. McCammick said he would talk to Ray about the call he had received from Dr. Carmen, and he would update the superintendent after that conversation.

Immediately after putting down the telephone, Mr. McCammick stormed into Ray's office and told him about his conversation with Dr. Carmen. "You promised that you would stay in Bentonville for at least five years. Today I find out that you're trying to leave already. Do you have an explanation for your behavior?"

"I never promised I would stay here for five years. I said I wanted to work under a highly experienced principal for five years. The opportunity in suburban Chicago is not something I directly pursued. I'm getting engaged in a few months and my future fiancée accepted a teaching position in Dr. Carmen's school. She told Dr. Carmen about me and things just evolved from that point. So I didn't have some grand plan to deceive you. If I don't get the job in Illinois, I'll stay here and do my best."

Mr. McCammick was not pleased with Ray's response. "If you don't withdraw your candidacy for this job, you'll never get a good evaluation from me. Integrity is very important and I will tell prospective employers that you lied to me. You have until tomorrow to give me an answer." Without waiting for a reaction, the principal turned and slammed the door as he left Ray's office.

PROBLEM FRAMING

1. Assume you are Ray. Describe what you would want to accomplish in dealing with the situation described in this case.

2. Based on the evidence of contextual variables, describe the difficulty associated with achieving your objective.

QUESTIONS AND SUGGESTED ACTIVITIES

1. Share and critique the problem statements prepared by students in your class.

2. Discuss the legal dimensions of an administrator's employment contract, especially with respect to the rights of both the employer and employee.

3. Did Ray really promise to remain at the high school for at least five years? What evidence in the case supports your answer?

4. Identify possible factors contributing to the assistant principal's job dissatisfaction.

5. Divide into two groups and debate the advantages and disadvantages of employers demanding that assistant principals remain in that job for a specified period of time.

6. Should Ray have told the principal that he had applied for another job? Why or why not?

7. Assume you were the principal of Bentonville High School. Would you have responded differently to learning that Ray had applied for another job? Why or why not?

8. Should employers in rural districts weigh an individual's cultural background in making hiring decisions? Why or why not?

9. Assume that Ray does not get the job in suburban Chicago. What advice would you give him about remaining at Bentonville High School?

SUGGESTED READINGS

Calabrese, R. L., & Tucker-Ladd, P. R. (1991). The principal and the assistant principal: A mentoring relationship. *NASSP Bulletin, 75*, 67–74.

Fields, L. J. (2005). Patterns of stress and coping mechanisms for novice school administrators. *Essays in Education, 14*, 1–10.

Gerke, W. (2004). More than a disciplinarian. *Principal Leadership (Middle School Ed.), 5*(3), 39–41.

Glanz, J. (1994). Dilemmas of assistant principals in their supervisory role: Reflections of an assistant principal. *Journal of School Leadership, 4*(5), 577–590.

Goodson, C. P. (2000). Assisting the assistant principal. *Principal, 79*(4), 56–57.

Hart, A. (1991). Leader succession and socialization: A synthesis. *Review of Educational Research, 61*, 451–474.

Hartzell, G. N. (1993). When you're not at the top. *High School Magazine, 1*(2), 16–19.

Hibert, K. M. (2000). Mentoring leadership. *Phi Delta Kappan, 82*(1), 16–18.

Murray, K. T., & Murray, B. A. (1999). The administrative contract: Implications for reform. *NASSP Bulletin, 83*(606), 33–38.

Oliver, R. (2003). Assistant principal job satisfaction and desire to become principals. *Education Leadership Review, 4*(2), 38–46.

Tooms, A. (2003). The rookie's playbook: Insights and dirt for new principals. *Phi Delta Kappan, 84*(7), 530–533.

Winter, P A., & Partenheimer, P. R. (2002). *Applicant attraction to assistant principal jobs: An experimental assessment.* (ERIC Document Reproduction Service No. ED471 558)

Sutter, M. R. (1996). What do we know about the job and career satisfaction of secondary school assistant principals? *NASSP Bulletin, 80*(579), 108–111.

REFERENCES

Chen, K., Blendinger, J., & McGrath, V. (November, 2000). *Job satisfaction among high school assistant principals.* Paper presented at the Annual Meeting of the Mid-South Educational Research Association, Bowling Green, Kentucky.

Kowalski, T. J. (2003). *Contemporary school administration: An introduction* (2nd ed.). Boston: Allyn and Bacon.

Miklos, E. (1988). Administrator selection, career patterns, succession, and socialization. In N. Boyan (Ed.), *Handbook of research on educational administration* (pp. 53–76). New York: Longman.

Sutter, M. R. (1996). What do we know about the job and career satisfaction of secondary school assistant principals? *NASSP Bulletin, 80*(579), 108–111.

Weller, L. D., & Weller, S. J. (2001). *The assistant principal: Essentials for effective leadership.* Thousand Oaks, CA: Corwin Press.

CASE
14

A One-Trick Principal

Background Information

In the current context of school reform, principals are expected to be competent leaders as well as capable managers. Leadership primarily entails making or facilitating decisions focusing on *what* should be done to improve schools; collaborative visioning and strategic planning are examples. Management primarily entails making or facilitating decisions about *how* to implement improvement initiatives; controlling and deploying human and material resources are examples (Kowalski, 2003). During much of the last century, normative practice in school administration was dominated by managerial responsibilities. Even as late as the 1980s, the pursuit of school improvement was framed by an instrumental view, a philosophical perspective relegating principals and teachers to implementing changes mandated by policy elites (St. John & Daun-Barnett, 2007). Since approximately 1990, expectations have changed, both because intensification mandates had failed to meet expectations and because policymakers began to recognize that reform would be more likely if it were pursued locally (Bauman, 1996: Wirt & Kirst, 2001).

Greater emphasis on leadership has broadened the essential knowledge base for school administrators. Administration, a generic term that encompasses both leadership and management (Kowalski, 2003), is commonly characterized by three skill categories:

- *Technical skills.* This category includes knowledge related to certain procedures and methods essential to administering schools; application examples include managing fiscal resources and operating a school-based food service program.
- *Human relations skills.* This category focuses on knowledge of human behavior, motivation, attitudes, communication, and other facets of organizational life; application examples include school-community relations, conflict resolution, and communication.
- *Conceptual skills.* This category includes analytical and problem-solving skills that are primarily associated with leadership responsibilities; application examples include visioning and planning (Yukl, 2006).

A level of a practitioner's skills, however, is not determined solely by knowledge but rather by the application of knowledge in a specific context (i.e., the work environment in which the principal functions). Factors such as school climate, prevailing problems, community culture, and people exemplify contextual variables. The interaction of knowledge and context helps us understand why the effectiveness of a principal can vary over time. Either substantial contextual changes in a present assignment or a new assignment (transferring to a different school) can alter effectiveness, even substantially, if the principal's behavior remains constant (Gaynor, 1998).

Role conflict, tensions resulting from seemingly incompatible expectations, clearly influences a practitioner's ability to balance leadership and management (Hanson, 2003). This condition, prevalent across all types of organizations, occurs for a variety of reasons, but the following three are quite common in schools:

- Principals discover that their supervisors and employees have different expectations of them. As an example, a superintendent may expect principals to treat teachers as subordinates, whereas the teachers expect principals to treat them as professional peers.
- Principals find that their personal needs conflict with job expectations. As an example, some principals have a high need to be liked and accepted by teachers, students, and parents; the position, however, directs them to be task-oriented, stern, and unemotional.
- Principals confront differing expectations regarding their approach to practice. The two most notable examples are between being autocratic and being democratic and between being transactional versus being transformational.

In this case, an experienced high school principal, considered to be highly effective in the area of community relations, accepts a new assignment. He sustains the behaviors that have served him well in the past; that is, he devotes much of his time and energy to engaging parents and participating in community activities. The superintendent and the associate superintendent applaud his efforts, but the senior assistant principal at the school has a very different perspective. The assistant believes that she and the other two assistant principals (both males) are being mistreated by a narcissist who uses subordinates to do his work.

Key Areas for Reflection

1. Principal responsibilities in a large high school
2. Community and school district cultures as determinants of ideal and real roles
3. Role conflict
4. Male and female administrator relationships
5. School public relations

The Case

Wellington

One of Peter Farley's earliest memories of Wellington involved a demolition project in the downtown area, a scene he observed on his first trip to this city. He was there to interview for the job of high school principal. As he drove down Main Street searching for the district administrative office, he saw two large stores, each more than 100 years old, being flattened by a swinging steel ball.

Wellington, an industrial community that fell on hard times during the 1980s, is one of the larger cities in this New England state. Recently, however, the city's fortunes have been changing. An upward economic trend started about the time that Dan Shea was elected mayor. An energetic and popular attorney who previously served two terms in the state legislature, Mayor Shea campaigned on the promise that he would bring new businesses to the city. Since being in office, he has claimed responsibility for attracting two technology-based corporations to the city and for launching a downtown renewal program. His popularity is unchallenged; he was reelected to a second four-year term, defeating his opponent by a margin of 62 percent to 38 percent.

Wellington School District

Mayor Shea directly involved himself in the local public schools almost immediately after taking office. At the same time he was elected mayor, a law partner, John O'Dell, and close political ally, Jennifer Scott, were elected to the school board. Two years later, two other political allies were elected to the school board, giving the mayor indirect control of four of the five board members. The first decision made by the new majority was not to renew the contract of the superintendent who had been in office for seven years. The search for a new chief executive was shaped by two convictions the mayor had shared with the school board: The city's revival would be enhanced if the image of public schools improved, and changing the school district's image depended on having a politically astute superintendent who would be highly active in the community. As a result, the board made statesmanship and public relations the two primary employment criteria.

After a two-month search, the board employed Dr. Daniel French to be the new superintendent. He had been the superintendent in a 12,000-student district in Michigan, where he supposedly improved the image of one of the state's lowest performing districts. Since coming to Wellington, Dr. French and Mayor Shea have worked closely together and have become friends.

Wellington High School

Dr. French spent the first year in Wellington closely observing the performance of his administrative staff and soliciting comments about their performance from influential citizens. As is the case in virtually all school districts, the high school was the center of attention for local residents, and consequently the superintendent concluded that changing the district's image had to begin by changing the high school's image.

Wellington High School is large, serving about 2,300 students. Superintendent French believed that changing leadership in the school would be risky because he was not fully aware of political affiliations among the principal, staff, and community. Nevertheless, information he collected led him to believe that the principal was part of the school's image problem. Just six months after becoming superintendent, he made a bold decision: He informed the principal that he could either resign or be dismissed.

The principal had been in office for only four years but previously had served as an assistant principal in the school for eleven years. Though well liked by teachers and staff, he was not especially popular with parents or students, many of whom viewed him as being unreasonable and dictatorial. After being elevated to the principalship, he realigned the duties of the three assistant principals so that he could continue to devote much of his time to managerial responsibilities, most notably handling student discipline and personnel issues. The principal was not directly involved in community activities, nor did he spend much time away from the school—factors that were central to the superintendent's decision to replace him. Recognizing that the superintendent had the backing of the school board and mayor, the principal resigned.

Search for a New Principal

After conferring with the mayor and school board members, Superintendent French initiated a national search for a new high school principal. An impressive brochure listing the following qualifications was sent to universities, professional associations, and search consultants:

- Because the principal of Wellington High School represents the district and school to multiple publics, candidates for the position must possess outstanding public relations and communication skills.
- Candidates must be able to relate effectively to diverse community groups.
- Candidates must be committed to working closely with local governmental agencies.
- Candidates must take an active role in community activities.
- Candidates must be committed to school improvement.

Though other qualifications were mentioned, the brochure unambiguously transmitted a message that the new principal had to be highly involved with the community.

The superintendent appointed himself and three other individuals to the search committee. The other members were Dr. Susan Mays, the associate superintendent; Mr. O'Dell, a school board member; and Mrs. Constance Goldman, chair of the English department at the high school. The committee interviewed six candidates and then invited two of them to return for second interviews. One of the two finalists was Peter Varber, principal of smaller high school located in an affluent suburb of New York City.

Mr. Varber was initially apprehensive about applying for the vacancy at Wellington High School, largely because he knew about the community and its past economic struggles. His hesitation was countered, however, but the fact that he could retire in New York, though he was only 52, and then establish a new pension program in another state. As a result of his initial interview, he became highly interested in the

Wellington High School position. When he arrived for the second interview, he was accompanied by his wife. On the evening they arrived, they were the guests of Mayor Shea and his wife for dinner. The next morning, Mrs. Varber was taken on a community tour by a realtor as Mr. Varber met the high school faculty at a reception. Later in the morning, he met with the school's administrative staff and counselors. The interview concluded with a working lunch hosted by the selection committee. By 3 P.M., the Varbers were driving back to New York.

The search committee discussed the two finalists the next day. As soon as the meeting started, John O'Dell told the other members that Mayor Shea definitely favored Peter Varber. Dr. French then said that he too believed that Peter was the better candidate. At that point, the remaining committee members voiced a preference for Peter. One week later, Peter accepted the invitation to become Wellington High School's next principal.

New Principal Arrives

Mr. Varber arrived in his new office on July 1 and immediately met with the assistant principals. Teresa Howard was the most senior of the three and the only one who had applied for the principal vacancy. Having worked at the school for twenty-three years, the last eleven as an assistant principal, she had been a staunch supporter of the previous principal. Mike Petrov has worked at the school for fourteen years; he was coach and physical education teacher before becoming an assistant principal six years ago. The third assistant was Ron Kazka; he was the youngest and least experienced administrator, having been an assistant for only two years.

During the meeting, Principal Varber asked his assistants to share their perceptions about the school, the district, and community politics. Based on what he observed and heard during the session, he concluded that the assistants were very guarded in making comments to him. Moreover, it was obvious to him that Mrs. Howard was the leader in this group; for example, whenever a seemingly controversial issue was raised, she usually spoke for the others or offered interpretations of their comments.

During the month of July, the four administrators met five more times, some of the meetings lasting more than four hours. At the last of these meetings, Principal Varber announced three decisions and emphasized that they were made in consultation with Superintendent French.

- Mrs. Howard's title would be changed to associate principal, pending school board approval. The purpose was to identify the assistant who would be in charge during the principal's absence from the school.
- Unlike his predecessor, he would be spending time on community relations. In particular, he planned to become involved in a service club and would be appointed to the city recreation board by the mayor.
- Under the direction of Mrs. Howard, the three assistants were to determine how administrative responsibilities would be divided among them.

A Successful Beginning

Both the mayor and the superintendent made sure that the new high school principal got community exposure. They arranged for him to speak to the service clubs and the Chamber of Commerce, and he was appointed to a vacancy on the city recreation board. The local media treated him very favorably, and after successfully negotiating a partnership venture involving the high school and three local businesses, he was praised in an editorial focusing on improvements at the high school.

The other high school administrators, teachers, and staff quickly discovered that Principal Varber was very different from his predecessor. Whereas the previous principal rarely left the school during the day, Mr. Varber seemed to be gone more than he was there. His absence was magnified by his behavior when he was at the school. The previous principal spent a great deal of time walking the halls, visiting classrooms, and spending time in the teachers' lounge. Mr. Varber spent most of the time on site working in his office; by Thanksgiving, for example, he had eaten in the school cafeteria only three times and visited the teachers' lounge only once. Recognizing that the principal had the support of the school board, superintendent, and mayor, few employees were willing to criticize him—at least not overtly.

During the first year at Wellington High School, Peter Varber worked hard to meet the objective of changing the school's image. The following initiatives exemplify his efforts:

- He personally took charge of the school newsletter, a publication that previously had been the domain of the English department. The number of issues per year increased from two to six and the volume of each issue increased by about 30 percent.
- Twice a month, twenty parents were invited to have coffee with the principal. Over the course of the school year, he met with 118 parents.
- He became active in the local Chamber of Commerce and conducted a follow-up study of high school graduates who were employed by local business and industry. This effort resulted in his being named the outstanding educator of the year by the Wellington Chamber of Commerce—a remarkable accomplishment given that he had been in the community for slightly less than a year.

Both Mayor Shea and Superintendent French were confident they had selected the right person to improve the image of Wellington High School.

Conflict Emerges

Every Monday morning, Principal Varber met with Mrs. Howard so that she could brief him on problems, opportunities, and so forth. The typical meeting lasted about 90 minutes. During the first year they worked together, Mrs. Howard considered the meetings advantageous because they were an opportunity to receive feedback on her performance. As the second year began, however, she became increasingly negative about the sessions; she believed that the principal used them to compensate for the considerable time he spent away from the school.

After school started in the fall, she boldly suggested to the principal that he was spending too little time at the school. She indicated that his presence was important to staff morale and reminded him that relationships in the school are at least as important as those outside the school. Principal Varber thanked her for her candor but then told her that he worked diligently both in an out of the school building.

"I'm not implying that you don't work hard. But you are not here at the school very often. The staff is cognizant of this fact, and they are saying some pretty unfavorable things. For instance, I overheard a teacher refer to you as the 'phantom principal.' The other assistant principals share my thoughts on this matter."

"Teresa, I've been a principal for a long time, and I think I know what I'm doing. Contrary to your comments, things are going well. That includes the performance of our administrative team here at the high school. You have excellent rapport with the teachers and the other assistants; you are a competent manager. I'm not going to change things just because a few teachers are displeased. And besides, if they are displeased, tell them to talk to me directly."

After the encounter, Mrs. Howard decided to drop the issue. Though she was convinced that the principal was erring in the areas of time management and staff relations, she did not want to jeopardize her own relationship with him. The previous year, for example, he gave her a glowing performance evaluation and recommended her for the maximum salary increase. Thus, the issue of the principal's presence was not discussed again—that is, until Mrs. Howard met with him to receive another performance evaluation.

The second annual evaluation looked much like the first one. The principal praised his associate for doing an outstanding job of managing the school and he again recommended a maximum salary increase. To his surprise, Mrs. Howard responded by saying that the evaluation was basically meaningless. She then told him that she was considering resigning.

"Why?" he asked. "Are you ill? What's the problem?"

"No. My health is fine. Answering your question appropriately would take time, and you're usually in a hurry to end meetings," she responded.

"Take as much time as you need. This is an important matter."

She was scheduled to meet with the department chairs in 45 minutes and therefore requested that they meet the next day to continue the discussion. The principal said he would meet with her, pointing out that he had to cancel another meeting in order to do so. He offered to take her to one of Wellington's finest restaurants so that they could have the discussion away from the school; she said she preferred to meet in his office.

When they met the next day, Principal Varber reiterated that he was pleased with her performance and surprised by the suggestion that she might resign. After listening politely, she began explaining why she was dissatisfied.

"I really don't know where to begin. But here goes. Staff members at the school are concerned—no, let me rephrase that. I am concerned that you don't get involved in critical administrative functions. I have to give you detailed briefings just so you have some inkling of what's going on at school. Your lack of visibility at school has spawned all types of rumors. In addition to calling you the 'phantom,' some teachers suggest that you are the mayor's and superintendent's puppet. Personally, I think they are being unfair, but they liked your predecessor, and they still think that Dr. French treated him unfairly."

Peter Varber reflected for a moment and then asked, "Is the concern about the time I spend at school being expressed by all or most of the staff—including administrators?"

"Yes. The other assistant principals and I would prefer to work with a principal who is more accessible and visible. When you're not at the school, the staff speculates about what you're doing, and they draw their own conclusions."

"What else are they, or you, concerned about?" he asked.

"I feel I'm running the school, and you're getting the credit. The Chamber of Commerce made you educator of the year after being here less than a year. When you received the award, you failed to acknowledge how much help you receive from your assistants. Then there's the matter of salary. I'm making $22,000 less than you, and I'm managing the school. If the tables were turned, would you consider such an arrangement fair? You may not know that I applied for your job. After all the years I have devoted to this community and this school, the school board did not even extend me the courtesy of having an interview."

"Teresa, I can't speak for others. As for my behavior, the superintendent and the school board have directed me to improve the school's image. Their instructions have not been a secret. From the very beginning of our association, I told you what I would be doing and what you would be doing. I never misled you, and I certainly have not taken advantage of you."

"I work very hard, Peter. Every day, I get here early and leave late. How many hours do you spend here each week? Some secretaries and most of the teachers have never had a personal conversation with you."

At that point Mrs. Howard lost her composure and turned away from the principal. He remained silent and after about a minute, she continued.

"I don't think a male associate would be treated the way I have been treated. I'm not worthy to interview to be principal but apparently I'm very competent to do all the difficult tasks related to operating the school. If you want me to continue as associate principal, two things must happen. First, I want a major salary increase—at least $10,000. Second, I want you to promise that you'll spend more time at school. You let me know your answer by the end of the week." Mrs. Howard then got up and left the office before the principal could respond.

Principal Varber did not want to lose his associate but he doubted that the superintendent would agree to her salary demand. In fact, he was confident that sharing the conversation with Dr. French would result in his recommending that she resign.

PROBLEM FRAMING

1. Assume you are the principal in this case. Describe what you would want to accomplish in dealing with this situation.

2. Based on the evidence of current conditions in the school, describe the difficulty associated with achieving your objective.

QUESTIONS AND SUGGESTED ACTIVITIES

1. Share and critique the problem statements prepared by students in your class.

2. Assistant Principal Howard implies that gender is an issue in relation to the way she is being treated. Do you agree with her? Provide a rationale for your response.

3. Identify communication problems that have contributed to the conflict between Principal Varber and Associate Principal Howard.

4. Discuss your perceptions regarding the manner in which most principals would deal with this situation. Identify factors that contribute to your perceptions.

5. Develop a characterization of an ideal high school principal and then compare that characterization to your assessment of Principal Varber.

6. Associate Principal Howard apparently believes that the principal of a large high school cannot be successful if he or she is away from the school campus nearly half the work day. Do you agree with her? Provide a rationale for your answer.

7. Clearly, Associate Principal Howard believes she has a grievance. Evaluate her approach to dealing with the matter from both professional and political perspectives.

8. As per evidence in the case, Associate Principal Howard applied to become principal but was not even interviewed. Should this fact influence the decision Principal Varber makes? Why or why not?

9. Apparently the mayor in this case has become involved in the school district directly and indirectly. In your opinion, is this a positive or negative factor for the school district? Explain your answer.

SUGGESTED READINGS

Armistead, L. (2000). Public relations: Harness your school's power. *High School Magazine*, 7(6), 24–27.

Black, B. (2002). An insider's view. *American School Board Journal*, 189(2), 37–38.

Carr, A. A. (1997). Leadership and community participation: Four case studies. *Journal of Curriculum and Supervision*, 12(2), 152–168.

Chirichello, M. (2003). Co-principals: A double dose of leadership. *Principal*, 82(4), 40–44.

Copland, M. A. (2001). The myth of the superprincipal. *Phi Delta Kappan*, 82(7), 528–533.

Denison, P. (2004, July 2). Anyone seen the head? *Times Educational Supplement*, (4590) p. 30.

Eckman, E. W. (2004). Similarities and differences in role conflict, role commitment, and job satisfaction for female and male high school principals. *Educational Administration Quarterly*, 40(3), 366–387.

Glanz, J. (1994). Dilemmas of assistant principals in their supervisory role: Reflections of an assistant principal. *Journal of School Leadership*, 4(5), 577–590.

Hale, R. P. (1994). Aspirations and frustrations of female secondary administrators. *Professional Educator*, 16(2), 45–50.

Hassenpflug, A. (1996). The selection of female secondary school assistant principals and transformational leadership. *Research in the Schools*, 3(1), 51–59.

Hibert, K. M. (2000). Mentoring leadership. *Phi Delta Kappan*, 82(1), 16–18.

Hines, R. W. (1993). Principal starts with PR. *Principal*, 72(3), 45–46.

Keesor, C. A. (2005). Administrative visibility and its effect on classroom behavior. *NASSP Bulletin*, 89, 64–73.

Marshall, C. (1992). School administrators' values: A focus on atypicals. *Educational Administration Quarterly*, 28(3), 368–386.

Mertz, N.T., & McNeely, S. R. (1999). *Through the looking glass: An up front and personal look at the world of the assistant principal.* (ERIC Document Reproduction Service No. ED435 124)

Reis, S. B., Young, I. P., & Jury, J. C. (1999). Female administrators: A crack in the glass ceiling.

Journal of Personnel Evaluation in Education, 13(1), 71–82.

Ripley, D. (1997). Current tensions in the principalship: Finding an appropriate balance. *NASSP Bulletin, 81*(589), 55–65.

Sutter, M. R. (1996). What do we know about the job and career satisfaction of secondary school assistant principals? *NASSP Bulletin, 80*(579), 108–111.

REFERENCES

Bauman, P. C. (1996). *Governing education: Public sector reform or privatization*. Boston: Allyn and Bacon.

Gaynor, A. K. (1998). *Analyzing problems in schools and school systems: A theoretical approach*. Mahwah, NJ: L. Erlbaum Associates.

Hanson, E. M. (2003). *Educational administration and organizational behavior* (5th ed.). Boston: Allyn and Bacon.

Kowalski, T. J. (2003). *Contemporary school administration: An introduction* (2nd ed.). Boston: Allyn and Bacon.

St. John, E. P., & Daun-Barnett, N. J. (2007). Public opinions and political contexts. In T. J. Kowalski (Ed.). *Public relations in schools* (4th ed.; pp. 51–72). Upper Saddle River, NJ: Merrill, Prentice Hall.

Wirt, F., & Kirst, M. (2001). *The political dynamics of American education* (2nd ed.). Berkeley, CA: McCutchan.

Yukl, G. (2006). *Leadership in organizations* (6th ed.). Upper Saddle River, NJ: Prentice-Hall.

C A S E
15
Even on Saturdays

Background Information

The legal doctrine of *in loco parentis* refers to assuming parental responsibility for a nonadult without legal adoption. In fact, the term means "in the place of parents." The concept was first applied to public education in colonial times. Rooted in English common law, the concept was interpreted to give school personnel authority over both education and moral development. Over time, legal challenges to the concept's application have weakened it, particularly as it relates to older students. During the 1960s, lawsuits regarding the authority of school officials to control pupil behavior resulted in legal precedent that students do not lose their constitutional rights at the schoolhouse door. The courts continued to permit the application of *in loco parentis*, however, but have limited the application of the concept to reasonable punishment in light of circumstances such as the nature of the infraction, the method of discipline, and the age of the student (Zirkel & Reichner, 1987).

This case is about a student initiation that took place on a Saturday away from a high school campus. Over forty students, mostly females, are arrested for underage drinking and several also for assault. The incident brings into question the legal responsibility of school officials to prevent and control such incidents since they are allegedly school-related but not school-sponsored.

Once the media become involved, school officials face a public relations nightmare. Incidents, even those away from campus and clearly not part of the school curriculum, can damage a school's reputation (Kowalski, 2007). In this case, the superintendent and principal take the position that neither they nor other school personnel are responsible for student behavior in this incident. They then declare that they will not comment further on the matter until the legal charges against the students are resolved. As is almost always the case, reporters are suspicious that their "no further comment" indicates that the administrators are attempting conceal vital information (Kowalski, Petersen, & Fusarelli, 2007). Failure to communicate effectively during a crisis situation often produces a second-level problem for school officials (Kowalski, 2002).

Key Areas for Reflection

1. Student discipline
2. Media relations
3. Dealing with a crisis situation
4. School public relations
5. Legal aspects of student punishment

The Case

Jim Marshfield and his wife, Angie, were attending a party at their daughter's sorority. It was parents' weekend, the Texas sun was shining, and everyone was celebrating the victory at the football game that had ended just hours earlier. Jim was putting the finishing touches on his second barbeque sandwich when his cell phone started vibrating.

Jim is principal of Melton High School, one of the most prestigious public schools in Texas. Located in an affluent suburb of Dallas, the school enrolls nearly 2,500 students; nearly 85 percent of the graduates enter a higher-education institution. Prior to becoming principal, Jim was an assistant principal at Melton High School for six years.

Opening his phone, Jim saw the call was from his superintendent, Dr. Rachel Gregory. He knew that there was a problem because he did not routinely get calls from the superintendent on weekends—and his instincts proved to be accurate. Dr. Gregory told him that forty-three Melton students, almost all junior and senior girls, had been arrested several hours earlier at a local state park. All were charged with underage drinking and several were also charged with assault. Jim immediately knew what had occurred.

For at least the last twenty-five years, a touch football game between the senior girls and the junior girls had become a Melton tradition. School officials, though aware of the contest, did not interfere because the game occurred on a Saturday morning away from the school's campus. In fact, Jim did not even know that the game had been held on that Saturday. School employees had been warned not to participate in this or other unsanctioned student events that occurred off school property.

In recent years, however, the touch football game had become a prelude to activities indicative of fraternity initiations prior to universities banning hazing. Though social clubs or sororities were not permitted at Melton, it was widely known that the annual touch football game was sponsored by an elite social clique. A group of approximately twenty-five senior girls who had been initiated the previous year challenged an equal number of junior girls to a touch football game. The initiation to upper-class standing, not the football game, was the primary activity. Though rumors about the ritual were widespread throughout the school and the community, school officials had ignored the activity because it occurred away from school and on a weekend.

Superintendent Gregory indicated that reporters were in a feeding frenzy about the arrests. She was even contacted by a national news service. She wanted to alert Jim because the reporters were asking how they could contact him. Apparently, there were several kegs of beer at the event, and some male students attended to cheer on the activities. The initiation turned into a minor riot. Several fights broke out, and a student was seriously injured when she tried to escape an assailant by climbing into a tree and then broke her leg in three places after she was pushed out of the tree.

The call for an ambulance brought police to the scene. They found several dozen students intoxicated. The junior girls were covered with honey and feathers and several had minor injuries ranging from bruises on the faces to cuts on their arms and legs.

Superintendent Gregory indicated that she was trying to reach the school board members to apprise them of the situation. She had told reporters that the initiation, while unfortunate and disgusting, was not a school-sponsored event. She added that school officials would investigate the matter and take disciplinary action if warranted. She also suggested that Jim return to Melton as soon as possible.

Jim and wife returned home at about 8:00 P.M. The answering machine was filled with messages, most from media representatives but some from angry parents. Less than 15 minutes later, Jim had his first conversation with a reporter about the incident. He reiterated what Superintendent Gregory had already told the media: The gathering at the state park was not a school-sponsored event, and school officials in no way condoned this or any previous initiation.

By Sunday evening, the story had made national news. One network had obtained a videotape from an unidentified male student who had left the scene before police arrived. The video shocked even Principal Marshfield. Several senior girls, obviously intoxicated, were repeatedly punching junior girls while they were constrained. The video also showed several students vomiting and making obscene gestures toward the camera.

On Monday morning, a special meeting of the school board was held in Superintendent Gregory's office, and Principal Marshfield was told to attend. The board members were outraged. Melton was an upscale community, and its high school had an outstanding reputation. The board members demanded to know how this could happen. Both the superintendent and the principal explained that the event was beyond their control. They argued that they could not be held accountable for student behavior that occurred on a weekend and away from campus. One board member asked if the school officials knew that the initiation would be taking place. Both administrators indicated that they had no such information.

After emotions subsided, the board members, at the urging of the two administrators, decided to schedule a press conference that afternoon. School officials would continue to take the position that the incident, though unfortunate, was not their responsibility. The superintendent and principal would tell reporters that they had no knowledge that the event was taking place and inform the media that they would refrain from further comments until the legal aspects of the case were resolved. At that point, they would decide if they would take disciplinary action against any of the students.

The press conference drew a huge crowd of reporters. Principal Marshfield read a prepared statement that had been approved by the school district's attorney and director of communication. The statement, only two paragraphs, summarized the decisions that had been made with the school board that morning. Reporters attempted to ask questions after the statement, but both the superintendent and the principal responded that they would have no further comment on the matter until the legal aspects of the situation were resolved.

Over the next twenty-four hours, media coverage was not kind to the school officials. Some reporters even hinted that the superintendent, principal, and school board were trying to cover up the matter. A Dallas newspaper reported that several unnamed teachers at Melton High School admitted that the initiation was a long-standing tradition at the school and many teachers, if not administrators, knew that it would be taking place.

Over the next week, media coverage of the initiation and arrests intensified. So did criticism of school officials. Several experts on school violence who were interviewed by reporters indicated that the principal should have taken steps to prevent the initiation because it centered on the school and affected the school's reputation and culture.

Exactly one week after they first met to discuss a strategy for dealing with the arrests, the school board met again. This time, several members directly criticized the principal for not having taken action to prevent the initiation and the superintendent for having mismanaged "the crisis after the crisis." The board then directed the superintendent to retain a public relations firm immediately so that they could advise school officials on further action related to the matter.

The public relations consultant assigned to handle the school district advised the superintendent and principal to make public statements admitting that some mistakes were made. More importantly, they would assure the public that steps were being taken to prevent any recurrence of such an incident. Both Superintendent Gregory and Principal Marshfield were displeased with the recommendation. They felt that they were being made scapegoats for a situation that was beyond their control and certainly beyond their scope of responsibility. Dr. Gregory telephoned the board president about the consultant's recommendation. The board president had been her staunchest supporter. This time, however, the board president said, "Rachel, you better do what you are advised to do. If not, be prepared to face the consequences. We are paying this PR firm a big fee. We have confidence in their advice."

After that conversation, Dr. Gregory telephoned Principal Marshfield and shared the board president's comments. The superintendent then said that she would prepare a statement indicating that school officials could have done more to prevent this situation. She advised him to consider a similar statement.

PROBLEM FRAMING

1. Assume you are Principal Marshfield. Describe what you would want to accomplish in dealing with the situation described in this case.

2. Based on the evidence of contextual variables, describe the difficulty associated with achieving your objective.

QUESTIONS AND SUGGESTED ACTIVITIES

1. What is the legal concept of *in loco parentis?* Why may this concept be relevant to this case?

2. Evaluate the position taken by the principal that an event occurring on Saturday away from the school campus is not the school's responsibility.

3. This case has both a legal dimension and a public relations dimension. What is the legal dimension?

4. What is the public relations dimension of this case?

5. Do you agree that school officials should not take any action against the students until the legal charges against the students are resolved? Why or why not?

6. Evaluate the press conference held by the superintendent and principal. Did they handle the situation properly? Why or why not?

7. Evaluate the advice given to the superintendent and principal by the PR consultant.

8. Determine if the school district in which you work or reside has policy that would have been relevant to situations such as the one described in this case. Discuss the policies in class.

9. Most of the students attending the initiation were arrested for underage drinking. Is such an arrest away from campus on a weekend grounds for expelling or suspending a student? Why or why not?

10. What actions could have been taken by the principal to prevent the initiation?

11. What actions can be taken by the superintendent, principal, and other school officials to repair the high school's reputation?

12. Is this incident likely to cause irreparable damage to the principal's relationship with the superintendent and school board? Why or why not?

13. Discuss possible lawsuits that may result from this incident. How might these lawsuits affect the school district, the superintendent, and the principal?

SUGGESTED READINGS

Eastridge, H. E. (1999). The do's and don'ts of coping with crises. *School Administrator, 56*(6), 31–32.

Dixon, M. (2001). Hazing in high schools: Finding the hidden tradition. *Journal of Law and Education, 30*(2), 357–363.

Kowalski, T. J. (2002). Working with the media during a crisis situation: Perspectives from school administrators. *Journal of School Public Relations, 23*(3), 178–196.

Kowalski, T. J. (2007). *Public relations in schools* (4th ed.). Upper Saddle River, NJ: Merrill, Prentice Hall (see Chapters 11 and 14).

Kowalski, T. J., Petersen, G. J., & Fusarelli, L. D. (2007). *Effective communication for school administrators: An imperative in an information age.* Lanham, MD: Rowman and Littlefield Education (see Chapter 9).

Lester, J. (2004). Crisis situations deserve more than a "no comment." *School Administrator, 61*(3), 34.

Rerrandino, V. (2002). Surviving a crisis. *Principal, 80*(4), 72.

Sharp, H. M. (2005). After the fact. *Principal Leadership (High School Ed.), 5*(5), 39–41.

Sharp, H. M. (2006). *When a school crisis occurs: What parents and stakeholders want to know.* Lanham, MD: Rowman and Littlefield Education.

Worley, V. (2003). The teacher's place in the moral equation: In loco parentis. *Philosophy of Education Yearbook,* 280–282.

Zirkel, P. A., & Reichner, H. F. (1986). Is the in loco parentis doctrine dead? *Journal of Law and Education, 15,* 271–83

REFERENCES

Kowalski, T. J. (2002). Working with the media during a crisis situation: Perspectives from school administrators. *Journal of School Public Relations, 23*(3), 178–196.

Kowalski, T. J. (2007). *Public relations in schools* (4th ed.). Upper Saddle River, NJ: Merrill, Prentice Hall.

Kowalski, T. J., Petersen, G. J., & Fusarelli, L. D. (2007). *Effective communication for school administrators: An imperative in an information age.* Lanham, MD: Rowman and Littlefield Education.

Zirkel, P., & Reichner, H. (1987). Is in loco parentis dead? *Phi Delta Kappan, 68*(2), 466–469.

Background Information

One of the primary responsibilities of local district school boards is to set policy. The power to perform this responsibility is granted by state government. However, this power is not unlimited; all board policy decisions must conform to the limitations of relevant constitutional provisions, statutes, federal and state regulations, and common law (Imber & Van Geel, 1993). Administrators have the responsibility of developing rules and regulations that are extensions of policy.

Over the past two decades, a series of violent acts perpetrated in schools across the country made the public aware of two facts. First, violence can and does occur in any school, public or private, and in any type of community, from small towns to large cities. The most publicized acts of violence have occurred in such places as Columbine, Colorado; Jonesboro, Arkansas; Paducah, Kentucky; and Lancaster, Pennsylvania. Beginning in the 1990s, an outraged public demanded that school officials take actions to ensure that schools are safe places. In response, many states either required or encouraged school boards to adopt "zero-tolerance" policies. Often these policies were promulgated with little consideration of their effectiveness and potential pitfalls (Holloway, 2002).

Student discipline policy may be influenced by federal and state laws, philosophy, politics, and professional guidance (i.e., direction from the district superintendent) (Kowalski, 2006). Frequently, policy regulating pupil conduct has sparked intense conflict because various publics comprising the school's community do not share the same philosophy about education and punishment. Some parents, for example, believe that discipline's primary purpose is to protect the school and broader community, whereas other parents believe it is to correct improper behavior (Rasicot, 1999). Such philosophical disagreement also occurs among professional personnel. Some teachers and administrators, for example, view zero-tolerance policies as being essential to school safety, whereas others see these policies as being unfair because they disregard a student's total record. Observing these tensions, some authors (e.g., Essex, 2000) argue that the challenge facing administrators and school board members formulating discipline policy and rules is to balance school safety and student rights.

In this case several African American males are initially expelled for two years for engaging in violent acts at a high school football game. Segments of the local community react negatively, claiming the punishment is excessive and biased. After being expelled, the teenagers are charged with criminal offenses. A national civil rights leader gets involved and tensions worsen in a city that has had a history of racial strife.

Key Areas for Reflection

1. Race relations
2. Race and student discipline
3. The appropriateness of zero-tolerance policies
4. Violence in schools
5. Managing political conflict
6. Using conflict to produce positive change

The Case

Lincoln

Lincoln is an industrial community with a population of approximately 76,000. The three primary employers are a chemical plant, a stamping plant that makes truck fenders, and a candy company. Approximately 15 percent of the city's residents are African American and approximately 3 percent are Hispanic. In the past two decades, the city's population has declined about 11 percent, primarily because of employment reductions at the stamping plant.

The city has a history of segregation in housing patterns. Virtually all African American families reside in two neighborhoods just south and west of the city's center; virtually all Hispanic families reside in a neighborhood just east of the city's center. Less than 100 new single-family dwellings have been built in Lincoln in the last twenty-five years.

Prior to 1975, registered Republicans outnumbered registered Democrats by nearly a two-to-one margin. Now, however, the voter registration records show an almost equal number of Republicans and Democrats. The current mayor is the first Democrat to be elected to that office in over twenty-five years. His political base is a coalition of minority groups and union members. Since taking office three years ago, he has created a special advisory committee on race relations and sponsored a number of improvements in both the African American and Hispanic neighborhoods. Several months ago, the most prominent leader in the African American community issued a statement indicating that race relations in Lincoln had improved and that the mayor was largely responsible. He told a reporter, "Things aren't as bad as they were twenty-five years ago. Racism was very obvious back then. We are still trying to deal with the lingering effects of institutional racism but things certainly have improved." Just two weeks after this interview, a white policeman shot and killed an African American male who had shot at him. Reactions to the incident differed along racial lines.

The School District

The Lincoln School District has a total enrollment of approximately 10,000. The peak enrollment, 12,300 students, occurred in 1985. The district operates twelve elementary schools (grades k–5), four middle schools (grades 6–8), and two high schools (grades 9–12).

There are two high schools in the district: Lincoln High School and Lincoln North High School. The former, built in 1955, is just blocks from the city's business district. The school enrolls about 2,000 students, of whom 46 percent are African Americans and 2 percent are Hispanics. The newer high school, built in 1979, is located in city's most affluent neighborhood just about a quarter mile from the city's northern boundary line. Enrollment at Lincoln North is about 1,800 students, of whom 18 percent are African American and 1 percent are Hispanic.

There are seven members on the district's school board; four elected from specific areas of the city and three elected at-large. Currently, two board members are African Americans. The superintendent, Dr. Thomas Yundt, and the principals of both high schools are white males. Dr. Yundt has been in his present position for three years, having moved to Lincoln after serving as superintendent in a smaller school district. One of the three assistant superintendents reporting to Dr. Yundt, Dr. Robin Daniels, is an African American.

The Incident

The two Lincoln high schools belong to different athletic conferences; however, they compete against each other in football. The annual game, always scheduled for the third Friday of September, draws a huge crowd. During the most recent game, a brawl broke out in the bleachers midway through the second quarter, causing the game to be stopped. A group of African American students appeared to engage in a fistfight, then the turmoil spread indiscriminately through the crowd. School officials, including the principals of both schools, and several law enforcement officers attempted to intervene. One of the students involved allegedly grabbed the principal from Lincoln High School by the shirt and hit him in the chest with his fist. Although there were no hospital reports of injuries, there were conflicting stories as to whether people had been hurt.

The Lincoln School District had adopted a zero-tolerance policy with regard to violence at school or school events eighteen months prior to the incident at the football game. The two principals identified nine African American teenagers whom they believed were part of the group initiating the fighting; seven of them were current students. The principals recommended a two-year expulsion for the seven students. Their recommendation was based on provisions in the board's zero-tolerance policy.

Separate due process hearings were set for the students. Only one of them attended his hearing. He and his parents requested that he be allowed to withdraw from school to avoid being expelled—an act that would protect his permanent record. The hearing officer recommended that the request should be honored but argued that expulsion recommendations for the six students who did not appear at their hearings should be upheld. Dr. Yundt concurred with all of the hearing officer's recommendations and so informed the school board. He pointed out that the period of the expulsion, two years, was based on the egregious nature of the offense. However, the students could seek reinstatement after only one year if they produced evidence of positive behavior, such as staying out of trouble, pursuing tutoring and counseling, or performing community service. The board voted six to one to approve the superintendent's recommendation; one of the black board members voted against the recommendation.

Fallout

During the weeks that followed the board's approval of the expulsions, police were careful not to label the brawl as "gang-related." Nevertheless, rumors flowed through the community that the fight was the continuation of an altercation that occurred between two groups of teenagers several days earlier. Eventually, criminal charges were filed against the nine teenagers identified as being part of the initial fight. Four were charged as adults with felony mob action and one of them, an 18-year-old, was also accused of aggravated battery and resisting a peace officer. The remaining five were charged in juvenile petitions.

Initially, many in the African American community believed that expelling the seven students for two years was excessive punishment. When the criminal charges were filed weeks later, their disapproval changed to anger. At that point, a national civil rights figure, Reverend Arnold James, became involved. He spoke at a rally held in Lincoln to protest the treatment of the students and to start a defense fund for them. Rev. James made the following points in his speech to the angry crowd:

- He condemned the action of the school board and superintendent, arguing that they had rushed to judgment and overreacted.
- He insisted that the key issue in this matter was fairness rather than race. He argued that black students had been disproportionately the subjects of harsh discipline; he cited a statistic indicating that of the six students expelled the previous year, five were black. He also noted that the board had expelled a white student who had committed what he considered to be a much more serious offense (sending a bomb threat note) for only one year.
- He contended that the punishment given to the students was excessive for a fistfight in which no weapons were involved.
- He condemned the filing of criminal charges, insisting that the school board was working in tandem with law enforcement. He noted that by making the students criminals, the board was in essence justifying the unusually long expulsions.

Within days of Rev. James's appearance in Lincoln the controversy was covered by the national media. The governor, the state school superintendent, and local elected officials were drawn into the matter. Unrest in the African American community was getting progressively tense, and Superintendent Yundt decided to close the schools for three days fearing an outbreak of additional violence.

In the midst of growing national interest, the board president issued a statement in which she noted, "I really resent the fact that we have outsiders telling us how to run our schools." The governor was able to get both sides to attend a day-long meeting that resulted in the school board's agreeing to reduce the punishment to an expulsion for the remainder of the school year. In addition, the expelled students would be allowed to attend the district's alternative high school program. Rev. James called the board's concession inadequate and pressured both the governor and state superintendent to intervene directly. Both declined, indicating that they would facilitate a solution but would not usurp the authority of the local school board.

Key figures on both sides were inundated with requests for media interviews. Leaders in the local African American community met with reporters and restated many of the claims that Rev. James made in his initial speech in Lincoln. School officials who previously refused to disclose any information about the students now made selected data available to the media and public. For example, Dr. Yundt, appearing on a national news show, revealed that three of the students were third-year freshmen and that collectively the seven students had missed 350 days of school the previous year. In addition, school officials made available an amateur videotape of the incident. The camera captured the last third of the brawl, showing spectators scurrying to get away from a group of teenagers throwing punches and tossing each other down the cement bleacher steps.

In the aftermath of the board's concession (reducing the length of the expulsion) and the viewing of the videotape, conservative media commentators and politicians criticized Rev. James for having misstated the facts and for having intensified tensions in Lincoln. They refuted Rev. James's contention that no one was hurt and declared that criminal activity was indeed an issue. They pointed to the video as clear evidence that Rev. James either erred in reporting the facts of this case or purposely misled the public.

Continuing Controversy

Despite the school board's decision to reduce the expulsion period, tensions did not subside. Rev. James and his supporters filed a thirteen-page civil rights complaint in U.S. District Court alleging that the school board had violated the students' constitutional rights in the following ways:

- By failing to have an explicit zero-tolerance policy in writing
- By labeling the conduct as "gang-related" without evidence
- By failing to notify the students about alternative education options
- By punishing them too harshly for a fistfight void of weapons

At the same time that anger lingered in the black community, many white residents criticized the school board and superintendent for having reduced the expulsion periods.

Rev. James repeatedly warned community officials and the media that the matter was not resolved just because the punishment was reduced. In addition, he now accused school officials of having violated privacy laws by disclosing information about the case to the news media. He vowed to continue his activities in Lincoln until the teenagers were cleared of criminal charges. He announced that he would lead a march through the city the following week. Clearly, the matter was not resolved, and the superintendent, school board, and other school officials continued to be criticized by leaders in the African American community.

PROBLEM FRAMING

1. Assume you are the superintendent. Describe what you would want to accomplish in dealing with the situation described in this case.

2. Based on the evidence of contextual variables, describe the difficulty associated with achieving your objective.

QUESTIONS AND SUGGESTED ACTIVITIES

1. Share and critique the problem statements prepared by students in your class.

2. What racial and political characteristics of the community and school district are relevant to the problem presented in the case?

3. Rev. James cited a case in which a white student had been expelled for just one year for a bomb threat. Do you agree with him that the fistfight was a lesser offense? Do you agree with him that the lesser penalty given to the white student was evidence of discriminatory discipline practices?

4. Debate the issue of zero-tolerance policy.

5. The one student recommended for expulsion who attending his hearing requested that he be permitted to withdraw from school instead of being expelled. The hearing officer, superintendent, and school board concurred.

Do you think this was a good decision? Why or why not?

6. Was Rev. James's claim of unequal treatment of black students nullified when the school board reduced the expulsion period? Why or why not?

7. In the aftermath of this incident, identify actions you would recommend with regard to increasing security at school-sponsored events.

8. Some educators believe that student discipline should be primarily punitive and others believe it should be primarily remedial. Which position do you favor? Provide a rationale for your response.

9. Discuss possible objectives of student expulsion. Identify the least and most important objective.

SUGGESTED READINGS

Baker, J. A. (1998). Are we missing the forest for the trees? Considering the social context of school violence. *Journal of School Psychology, 36*(1), 29–44.

Bock, S. J., Savner, J. L., & Tapscott, K. E. (1998). Suspension and expulsion: Effective management of students? *Intervention in School and Clinic, 34*(1), 50–52.

Casella, R. (2003). Zero tolerance policy in schools: Reationale, consequences, and alternatives. *Teachers College Record, 105*(5), 872–892.

Clark, C. (1998). The violence that creates school dropouts. *Multicultural Education, 6*(1), 19–22.

Costenbader, V., & Markson, S. (1998). School suspension: A study with secondary school students. *Journal of School Psychology, 36*(1), 59–82.

Edmonson, H. M., & Bullock, L. M. (1998). Youth with aggressive and violent behaviors: Pieces of a puzzle. *Preventing School Failure, 42*(3), 135–141.

Edwards, C. H. (2001). Student violence and the moral dimensions of education. *Psychology in the Schools, 38*(3), 249–257.

Gable, R. A., Quinn, M. M., & Rutherford, R. B. (1998). Addressing problem behaviors in schools: Use of functional assessments and behavior intervention plans. *Preventing School Failure, 42*(3), 106–119.

Gordon, J. A. (1998). Caring through control. *Journal for a Just and Caring Education, 4*(4), 18–40.

Haynes, R. M., & Chalker, D. M. (1999). A nation of violence. *American School Board Journal, 186*(3), 22–25.

Holloway, J. H. (2001). The dilemma of zero tolerance. *Educational Leadership, 59*(4), 84–85.

Hyman, I. A., & Perone, D. C. (1998). The other side of school violence: Educator policies and practices that may contribute to student misbehavior. *Journal of School Psychology, 36*(1), 7–27.

Jimerson, S. R., Brock, S. E., & Cowan, K. C. (2005). Threat assessment: An essential component of a comprehensive safe school program. *Principal Leadership (Middle School Ed.), 6*(2), 11–15.

McEvoy, A., Erickson, E., & Randolph, N. (1997). Why the brutality? *Student Intervention Report, 10*(4).

Morrison, G. M., & D'Incau, B. (1997). The web of zero-tolerance: Characteristics of students who are recommended for expulsion from school. *Education and Treatment of Children, 20*(3), 316–335.

Roper, D. A. (1998). Facing anger in our schools. *Educational Forum, 62*(4), 363–368.

Skiba, R. J., & Peterson, R. L. (1999). The dark side of zero tolerance: Can punishment lead to safe schools? *Phi Delta Kappan, 80*(5) 372–376.

Stefkovich, J. A., & Guba, G. J. (1998). School violence, school reform, and the Fourth Amendment in public schools. *International Journal of Educational Reform, 7*(3), 217–225.

St. George, D. M., & Thomas, S. B. (1997). Perceived risk of fighting and actual fighting behavior among middle school students. *Journal of School Health, 67*(5), 178–181.

Toby, J. (1998). Getting serious about school discipline. *Public Interest,* (133), 68–83.

Zirkel, P. A., & Gluckman, I. B. (1997). Due process in student suspensions and expulsions. *Principal, 76*(4), 62–63.

REFERENCES

Essex, N. L. (2000). Zero tolerance approach to school violence: Is it going too far? *American Secondary Education, 29*(2), 37–40.

Holloway, J. H. (2002). The dilemma of zero tolerance. *Educational Leadership, 59*(4), 84–85.

Imber, M., & Van Geel, T. (1993). *Education law.* New York: McGraw-Hill.

Kowalski, T. J. (2006). *The school superintendent: Theory, practice, and cases* (2nd ed.). Thousand Oaks, CA: Sage.

Rasicot, J. (1999). The threat of harm. *American School Board Journal, 186*(3), 14–18.

17 The Passive Principal

Background Information

After 1980, policymakers attempted to improve schools by first making students do more of what they were already doing and, second, by raising standards for preparing and licensing administrators. Though these actions had some positive effects, they failed to produce the desired levels of school improvement. Since approximately 1990, the strategy of intensification mandates has been replaced by efforts to restructure schools. The current approach is nested in two beliefs:

1. Reform is more effective when it is pursued at the district and individual school levels. Both state deregulation and district decentralization are manifestations of this prevailing improvement strategy.
2. Unless the basic structure of schools, including organizational culture, is adjusted to address the real needs of students, the outcomes of reform will be limited (Kowalski, 2003).

School-based management (SBM) is arguably the most recognizable product of contemporary school reform strategies.

The decentralization of authority and decision making in public education stems from several beliefs, including these:

- Teachers become more effective when treated as true professionals (Marzano, 2003).
- Instructional decisions are improved when teachers are empowered to tailor their classroom activities to the real needs of their students (Hoy & Miskel, 2005).
- School productivity improves when principals and teachers are not manacled by a seemingly endless list of policies and rules (Kowalski, 2006).
- Democratic decision making and community involvement in governance have a positive influence on school productivity (Kowalski, Petersen, & Fusarelli, 2007).

Flexibility and adaptability are primary decentralization objectives intended to allow individual schools to be reshaped based on the needs of students being served. Decentralization, however, has often elevated state accountability standards. As an example, some states have given local districts greater leeway to determine curriculum, but at the same time they require students to take state proficiency examinations intended to measure learning outcomes. This strategy is often called *directed autonomy* (Kowalski, 2006).

The principal is often the person most affected by decentralization (Brown, 1990). This is true for at least three reasons.

1. Principals assume greater leadership responsibility (i.e., determining what should be done) without a corresponding decrease in managerial responsibilities (i.e., being responsible for how things are done).
2. Engaging in shared decision making is often threatening to a principal if he or she remains personally accountable for group decisions.
3. Participatory decision making typically increases the frequency and severity of conflict, and principals must manage and resolve these tensions.

A summary of research on SBM does little to alleviate administrative apprehensions. Findings often indicate that this decentralization approach increases political activity, is time-consuming, is not always supported by teachers, and is not always adequately funded (Brown, 2001). Yet most scholars recognize the potentialities of SBM and continue to advocate its use (Kowalski et al., 2007).

This case is about an experienced principal who volunteers to participate in a first phase of implementing SBM. In creating a school council, he decides to permit council members to be elected by the groups they represent (teachers, parents, and staff), and although he too is a council member, he assumes a passive role. Teachers representing two factions of the school's faculty are elected to the council, and they vie for power. The principal's laissez-faire attitude in the context of this conflict angers the council chair, a parent and the president of the school's parent-teacher association (PTA).

Key Areas for Reflection

1. Problems associated with decentralized governance of schools
2. Social conflict among individuals and groups in schools
3. Dynamics of group decision making
4. Leadership style and participatory decision making
5. Leadership role in conflict resolution

The Case

Community and School District

Sunland is a prosperous city in a southern state. With a population of approximately 75,000, it has grown nearly 25 percent in the last twenty years. New industries and businesses continue to locate in or near the city, and population projections indicate that there will be 100,000 by the year 2012. Sunland also is the county seat for LaSalle County.

Serving the entire county, including the city of Sunland, the LaSalle County School District has three high schools, six middle schools, and nineteen elementary schools. Although population is increasing across the county, the growth has been the greatest and most rapid growth in Sunland. As a result, a new middle school and three new elementary schools have been built in the city in the past decade.

Superintendent and SBM

Three years ago, the school board employed Dr. Ursula Jones as superintendent. The 42-year-old administrator had been associate superintendent for instruction in a large-city school system in an adjoining state. Prior to coming to LaSalle County, Dr. Jones had established a reputation as a change agent. When the newspaper announced her employment, her former superintendent was quoted as saying, "LaSalle County is getting a top-notch superintendent. Dr. Jones is one of the most creative and bold administrators I have known."

During her first year as superintendent, Dr. Jones developed a decentralization plan for the district. It called for the adoption of SBM. The initial phase involved implementation in one to three elementary schools. Selection of the schools was based on interviews of principals who had expressed an interest in becoming part of the first phase. Six principals were interviewed, and the superintendent then selected three of them.

Financial support was provided for the three participating schools. This included funding for the principals to attend a two-week seminar during the summer to help them implement the process and a $20,000 allocation for staff development. The only restriction placed on the staff development funds was that they had to be used for SBM-related activities. In addition, the principals were given budgetary control over two critical areas: supplies/equipment and staff travel.

Elm Street Elementary School

Elm Street Elementary is one of the district's newest buildings. It opened just four years ago to accommodate the growing population of students in Sunland. The school has three sections per grade level in grades K–5, but there are plans to add a fourth section at each grade level if the enrollment projections prove to be accurate. When the school was opened, teachers from across the district had an opportunity to apply for a transfer to the new building; consequently, about 70 percent of the teachers were already employed in the district.

The Principal

Albert Batz had been the principal of a small elementary school in LaSalle County when he was selected as Elm Street's first principal. An outgoing, friendly individual, he relates well to students, staff, and parents. Prior to becoming an administrator he had taught fifth grade for twelve years.

As principal of Elm Street, Mr. Batz spends virtually all of his time walking the halls. He enjoys interacting with teachers, students, and other school personnel. It is not uncommon for him to walk into a classroom and join whatever activities are taking place. He usually makes two or three trips a day to the teachers' lounge, and one of his favorite midmorning hideaways is the kitchen. Teachers often comment that they don't know if he is more interested in getting the latest gossip from the cooks or in sampling that day's dessert. He considers himself a disciple of the concept known as "managing by walking around."

Teachers view Albert as a unique principal. He would rather be seen as just another teacher than as the boss. When he came to Elm Street, he brought his secretary, Mrs. Lumans, with him because she is capable of handling many of the routine management tasks that he dislikes.

Implementing SBM

When Dr. Jones announced that three elementary schools would be selected for the first phase of SBM implementation, Albert Batz was the first to contact her expressing interest in participating as a pilot site. He believed in democratic decision making and unlike some of his peers, maintaining power over teachers was not an issue. Before contacting the superintendent, however, he had asked for and received overwhelming support from the school's employees to do so.

In addition to being in philosophical agreement with the superintendent's plan, Albert had another motive for making Elm Street an SBM pilot site. When he came to the new school, he encountered what was for him a novel problem. Two factions divided the faculty. One consisted of four teachers who previously had taught at Harrison Elementary School, an older school in Sunland. The spokesperson for this group was Jenny Bales. The other consisted of three teachers who previously taught at Weakland Township Elementary School, one of the district's rural schools. The designated leader of this group was Leonard Teel. While neither faction was very large, they constantly vied for political support from the remaining faculty members.

Albert concluded that Mrs. Bales and Mr. Teel had similar traits and needs. In their previous schools, each had been the "alpha" teacher—that is, the teacher in the school who had the greatest power to influence others. Now each was attempting to establish the same stature at Elm Street Elementary School. For the most part, the fifteen teachers not aligned with either faction tried to remain neutral.

After Elm Street was selected to be an SBM pilot site, Mr. Batz had to establish a governance committee. The size and composition of the committee was not specified by the superintendent. He opted to have an eleven-member committee consisting of six teachers, three parents, one other school employee, and himself. Rather than appointing the members, he asked the faculty, the PTA, and the school's nonteaching staff to select their representatives.

The faculty decided to hold an election to select its representatives. All teachers were eligible to be candidates. All seven members of the two factions announced that they wanted to be on the council. Two other faculty members did likewise. Thus, nine teachers competed for the six council positions. Each teacher could vote for up to six candidates.

Amy Raddison and Tim Paxton, the two not aligned with either faction, received the most votes. The other four successful candidates were Jenny Bales, Arlene Mc-Fadden (aligned with Mrs. Bales), Leonard Teel, and Lucille Isacson (aligned with Mr. Teel). Both Ms. Raddison and Mr. Paxton were relatively young and inexperienced teachers.

Mr. Batz had hoped that being on the school council would satisfy the egos of both Mrs. Bales and Mr. Teel. He even thought that the two might reconcile their differences by interacting more frequently. After just four months, however, he realized that his hopes would not likely be realized. The adversarial relationship between the two teachers and their factions actually became more intense because the council provided a formal arena for their battles.

A dispute over an agenda item at the December council meeting provided an example of the power struggle that was occurring. A request to send a team of five teachers to a mid-January conference on SBM was submitted for approval. Among the five teachers who would be attending were Mr. Teel and another teacher politically aligned with him. Mrs. Bales spoke against approving the request.

"Just because we have a budget for staff development doesn't mean that we should send people to California to learn about SBM."

Leonard Teel shot back immediately, "This conference focuses on model SBM programs. Teachers from all over the United States will be there. We can learn a great deal by participating. It's not my decision to have the conference in California. Why do you care where it is held?"

Mrs. Bales answered. "There are plenty of good programs closer to home. And for that reason, I urge everyone to vote against this request."

Barbara Whitlow, president of the PTA and a parent representative to the council, had been elected as the council's chair. Having to preside over yet another fight between Mrs. Bales and Mr. Teel frustrated her. She turned to Mr. Batz and asked him if he favored approval of the travel request.

He answered, "You know that I don't like to take sides. As principal, I need to be neutral. I have to work closely with all teachers. This is probably a good conference but there are also good conferences and workshops closer to home."

The principal's role on the council had been questioned on a number of occasions by Mrs. Whitlow. She had asked Mr. Batz several times to explain how his role as principal interfaced with his role as council member. His consistent response was that he was just like all the other council members and should be treated as such. Mrs. Whitlow considered his answer evasive, and in front of the other council members, she told him so. When the council was first formed, she had assumed that the principal would be the chair. When he declined to serve in this capacity, the other members did not object to his decision.

Both Mrs. Bales and Mr. Teel had consistently supported Mr. Batz's decision not to assume leadership of the council. Mrs. Whitlow concluded that the two actually preferred the principal's passive role.

After Mr. Batz evaded the question of whether he recommended approval of the conference request, Mrs. Bales made a formal motion to deny approval. The motion was seconded by Mrs. McFadden, the council member politically aligned with her. Mr. Teel requested that the vote on the motion be taken by secret ballot. The council was increasingly taking secret votes, and Mrs. Whitlow saw this process as counterproductive to building team spirit. The two other parents on the council were becoming increasingly disgruntled as well because most meetings were immersed in conflict.

The motion made by Mrs. Bales was defeated by a one-vote margin. One of the parents then made a motion to approve the travel request, and it passed. The dispute, however, had an obvious negative effect on the council.

The next day, Mrs. Whitlow met with Mr. Batz at her request. She wanted to know why he had repeatedly refused to provide leadership on the council.

"I just don't understand how you can sit back and allow Mrs. Bales and Mr. Teel to constantly be at each other. Don't you understand the destructive nature of their behavior?" she asked.

"Barbara, I still hope that those two will reconcile their differences and learn to cooperate. And even if I intervene, they will interpret my intervention as taking sides."

Mrs. Whitlow was irritated with Mr. Batz's refusal to be a leader and told him that unless he became a more active council member, she would resign. "You know, Albert, I have plenty to do besides spending ten to twelve hours a week here at the school. I'm more than willing to volunteer my time; however, only if we start making progress. And right now, that is not happening. All the council members have done is sit and listen to petty arguments. If this is SBM, I say we get rid of it. As principal, you have a responsibility to do something about this negative behavior."

Mr. Batz pleaded with Mrs. Whitlow to be patient. He told her that her continued leadership was essential to the council. Yet, he again sidestepped making a commitment to change his behavior. He told Mrs. Whitlow that he would think about becoming more vocal at the meetings.

Two days after visiting the principal, Mrs. Whitlow wrote a letter to Mr. Batz resigning from the council. Copies were sent to the superintendent, Dr. Jones, and each member of the LaSalle County school board. In her letter, she suggested that the potential of SBM was being undermined. She wrote:

> . . . If schools are given leeway and added resources, we need to be certain that proper leadership is provided by administrators. Simply sharing power and authority does not ensure that our children will receive a better education. I am resigning from the Elm Street Elementary School Council because I'm frustrated. Frustrated that I was unable to accomplish more as council chair and frustrated that the ambiguities concerning the principal's role on the council have not been resolved. At least at Elm Street Elementary School, SBM has not been productive.

After reading the letter, Mr. Batz put it in his top desk drawer and thought about how the superintendent, school board, and Elm Street faculty would react. After about a minute, he left his office walking toward the school cafeteria. A smile came over his face as he got close enough to smell the freshly baked cookies.

PROBLEM FRAMING

1. Assume you are the superintendent. Describe what you would want to accomplish in dealing with the situation described in this case.

2. Based on the evidence of contextual variables, describe the difficulty associated with achieving your objective.

QUESTIONS AND SUGGESTED ACTIVITIES

1. Evaluate the process used by the superintendent to implement SBM in this school district. Identify other alternatives that could have been used to implement the program.

2. Do you agree with the principal's decision to permit council members to be elected? What other options could he have used to select council members?

3. The superintendent could order the principal to remove the four teachers who are members of the competing factions from the council. What are the advantages and disadvantages of this decision?

4. Were members of the school council adequately prepared to assume their responsibility? What evidence do you have to defend your response?

5. What role do you believe a principal should play on an SBM council?

6. Does Mr. Batz exhibit a democratic leadership style? If yes, what evidence supports your response? If no, describe his leadership style.

7. To what extent is the superintendent responsible for the conflict that emerges in this case?

8. Power is commonly defined as the ability to influence behavior in others. Often school employees other than the principal possess power. How do they acquire it?

9. One could argue that interventions by the superintendent would be contrary to the guiding philosophy of SBM. Do you agree? Why or why not?

SUGGESTED READINGS

Bergman, A. (1992). Lessons for principals from school-based management. *Educational Leadership*, *50*(1), 48–51.

Blasé, J. R., & Blasé, J. (1999). Shared governance principles: The inner experience. *NASSP Bulletin*, *83*(606), 81–90.

Conway, J. (1984). The myth, mystery, and mastery of participative decision making in education. *Educational Administration Quarterly*, *21*(1), 11–40.

Delaney, J. G. (1997). Principal leadership: A primary factor in school-based management and school improvement. *NASSP Bulletin*, *81*(586), 107–111.

Epp, J. R., & MacNeil, C. (1997). Perceptions of shared governance in an elementary school. *Canadian Journal of Education*, *22*(3), 254–267.

Ferris, J. (1992). School-based decision making: A principal-agent perspective. *Educational Evaluation and Policy Analysis*, *14*(4), 333–346.

Fraze, L., & Melton, G. (1992). Manager or participatory leader. *NASSP Bulletin*, *76*(540), 17–24.

Golarz, R. (1992). School-based management pitfalls: How to avoid some and deal with others. *School Community Journal*, *2*(1), 38–52.

Henkin, A. B., Cistone, P. J., & Dee, J. R. (2000). Conflict management strategies of principals in school-based managed schools. *Journal of Educational Administration*, *38*(2), 142–158.

Kowalski, T. J., Petersen, G. J., & Fusarelli, L. D. (2007). *Effective communication for school administrators: An imperative in an information age*. Lanham, MD: Rowman and Littlefield Education (see Chapter 11).

Kowalski, T., Reitzug, U., McDaniel, P., & Otto, D. (1992). Perceptions of desired skills for effective principals. *Journal of School Leadership*, *2*(3), 299–309.

Lange, J. (1993). School-based, shared decision making: A resource for restructuring. *NASSP Bulletin*, 76(549), 98–107.

Laud, L. E. (1998). Changing the way we communicate. *Educational Leadership*, 55(7), 23–25.

Leithwood, K., & Menzies, T. (1998). A review of research concerning the implementation of school-based management. *School Effectiveness and School Improvement*, 9(3), 233–285.

Lovely, S. D. (2005). Making the leap to shared leadership. *Journal of Staff Development*, 26(2), 16–21.

Miles, W. (1982). The school-site politics of education: A review of the literature. *Planning and Changing*, 12(4), 200–218.

Minor, J. T., & Tierney, W. G. (2005). The danger of deference: A case of polite governance. *Teachers College Record*, 107(1), 137–156.

Rodriguez, T. A., & Slate, J. R. (2005). Site-based management: A review of the literature part II: Past and present status. *Essays in Education*, 15, 186–212.

Smylie, M. (1992). Teacher participation in school decision making: Assessing willingness to participate. *Educational Evaluation and Policy Analysis*, 14(1), 53–67.

Sorenson, L. D., & Evans, R. D. (2001). Superintendent use of site-based councils: Role ambiguity and accountability. *Planning and Changing*, 32(3/4), 184–198.

Turk, R. L. (2002). What principals should know about building and maintaining teams. *NASSP Bulletin*, 87, 15–23.

Watkins, P. (1990). Agenda, power and text: The formulation of policy in school councils. *Journal of Education Policy*, 5(4), 315–331.

REFERENCES

Brown, D. J. (1990). *Decentralization and school-based management*. London: Falmer Press.

Brown, F. (2001). School-based management: Is it still central to the school reform movement? *School Business Affairs*, 67(4), 5–6, 8–9.

Hoy, W. K., & Miskel, C. G. (2005). *Educational administration: Theory, research, and practice* (7th ed.). New York: McGraw Hill.

Kowalski, T. J. (2003). *Contemporary school administration: An introduction*. Boston: Allyn and Bacon.

Kowalski, T. J. (2006). *The school superintendent: Theory, practice, and cases* (2nd ed.). Thousand Oaks, CA: Sage.

Kowalski, T. J., Petersen, G. J., & Fusarelli, L. D. (2007). *Effective communication for school administrators: An imperative in an information age*. Lanham, MD: Rowman and Littlefield Education.

Marzano, R. J. (2003). *What works in schools: Translating research into action*. Alexandria, VA: Association for Supervision and Curriculum Development.

A Disillusioned Assistant Principal

Background Information

Behavior in schools is determined by a combination of personal, professional, and contextual variables. One of the most influential factors is socialization, a process that begins during preservice professional preparation. During this period, professors usually advocate values and beliefs commonly accepted by the profession and expressed in the formal knowledge base. Examples include advocating that educators place students above all else and promoting the idea that professionals have a commitment to be lifelong learners. Socialization continues during student teaching; however, once a teacher is actually employed in a school, prevailing culture of the workplace intensifies the process (Aiken, 2002). This cycle of socialization recurs when a teacher makes a transition to school administration.

School culture represents the shared values and beliefs of those who work in the school. Over time, these values and beliefs represent accepted behavioral norms, especially in relation to the manner in which teachers and administrators should solve problems (Hanson, 2003). A school's culture may be weak or strong; strength describes the extent to which members of the school's culture adhere to the same values and beliefs. A culture may also be negative or positive; positive cultures are those in which the shared values and beliefs are congruous with the professional knowledge base (Kowalski, 2003).

School administrators do not adapt to socialization uniformly. Though most conform and accept the dominant values of their workplace, a few reject them, thus risking negative repercussions (Heck, 1995). Given these options, conformity appears to be a prudent choice; however, that is not always true. If the employing district or school has a negative culture, principals and teachers are guided by invalid assumptions (Kowalski, 2006). As an example, a principal socialized in a negative culture may come to believe that corporal punishment is effective when, in fact, research suggests otherwise.

Within a relatively short period of time, typically one or two years, the outcome of socialization is apparent. Those successfully enculturated typically are rewarded (e.g., they are rehired or given salary increases), and those who are not typically are penalized (e.g., they receive poor evaluations, they are recommended for dismissal, or they are shunned by their colleagues) (Kowalski, 2003).

This case is about a female teacher who becomes an assistant principal. As a novice administrator, she quickly discerns that she and the principal have different values and beliefs—a factor that is affecting her self-confidence and her relationship with the principal. Moreover, she recognizes that the principal's philosophy is shared by most, if not all, the teachers at the school. She begins to weigh four possible options: (a) learning to live with the conflict so she can remain in her current position, (b) accepting the principal's values and beliefs, (c) seeking an administrative position in another school, or (d) returning to teaching.

Key Areas for Reflection

1. School culture
2. Socialization in organizations
3. Problems encountered by novice administrators
4. Professional knowledge, personal values, and ethical behavior
5. Determinants of administrative behavior

The Case

Amber Jackson sat in her office at Polk Middle School trying to finish work assigned by the principal. At nearly 9:30 P.M., the three night custodians were the only other people still in the building. Amber was tired and frustrated, making it difficult for her to focus on the work she wanted to complete. As she continued to stare at the clock, she concluded that she was not going to get much sleep that evening.

Amber had started teaching English and physical education at a middle school in southern California at age 22. Two years later, she began coaching volleyball and enrolled as a part-time student in a master's degree program at a local state university. She selected educational administration as a major because she wanted to be a school principal. Dr. Tom Appleton, formerly a principal in a suburban school district near San Diego, was her adviser. During her master's program, Amber completed two of his classes: "School Public Relations" and "The School Principal." He considered her to be the best student he had encountered since becoming a professor four years earlier.

As Amber was nearing the end of her master's program, Professor Appleton told her that she could be a highly successful administrator. "You are intelligent and your work ethic is great. I think you should start applying for assistant principal jobs. And once you find the right position, you should apply for admission to our doctoral program."

Professor Appleton's career advice was flattering and the idea of becoming an assistant principal and a doctoral student was inviting. Amber, however, was hesitant to follow the advice because she had only five years of teaching experience and she had recently gotten engaged.

Amber told Professor Appleton that she had decided to wait at least a year before applying for administrative positions. "I'm getting married in November, and my fiancé is an Air Force pilot currently stationed in Texas. His tour of duty will be over in about eight months, and then he plans to seek employment as a commercial pilot. Therefore, I'm not sure where I'll be living a year from now. Once we get settled and he has a job, I would be more comfortable seeking an administrative position and entering a doctoral program."

Over the course of the following year, Amber did get married and her husband became employed as a pilot for an air freight company based in Chicago. They rented an apartment in a suburb about 20 minutes north of the city. Amber applied for both teaching and administrative positions in the Chicago area. In less than a month, she had two job offers: one a teaching position in an affluent suburban district and the other a middle-school assistant principal position in a far less affluent suburban district. She accepted the administrative position.

Polk Middle School, constructed in the early 1960s, enrolls approximately 800 students in grades 7 and 8. Twenty-eight percent of the students are identified as racial or ethnic minorities, equally divided between African American and Hispanic students.

Two other administrators are employed at Polk Middle School. Emil Denko, the principal, has been in his position for fourteen years, and he is a white male. Ernest Tarver, an assistant principal, has been in his position for twelve years, and he is African American. Both Mr. Denko and Mr. Tarver plan to retire together in three years.

Amber found Polk Middle School to be substantially different from the middle school where she had previously been employed as a teacher. Given the differences in the communities served, she correctly assumed that there would be more academic and discipline problems at Polk. She did not anticipate, however, that relationships among teachers and administrators at the two schools would be quite dissimilar. At her previous place of employment, the administrators had a collegial relationship with the teachers, and teachers were routinely involved in important decisions, especially those relating to curriculum and instruction. At Polk, relationships between teachers and administrators were primarily adversarial.

Conflict at Polk Middle School, which was pervasive both between administrators and teachers and among teachers, was almost always resolved in one of two ways. Either the principal brokered a negotiated settlement, or the dispute was adjudicated in accordance with the grievance procedures contained in the teachers' union master contract. Despite frequent disagreements with faculty, Mr. Denko and Mr. Tarver seemed to be friendly with many of the teachers outside of the school. It was as if the administrators and teachers agreed to play by two sets of rules: one set in effect inside the school and one set in effect outside the school.

Amber was also disappointed to find that many teachers at Polk set low expectations for their students. For example, on several occasions she heard teachers comment that a third of the students in the school would never be successful academically. Even more disturbing, Principal Denko repeated this conviction directly to her during a conversation they were having about student homework. She asked him to explain the basis for this judgment. He told her that many of the students came from families that placed little importance on education. Only 24 percent of the high school graduates in the district enrolled in post-secondary education and nearly 20 percent of the high school students dropped out before graduating.

After three months of being an assistant principal at Polk Middle School, Amber was dissatisfied with her job. Almost all of her assigned duties involved student discipline and routine management, and she wanted to be more involved in instructional issues. By the end of the first semester, she wrote a letter of resignation.

Before actually resigning, Amber telephoned her former professor, Dr. Appleton. She shared her impressions of Polk Middle School and her doubts about continuing in her current position. After listening for nearly 10 minutes, he responded.

"Before you decide to resign or continue, you need to have this type of conversation with the principal. Share your impressions of the school and express your desire to be more involved with instructional programs. If he reacts negatively or if he is indifferent, maybe you need to find another job. Regardless of the outcome of your conversation, I don't think you should quit immediately. Leaving in the middle of a school year may make it difficult for you to find another administrative position."

Heeding Dr. Appleton's advice, Amber met with Mr. Denko and shared her concerns. She told him, "I don't understand why teachers have such a low opinion of students at this school. They appear to be giving up on students who most need their help. High expectations usually affect students positively. One of my former professors said that it was especially important for administrators to believe that students could succeed."

Mr. Denko was surprised by her words but astonished that she was dissatisfied with her position. He thought a young female educator like Amber should be ecstatic about being an assistant principal so early in her career.

"How could you be dissatisfied? Here you are, not even 30 years old and you're already an administrator. You're making nearly twice as much as most teachers your age. Personally, I think you're doing a good job. Is there something else bothering you that I don't know about?"

Amber replied. "No. There is nothing else. I just feel uncomfortable in this school. Everyone seems negative about students and more often than not, people are fighting with each other rather than collaborating. Many of the teachers can't wait to leave school at the end of the day, and they don't seem to be proud of the school. The negative attitudes around here are depressing."

"Given what you have told me about the California school in which you taught previously, the differences you are seeing may be more community-based than school-based. Polk serves kids who don't come from wealthy families and in many instances, they don't come from healthy families. People who have not worked in these conditions, people like your former professor, find it easy to prescribe solutions because they don't have to deal with the issues. But being here, working with these problems day after day results in a different perspective. Did you ever consider the possibility that the teachers here are being honest? Many of them are dedicated to their students, but they have to let off steam every so often. About one-fourth of our students won't graduate from high school—at least not before they become adults. I have lived in this type of community all my life. I too once dreamed that every student would go to college and eventually become successful. Unfortunately, the brutal truth destroys such dreams. Years ago, I also listened to idealistic professors. The problem then and now is that many of them are unaware of what it is like to be a teacher or principal in a school like Polk."

Amber was not especially pleased with his response but instead of rebutting, she moved to her second concern.

"Emil, I'm also bothered by the fact that I have had no opportunity to work directly with teachers on instructional matters. I don't mind handling discipline problems, and I don't mind doing things like supervising students getting on and off buses. I expected to have these responsibilities—I just didn't expect them to be my only duties. I wanted to become an administrator so I could work closely with teachers. As a teacher, I benefited from the counsel of my principal; she always exhibited interest in my professional growth. She was a terrific role model. Several of my graduate classes focused on instructional leadership, and I believe I can make a meaningful contribution in this area."

"I'm sure you can," Mr. Denko answered. "And maybe next year, you can be assigned to evaluate several of the teachers, especially in language arts. Right now, I don't think that is a good idea. You're younger than most of the teachers, and some of the veterans might resent you doing their evaluations. In addition, teachers in this district don't expect us to supervise their teaching regularly, largely because they don't want us to do that."

"Why would they not want to receive supervision?"

"Because that's the way it's always been here. If teachers become dependent on administrators, the union leaders fear they'll quit the union. The doubts you're having will fade with time. Teachers who move from the classroom to administration usually have grand ideas about saving poor teachers and helping troubled students. But they quickly discover that dream is unattainable. Reality sets in, and you realize that your job is to keep the school operating efficiently and safely. That's the way it was when I started teaching in this district thirty-four years ago and that's the way it is today. You probably miss being with students in the classroom. In a couple of months, things will look different. Trust me. You play your cards right, and you could be next principal three years from now."

Now sitting at her desk trying to finish the monthly student discipline report, Amber's thoughts kept drifting back to the conversation she had with Principal Denko earlier in the day. She felt more dissatisfied than ever. The thought that she might become principal in a few years did nothing to reduce her frustration.

At 10:15 that evening, Amber managed to finish the report and left school. As she drove home, she again compared Polk to the middle school in California where she had previously been employed. She reached for her cell phone and called Dr. Appleton. She told him that she had followed his advice and met with the principal. She then conveyed the principal's comments.

"Clearly, these were not the answers you wanted," he told her. "Even so, I think you need to finish the school year at Polk before moving to another position."

PROBLEM FRAMING

1. Assume you are Amber. Describe what you would want to accomplish in dealing with the situation described in this case.

2. Based on the evidence of contextual variables, describe the difficulty associated with achieving your objective.

QUESTIONS AND SUGGESTED ACTIVITIES

1. Do you believe that Amber has a realistic perspective about her role as assistant principal? Why or why not?

2. Should Amber follow Professor Appleton's advice and remain at Polk until the end of the school year? Why or why not?

3. Principal Denko believes that college courses and professors are idealistic when it comes to prescribing teacher and administrator behavior. Do you agree? Why or why not?

4. Based on high school graduation rates and college enrollment figures, the staff at Polk Middle School assumes that approximately one-third of their students will not be successful academically. Is this a valid assumption? Is it an ethical assumption?

5. Assume that Amber pretends that she has been socialized, hoping that she becomes principal in three years. Her primary motive

is to change the school's culture after becoming principal. Is this an effective strategy? Why or why not?

6. In your opinion, is the nature of the community a factor that has produced the school's culture? Or is the community unfairly blamed for a culture created by the school's employees?

7. Identify some assumptions that would be associated with a negative school culture.

8. Why does school culture depend on socialization?

9. One could argue that Amber should have made a greater effort to identify the culture at Polk before accepting an administrative position there. Is this a valid argument? Why or why not?

10. To what extent is Principal Denko responsible for the climate at Polk Middle School?

SUGGESTED READINGS

Cantwell, Z. M. (1993). School-based leadership and the professional socialization of the assistant principal. *Urban Education*, 28(1), 49–68.

Derpak, D., & Yarema, J. (2002). Climate control. *Principal Leadership*, 3(4), 42–45.

Glanz, J. (1994). Dilemmas of assistant principals in the supervisory role: Reflections of an assistant principal. *Journal of School Leadership*, 4(5), 577–590.

Glanz, J. (2004). *The assistant principal's handbook: Strategies for success.* Thousand Oaks, CA: Corwin Press.

Golanda, E. L. (1991). Preparing tomorrow's educational leaders: An inquiry regarding the wisdom of utilizing the position of assistant principal as an internship or apprenticeship to prepare future

principals. *Journal of School Leadership*, 1(3), 266–283.

Goldring, L. (2002). The power of school culture. *Leadership*, 32(2), 32–35.

Hanna, J. W. (1998). School climate: Changing fear to fun. *Contemporary Education*, 69(2), 83–85.

Hartzell, G. N. (1993). When you're not at the top. *High School Magazine*, 1(2), 16–19.

Hausman, C., Nebeker, A., McCreary, J., & Gordon D. (2002). The worklife of the assistant principal *Journal of Educational Administration*, 40(2), 136–157.

Keedy, J. L., & Simpson, D. S. (2001). Principal priorities, school norms, and teacher influence: A study of sociocultural leadership in the high school. *Journal of Educational Administration and Foundations, 16*(1), 10–41.

Koru, J. M. (1993). The assistant principal: Crisis manager, custodian, or visionary? *NASSP Bulletin, 77*(556), 67–71.

Marshall, C. (1985). Professional shock: The enculturation of the assistant principal *Education and Urban Society, 18*(1), 28–58.

Marshall, C., & Greenfield, W. D. (1985). The socialization of the assistant principal: Implications for school leadership. *Education and Urban Society, 18*(1), 3–6.

Marshall, C., & Hooley, R. M. (2006). *The assistant principal: Leadership choices and challenges.* Thousand Oaks, CA: Corwin Press.

Michel, G. J. (1996). *Socialization and career orientation of the assistant principal.* (ERIC Document Reproduction Service No. ED 395 381)

Peterson, K. D. (2002). Positive or negative. *Journal of Staff Development, 23*(3), 10–15.

Picucci, A. C., Brownson, A., & Kahlert, R. (2002). Shaping school culture. *Principal Leadership (Middle School Ed.), 3*(4), 38–41.

Toth, C., & Siemaszko, E. (1996). Restructuring the assistant principalship: A practitioner's guide. *NASSP Bulletin, 80*(578), 87–98.

Weller, L. D., & Weller, S. J. (2002). *The assistant principal: Essentials for effective school leadership.* Thousand Oaks, CA: Corwin Press.

REFERENCES

Aiken, J. A. (2002). The socialization of new principals: Another perspective on principal retention. *Education Leadership Review, 3*(1), 32–40.

Hanson, E. M. (2003). *Educational administration and organizational behavior* (5th ed.). Boston: Allyn and Bacon.

Heck, R. H. (1995). Organizational and professional socialization: Its impact on the performance of new administrators. *Urban Review, 27*(3), 31–49.

Kowalski, T. J. (2003). *Contemporary school administration: An introduction* (2nd ed.). Boston: Allyn and Bacon.

Kowalski, T. J. (2006). *The school superintendent: Theory, practice, and cases* (2nd ed.). Thousand Oaks, CA: Sage.

19 Who Needs Career-Technical Education?

Background Information

Career centers (CCs), called vocational schools, technical schools, or trade schools in some states, are found across the country. Though these institutions share a common mission—providing career related and technical curricula—the manners in which they are funded and governed are not uniform. Some centers are part of a statewide network (e.g., as in Delaware), some serve students only in a single district, but most are operated by a joint service agency—basically confederations of local school districts that are independent or quasi-independent cooperatives structured under state laws (e.g., as in Indiana and Ohio) (Kowalski, 2006). Even among confederation-operated schools, differences are found in the following areas:

1. *Funding.* In some states, the confederations are allowed to levy taxes independently; in other states, revenues are generated by charging member districts fees.
2. *Organization.* Some CCs are independent of area high schools, enroll only full-time students, and grant their own diplomas; others are legally attached to one or more regular high schools, enroll only part-time students, and do not grant diplomas (diplomas are granted by the student's home high school).
3. *Scope of programming.* Some CCs offer only vocational programs and courses; others offer a broader curriculum (e.g., offering both vocational programs and remedial programs in the basic subjects).

As the school reform movement gained energy during the 1980s, a number of questions were raised about the continued need for and value of vocational high schools. Ernest Boyer (1983) charged that vocational education did not provide students with a sufficiently broad education and did not prepare them adequately for careers. John Goodlad (1984) pointed out that the purposes of these schools were no longer valid in an information-based society. Others (e.g., Oakes, 1985) claimed that vocational schools essentially perpetuated student tracking, a concept that separates students into groups so that they can receive a curriculum deemed to be based on their ability and interests. Critics of tracking (e.g., Brewer, Argys, & Rees, 1995; Oakes, 1985) claim that the practice has been especially detrimental for minority and low-income students.

Arguably, modern CCs are different from traditional vocational schools. As examples, the curricula are usually more comprehensive and academically challenging in CCs. Nevertheless, many of the criticisms that were levied at vocational schools continue to be directed at CCs. Proponents have responded by emphasizing that these schools provide at least three benefits for society:

1. Many students who attend CCs would otherwise not complete high school. Consequently, these schools reduce dropout rates and increase high school graduation rates.
2. The academic skills of students attending CCs do not deteriorate; their scores on standardized academic tests have been found to be no different from students at the same ability level attending traditional high schools.
3. Area employers are strongly supportive of CCs and view them to be successful. Demands for skilled workers are increasing, not decreasing.

Despite these counterarguments, the future of CCs in some states remains uncertain.

This case is about conflict among superintendents and principals who are members of a confederation operating a CC. The conflict intensifies to the point that the future of the confederation, and the school it operates, is placed in doubt.

Key Areas for Reflection

1. Collaboration among school districts
2. Ethical, moral, and legal obligations
3. Career-technical education
4. Reform in high schools

The Case

Medford Area Career Center (MACC) has a proud history. Established in southern Indiana in the early 1960s, it often has been cited as a model school. Located in a serene rural setting, the school still serves nearly 600 students coming from fifteen school districts and nineteen high schools across six counties; all of them attend the CC on a half-time basis. The school's governing board consists of the superintendents from each of the participating districts, and the nineteen high school principals are members of the school's curriculum advisory council.

Prior to the early 1990s, virtually no dissatisfaction had been voiced about the MACC. In its first thirty years of operation, the school had only two principals; the third and current principal, Roscoe Downey, was not employed until 1995. He had been a teacher and assistant principal at the center before being promoted. After becoming principal, he reported several problems to the governing board (the principal reported directly to a governing board composed of fourteen school district superintendents):

1. Enrollment had been declining steadily at a rate of about 1 percent per year for the previous six years.
2. The facility, constructed in 1963, had not been renovated or improved, and some areas were now in poor condition.
3. Much of the equipment was outdated and needed to be replaced.
4. The curriculum had not changed very much since the school first opened.
5. Some high school principals were reporting increased parental resistance to enrolling their children in the MACC. The principals attributed the resistance to a perception that the center served only low-ability, underachieving, or disruptive students.

Principal Downey recommended that the board retain a consultant to examine all five problems. Only two of the superintendents on the board, however, supported the recommendation; the others were unwilling to act on the recommendation but for varied reasons. Two openly indicated that they did not believe the problems were valid, three commented that the prevailing economic and political climates in their school districts were not conducive to addressing the problems, and the remaining six indicated that they were unwilling to address the problems unless the future of the center was more clearly established.

Five years later, nothing had been done to address the problems Principal Downey had presented to the governing board. The center's enrollment was now below 600 for the first time since 1965. Several letters critical of the center had been published on the local newspaper's editorial page. The authors noted that the facility had become outdated and as a result, badly needed programs could not be added to the curriculum. Moreover, tensions between the principals on the curriculum advisory board and MACC staff members were intensifying. Conflict was more evident in two areas: student discipline and decisions regarding teaching some MACC courses in the participating high schools. The first issue centered on disputes over how students should be disciplined for infractions that occurred at the MACC. Since the students were still officially enrolled in their home high schools, the principals of those high schools felt they had to approve of any disciplinary action authorized by the MACC staff. Until recently, all the administrators honored an unwritten agreement that the principals would honor punishment administered by the center's personnel. Responding to pressures from parents, three high school principals on the curriculum advisory committee wanted the practice changed. The second issue was more complex but no less contentious. Some districts (and high schools) in the confederation had lost considerable enrollment in the previous ten years, and their administrators wanted to establish MACC satellite centers in their schools. Doing so would provide needed revenue (the MACC paid host schools a fee for housing a course) and fill empty space. Two other districts (and their high schools) were experiencing the opposite problem—they were growing. Their administrators wanted to establish independent operations in high-enrollment programs provided at the MACC; the two most notable were electronics and building trades. In essence, these two districts were seeking to reduce their level of participation in the confederation without withdrawing from it.

Principal Downey decided to make another attempt at addressing the center's worsening problems. The governing board had experienced considerable change since Mr. Downey became principal, and he was hopeful that the superintendents new to the board would be more willing to address the problems than were their predecessors. Additionally, he anticipated that the board members might be cooperative because tensions between the high school principals and center personnel regarding discipline authority had lessened.

The governing board's current chair, Madeline Watkins, was superintendent of the second-smallest school district in the confederation. She was a staunch supporter of MACC and of Principal Downey. Though she wanted to improve the facility and update curricula and equipment, she did not know if the other board members shared her disposition. Therefore, she spoke privately to each of them. The responses were mixed. Only five superintendents said they would or probably would support efforts to resolve the problems. Among the remaining nine, three were definitely opposed to moving forward and six were undecided.

At the November governing board meeting, Principal Downey made a detailed report on the center and its lingering problems. He recommended that the board retain a planning consultant to study the problems, including continuing tensions about the development of independent programs and satellite courses. After a lengthy discussion, a motion to approve the superintendent's recommendation passed by a vote of eight to three with four members abstaining.

A university professor was retained to conduct the study. Over the next six months he interviewed over 160 people, including parents, students, staff, home school administrators, board members, and advisory council members. In addition, data were collected from over thirty local employers regarding their satisfaction with MACC graduates and their future employment needs.

The consultant presented his findings, conclusions, and recommendations to the governing board in late June. A summary of his report follows:

- The center's curriculum needed to be revamped so that there would be a greater emphasis on technology-based courses and programs. Conversely, several existing programs needed to be eliminated because of low enrollment, low demand for graduates, or both.
- After curricular revisions are completed, the facility should be completely renovated and new spaces created to accommodate the new technology-based courses/programs.
- The center's staff should develop and execute a public relations plan to increase communication with external publics and to enhance the school's image.
- Member high schools should not be allowed to develop duplicate programs and programs now housed at the center should not be relocated to member high schools. Making such decisions on an ad hoc basis could create political and economic problems that might destabilize the confederation.
- A long-term equipment replacement plan must be developed and coordinated with program changes and facility improvements.

- Disputes over authority to discipline students must be addressed. Though tensions had lessened, the problem had not been resolved. Any disciplinary action involving suspension or expulsion should be approved by the home school principal.

All fifteen superintendents and Principal Downey were present when the consultant presented his report to the board. Several superintendents asked technical questions about data but none challenged the report or commented on its outcomes. Superintendent Watkins urged the board members to study the report over the next month and to contact the consultant or Principal Downey if they had questions. None of the superintendents contacted the consultant.

Because it was late June, most center employees were not working. Nevertheless, Principal Downey arranged for the consultant to make a second presentation to the center's employees and to the chairs of the various program advisory committees. Approximately half of the employees attended and all but one of the advisory committee chairs attended. After listening to the consultant's report, Principal Downey told the center staff members that he was pleased with all the recommendations. The advisory committee chairs, all representatives of local businesses or trades, also expressed support for the recommendations. The center staff supported the recommendations except for the one pertaining to discipline authority.

Principal Downey and Superintendent Watkins had hoped that the governing board would make a decision on the consultant's report at its July meeting. However, the meeting was cancelled because six superintendents said they would be unable to attend, and they were opposed to the report's being discussed in their absence. Prior to the August board meeting, Superintendent Watkins attempted to speak with the other fourteen superintendents, either face to face or via telephone. She learned that the superintendents were still divided. Clearly, the most controversial issue was the recommendation to renovate the center's facility. Under state law, all of the member districts in the confederation had to share in the cost of construction. A school district's portion of the cost was based on its percentage of district enrollment in relation to the aggregate district enrollment in the consortium. Hence, higher-enrollment districts would pay a greater percentage of the construction cost. If the governing board voted to proceed with construction, the superintendents would have to gain approval from their respective school boards to raise the needed revenue for debt service. In this vein, the proposed renovation of the center was highly political because most districts had other needs requiring additional tax revenues.

Six superintendents told Mrs. Watkins that they would definitely vote against a recommendation to renovate the facility. Four argued that the center's future was in question for at least two reasons. First, there was a distinct possibility that the center would be unable to sustain sufficient enrollment to continue operating. Second, federal and state mandates related to school reform were not especially friendly to career-technical education. Therefore, pressures to increase academic performance might lead to the center's demise. Two superintendents opposed to renovating the facility indicated that their school boards would never support a tax increase to fund construction.

Four superintendents said they would support all of the consultant's recommendations, including the one pertaining to renovation. The remaining five superintendents said they were undecided and wanted to hear what the other superintendents had to say at the August board meeting.

When Superintendent Watkins told Principal Downey how the other superintendents had responded, he was dejected. Over the years, he had observed political relationships among the superintendents, and he concluded that the six superintendents opposing construction would influence at least three and maybe all of the undecided board members.

Principal Downey also faced another problem. Most of his staff were opposed to the consultant's recommendation regarding discipline authority. He was convinced, however, that he could persuade them to support the recommendation if they were assured that the other recommendations would be implemented. The August governing board meeting was several weeks away. Superintendent Watkins had indicated that she would continue to support the recommendations and would urge other board members to do the same. She told Principal Downey, however, that defeat appeared likely. She questioned whether they should insist that the board vote on the matter. She said that delaying action for six months or a year might be a better alternative. Principal Downey was unsure if he agreed. The center clearly needed to update its curriculum and doing this was unlikely if facility and equipment problems were not resolved. Superintendent Watkins and Principal Downey agreed that they would make a decision within a week on whether to include the consultant's recommendations at the August board meeting.

PROBLEM FRAMING

1. Assume you are Principal Downey. Describe what you would want to accomplish in dealing with the situation described in this case.

2. Based on the evidence of contextual variables, describe the difficulty associated with achieving your objective.

QUESTIONS AND SUGGESTED ACTIVITIES

1. Evaluate the approach Principal Downey used to address problems at the center.

2. Mr. Downey presented the governing board members with a list of problems shortly after becoming the center's principal. The board members refused to take action at that time. Five years later, the problems had gotten worse, and Principal Downey again raised

them with the board. Was it prudent for him to wait this long? Why or why not?

3. The chairs of the program advisory committees support the center and the recommendations to improve it. These individuals represent local businesses and trades. To what extent should Principal Downey involve them in trying to persuade the governing

board members to support the consultant's recommendations?

4. Discuss the governance structure for the center. Is this a positive or negative structure for the (a) principal, (b) center staff, (c) students, and (d) districts in the confederation?

5. Several superintendents opposed to renovating the center argued that the center's future was in question because of federal and state reforms. Do you agree? Why or why not?

6. No mention is made in the case of a vision statement. What is a vision statement? What is the relationship between the center's mission and a vision statement? To what degree would such a statement have

been beneficial to resolving the problems the center faces?

7. Principal Downey has the option of removing the consultant's recommendation from the August governing board agenda. What are the advantages and disadvantages of doing so?

8. What is the status of career-technical education in your state? Do teachers and administrators support centers such as the one described in this case?

9. Over the past few decades, efforts to integrate career education and academic courses have increased. To what extent have these efforts been successful in your state? To what extent have these efforts affected traditional high schools?

SUGGESTED READINGS

Bamford, P. J. (1995). Success by design: The restructuring of a Vo-Tech center. *Tech Directions, 54*(7), 15–17.

Dembicki, M. (2000). He's got the hook. *Techniques: Connecting Education and Careers, 75*(3), 28–31.

Harkins, A. M. (2002). The futures of career and technical education in a continuous innovation society. *Journal of Vocational Education Research. 27*(1), 35–64.

Jenkins, J. M. (2000). Looking backward: Educational reform in the twentieth century. *International Journal of Educational Reform, 9*(1), 74–78.

Lynch, R. L. (2000). High school career and technical education for the first decade of the 21st century. *Journal of Vocational Education Research, 25*(2), 155–198.

MacIver, M. A., & Legters, N. (2001). Partnerships for career-centered high school reform in an urban school system. *Journal of Vocational Education Research, 26*(3), 412–446.

Reese, S. (2001). High school career tech at the crossroads. *Techniques: Connecting Education and Careers, 76*(7), 33–35.

Reese, S. (2005). The new career and technical school. *Techniques: Connecting Education and Careers, 80*(7), 16–17.

Ries, E. (1999). Packed by popular demand. *Techniques: Making Education and Career Connections, 74*(3), 22–25.

Seccurro, W. B., & Thomas, D. W. (1998). School improvement through tech prep: How one vocational school changed its program and image. *Tech Directions, 57*(8), 22–23.

Shibley, I. A. (2005). One school's approach to No Child Left Behind. *Techniques: Connecting Education and Careers, 80*(4), 50–53.

Shumer, R. (2001). A new, old vision of learning, working, and living: Vocational education in the 21st century. *Journal of Vocational Education Research, 26*(3), 447–461.

Stasz, C., & Bodilly, S. (2004). *Efforts to improve the quality of vocational education in secondary schools: Impact of federal and state policies.* Arlington, VA: RAND Corporation.

REFERENCES

Boyer, E. L. (1983). *High school*. New York: Harper.

Brewer, D. J., Argys, L. M., & Rees, D. I. (1995). Detracking America's schools: The reform without cost? *Phi Delta Kappan*, 77, 210–12.

Goodlad, J. I. (1984). *A place called school*. New York: McGraw-Hill.

Kowalski, T. J. (2006). *The school superintendent: Theory, practice, and cases* (2nd ed.). Thousand Oaks, CA: Sage.

Oakes, J. (1985). *Keeping track: How schools structure inequality*. New Haven, CT: Yale University.

20 Illegal Drugs, In-School Suspension, and the Novice Principal

Background Information

Experts often disagree about the causes of substance abuse problems and how they should be handled. Some see this problem largely as a criminal matter; these individuals typically advocate zero-tolerance policies that call for offenders to be excluded from the traditional school environment. Others view the problem as a physical, emotional, or psychological problem; these individuals are more prone to allowing offenders to remain in school provided they receive counseling and other prescribed therapies. Disagreement over the issue of illegal drug use is evidenced by the fact that zero-tolerance policies established by school boards have been the subject of litigation (Henault, 2001; Zirkel, 1999).

Suspension from school is commonly used as a disciplinary measure in high schools for a variety of violations to student conduct rules. Such punishment can occur in several ways:

- The student is not allowed to attend school for a specified period of time.
- The student is not allowed to attend his or her regular school for a specified period of time but is permitted to attend an alternative program while suspended.
- The student is placed in an in-school suspension program—a program that isolates him or her from the main population while requiring continued attendance in school.

Both alternative programs and in-school suspension programs are often designed to be punitive, but some are structured to provide either academic or behavioral remediation (Sheets, 1996). Often alternative programs are not feasible for suspensions because the timeframe is usually ten days or less. Critics of in-school programs argue that this option does not provide a sufficient punishment and allows students exhibiting dangerous behavior to jeopardize the welfare of the school's general population.

This case is about an inexperienced principal who establishes an in-school suspension program in a large high school. The school has had high expulsion and dropout rates. Detractors of the new program become outraged after two students who were given in-school suspensions are arrested selling crack cocaine in the school's parking lot. The ensuing conflict causes this second-year principal to question her judgment and her desire to continue as the school's principal.

Key Areas for Reflection

1. Inexperienced principals
2. Job satisfaction
3. Pupil conduct and discipline
4. Job-related stress
5. Principal and staff relationships
6. Zero-tolerance policy

The Case

Setting the Stage

"Are you serious?" Lowell Tatum asked his wife as the two were having dinner at their favorite San Francisco restaurant. "Now let me get this straight. You want to leave your job as coordinator of English education to become a high school principal? You ought to think about this. You know what high school students are like, and you should know that being a principal is not going to be easy."

Patricia Tatum has met challenges successfully throughout her life. Reared in a low-income family, she is the oldest of six children. Though neither of her parents graduated from high school, they provided a warm, caring family environment where high expectations were the norm, especially for education.

Even in elementary school, Patricia was a good student and a leader. In high school, she was a member of the girls' track team, a cheerleader, and president of the student council. When she graduated from high school, her class rank was 6 out of 389. After graduating, she attended a private college on an academic scholarship. She finished her degree in four years and graduated cum laude.

While a college student, Patricia worked part-time as a teacher's aide in a parochial elementary school. That experience influenced her to change her major from pre-law to English education; she had decided to become a high school English teacher.

After graduating, however, Patricia accepted a job as copyeditor with a small publishing firm, largely because the salary was higher than what she could earn as a beginning teacher. Over the next two years, however, she completed her master's degree in English education and did not abandon her original goal of being a teacher. During this period, she also met and married Lowell Tatum, an executive with a San Francisco–based brokerage firm. After completing her master's degree, Patricia accepted a job teaching in a public suburban high school.

Four years later Patricia gave birth to a baby girl and resigned from her teaching position. A year later, she had a second child. For the next six years, she devoted her time to her children and attended graduate school. Initially, she enrolled in evening classes with the intention of completing the requisite courses for a principal's license. After completing her second class, she applied for and was admitted to a doctoral program in educational administration.

After completing the doctoral program and with her children now in school, Patricia wanted to return to a full-time position in education. She applied for assistant principal vacancies, two of which were in the school district where she had taught previously. Several weeks after applying, that district's personnel director contacted her via telephone. He remembered having met Patricia years before but did not know her well. Patricia assumed that he was contacting her about one of the assistant principal positions, but she quickly learned otherwise.

"Dr. Tatum," he said, "I'm actually calling about another administrative vacancy. Just a few days ago, Bob Hobart, our English coordinator, resigned. We're just about six weeks away from starting school and we don't have a great deal of time to fill this vacancy. I know you applied for assistant principal positions but I'm inquiring about your possible interest in the English coordinator vacancy."

Subject area coordinators are staff administrators; that is, they facilitate the work of principals and teachers but do not directly supervise them. She had worked with Bob Hobart when she was previously employed in the school district.

"I know Bob Hobart," she told the personnel director, "but I haven't talked with him for over six years. Presuming the job is still what it was then, I certainly would be interested."

Two weeks later, Patricia and one other applicant were interviewed by a selection committee consisting of the associate superintendent for instruction, the personnel director, two principals, and two English teachers. She was the committee's choice, and without hesitation she accepted the position.

Dr. Tatum felt good about her new position. The responsibilities allowed her to renew acquaintances with former colleagues and to spend time in schools. By the end of the school year, however, she questioned whether she would prefer being a principal. Being in the schools and working directly with teachers accounted for only about 35 percent of her work time—but it was this aspect of her job that she most enjoyed. She raised the possibility of becoming a principal with her immediate supervisor, Dr. Ernesto Javier, the associate superintendent for instruction, during her final performance evaluation conference.

"I don't want you to think I'm unhappy, because I'm not," she said. "It's just that I really like being in a school. I can't explain it. If I were a principal, or even an assistant principal, I could spend even more time working with teachers and students. Being a principal was my career goal after finishing my graduate studies—and it still is."

Dr. Javier had been a high school principal for fourteen years before becoming an associate superintendent. He understood Patricia's feelings because he too had struggled with the choice of being a principal or being a district-level administrator.

"I don't think there will be any assistant principal vacancies in the near future. We just filled two such positions last summer. I think you are doing a terrific job as English coordinator, and I want you stay in the position. However, you have to make your career decisions, not me. If you are certain that you want be an assistant principal or a principal, you can identify me as a reference."

Dr. Tatum did not tell her husband about the conversation with Dr. Javier and decided to wait until school term finished in about three weeks before deciding whether to apply for vacancies in another district. She was torn between her desire to continue working with Dr. Javier and her desire to be a building-level administrator. Unfortunately, it did not appear that she could do both.

A few days before the school year ended, Dr. Javier contacted Patricia and asked her to meet with him later that day. He told her the purpose was to discuss a possible job opportunity. After she put down the telephone, she realized that she had not asked if the opportunity was for him or for her. The two met at 3:30 that afternoon.

"Pat, Hank Malovidge at Western Valley High School just resigned because he accepted a job in the Seattle area. I met with the superintendent and personnel director this morning. We decided that given the timing of this resignation, it is best to name an interim principal—at least for the first semester of next school year. Given our previous conversation, would you be interested in that assignment?"

Patricia was surprised. She had not yet applied for other jobs and was still uncertain if she would do so. Before she could respond to Dr. Javier's question, he spoke again.

"Before you answer, you should know your options. As you know, you can say no and remain in your current position. If you become interim principal, you would have to decide if you would apply to be the permanent principal. If you do not, you can return to your English coordinator job. If you apply and are not selected, you can still return to your current position. It really is a no-lose situation for you."

"I must admit, Dr. Javier, I'm surprised that you are considering me for this assignment. There are three assistant principals at Western Valley and two of them are highly experienced. Why not appoint one of them as the interim principal?"

"I don't want to go into details, partly because some of them involve Hank. I can tell you that the superintendent and I want to see changes at Western Valley. Hank did not respond favorably to our position. He wasn't fired, but the demand for changes probably encouraged him to resign. I think both of the more experienced assistants want to replace him. Picking one over the other could divide the faculty and staff. More important, however, the superintendent and I are concerned that neither will pursue the improvements we seek enthusiastically. We want leadership and fresh ideas."

Though she wanted to say yes immediately, Dr. Tatum decided that it would be best to discuss the issue with her husband to reflect on her options before making a decision. She requested and was granted several days to make her decision. Before she left Dr. Javier's office, she asked him to clarify if she would have an opportunity to become the permanent principal.

"Certainly, you would have this opportunity. If you perform as I think you will, you have an excellent chance of being named the permanent principal. At this point, we plan to conduct a formal search in November. By that time, you should know whether you want to be an applicant."

Lowell Tatum was not especially thrilled by the prospect of his wife's becoming a high school principal. His impression of this assignment was shaped largely by his memories of his high school principal—an unpopular, autocratic administrator who always looked like he had stomach cramps. He was concerned that his wife would be viewed unfairly the same way, and knowing her well, he assumed she would be miserable. Moreover, he was concerned how this assignment would affect their family life. Yet he judged that she had already made up her mind to accept the appointment.

Life as an Interim Principal

Western Valley High School serves about 2,300 students in grades 9 through 12. The student population is diverse, both economically and racially. Most students come from middle-class homes and about 55 percent of the graduates enroll in four-year institutions of higher education.

Dr. Tatum, in her capacity as English coordinator, had been to Western Valley High School about a dozen times the previous year. She knew the English teachers and Joe Baldwin and Bill Fine, the two more experienced assistant principals. She had only met the third assistant principal, Sally Farmer, once.

When the superintendent announced that Patricia Tatum would be the interim principal at Western Valley, employees at the school were stunned, largely for two reasons. First, they expected that either Joe Baldwin or Bill Fine would be appointed; second, they did not expect a relatively young and inexperienced female to be appointed. The one person who felt relieved by the announcement was Sally Farmer. She feared that the appointment of either of her colleagues would have placed her in a very difficult political position.

In the first meetings with the assistant principals after becoming interim principal, Dr. Tatum outlined expectations for the next year. Most notably, there were three objectives:

1. Reduce the school's dropout rate.
2. Find more effective ways to deal with student discipline.
3. Increase student scores on the required state achievement tests.

She stressed that these goals were supported by the superintendent and associate superintendent for instruction.

Principal Tatum then told the assistants that four of them would function as a team, each with designated responsibilities. After considerable discussion, they decided that Dr. Tatum and Ms. Farmer would have primary responsibility for the instructional programs. Mr. Baldwin would be responsible for most managerial functions, such as food services, course scheduling, the school budget, and building maintenance. Mr. Fine would be responsible for supervising extracurricular programs, including athletics. Student discipline, the assignment none of them wanted, would be shared by all four. Each was assigned to oversee discipline for a given grade level, with Principal Tatum being responsible for seniors.

After school started in late August, Dr. Tatum realized that spending considerable time with instructional programs was going to be difficult if not impossible. No matter how meticulously she planned, her intentions were thwarted by unanticipated day-to-day problems, especially difficulties involving student discipline. Though she was responsible for seniors, she quickly discovered that all serious matters, regardless of grade level, ended up in her office.

The former principal had taken a hard line toward illegal drugs; students caught possessing, using, or selling drugs were recommended for expulsion. As a result, Western Valley had the highest expulsion rate among the district's four high schools. The assistant principals had not opposed this zero-tolerance rule even though it spawned criticism and legal challenges. Given the objectives promoted by her supervisor and her own philosophy, Dr. Tatum considered the rule too inflexible. She preferred to judge individual cases on their merits. As an example, she believed that a first offense for possessing marijuana should not be treated the same as either a second offense or a first offense involving selling drugs.

Shortly after becoming interim principal on July 1, Principal Tatum attempted to revise the school's rule on illegal drugs. The assistant principals, however, resisted. Not dissuaded, she appointed an ad hoc committee to examine the issue; members included two parents, one a social worker and the other a clinical psychologist; a counselor at Western Valley; Mr. Fine; and three Western Valley teachers. The committee was given one month to make a recommendation.

The committee examined rules used by the district's other schools and by schools in neighboring districts. The members also heard testimony from several experts, including narcotics officers, substance-abuse specialists, and a local juvenile judge. The committee members unanimously agreed that the district's zero-tolerance policy concerning selling illegal drugs should not be changed; students found guilty of this offense are expelled. They were deeply divided, however, over disciplinary action for students found guilty of possessing or using illegal drugs. A majority of four members (the two parents, the school counselor, and one of the teachers) voted to support two recommendations; the remaining three members voted against them, indicating they preferred to maintain the current rule. The majority's two recommendations were:

1. An in-school suspension program should be established at Western Valley High School. The program should be designed to reduce the number of out-of-school suspensions and expulsions. Students found guilty of possessing or using illegal drugs for the first time would be placed in this program. The length of suspension would depend on the nature of the drug and the student's overall discipline record. Students placed in the in-school suspension program for possessing or using illegal drugs would be required to undergo counseling.
2. Students found guilty of possessing or using illegal drugs a second time should either receive an out-of-school suspension or be expelled. Students suspended for this offense would be required to undergo and complete a substance abuse program.

Mr. Fine was the most vocal opponent of the committee's two recommendations. He told Dr. Tatum that she would be making a big mistake if she accepted it.

Dr. Tatum discussed the committee's recommendations with Dr. Javier after receiving them. District policy did not stipulate a specific penalty for first-time possession or use violations; it did, however, require that second-time offenders be expelled.

Members of the ad hoc committee recognized that their second recommendation conflicted with existing policy. They presented it anyway hoping that the school board would either grant a waiver to Western Valley for this provision or rescind it. Dr. Javier immediately indicated that the superintendent was unwilling to recommend changing the existing district policy on illegal drugs. He also said he would support the creation of an in-school suspension program.

School was opening in about two weeks and Principal Tatum could wait no longer to decide if she would recommend a change in the school's rule on illegal drugs and create an in-school suspension program. She decided to act on implementing the committee's first recommendation. She modified the school's rule on illegal drugs, revised the student handbook, and the revision was approved by the school board a week before school started. Her plan for establishing an in-school suspension program was approved by the superintendent and school board approximately one month later.

During the first semester of operation, the in-school suspension program ran smoothly. Only two students were affected by the change in the school's rule and all completed the suspension without controversy.

Life as Permanent Principal

Dr. Tatum applied to become the permanent principal in early November and was selected for the job. Her status changed at the beginning of the second semester. At the closing faculty meeting in late May, she declared that the in-school suspension program had been highly successful. She reported that a total of twenty-seven students had been placed in the program, only five for drug-related offenses. All twenty-seven students completed their suspensions without incident. Even more noteworthy, she told the faculty, the school's dropout rate had declined 13 percent and the expulsion rate declined 22 percent.

During the first two months of the next school year, a total of twelve students were found guilty of drug-related offenses. Five were expelled and the remaining seven were given an in-school suspension. The number of incidents of illegal drug offenses had increased from the previous year and this fact started to create a problem. Dr. Tatum received complaints from several faculty and parents who blamed the in-school suspension program for the increase in drug-related offenses. One parent wrote the following letter to her:

> Dear Dr. Tatum:
>
> This letter is written to object to your policy of allowing students found guilty of using drugs to stay in school. As parents, my wife and I think this policy sends the wrong message to students. We urge you to discontinue the in-school suspension program and to re-adopt the rules that were in place prior to your appointment as principal.

Though all three assistant principals had opposed a change in the school's rule on illegal drugs, Bill Fine was the most vocal critic. He made it clear to teachers, students, and parents that he opposed the in-school suspension program and any penalty less than expulsion for drug-related offenses. Recognizing that their colleague's overt criticism could result in political problems, Joe Baldwin and Sally Farmer began taking a neutral position on in-school suspensions.

Midway through the first semester, two students who had been given in-school suspensions for possessing marijuana were arrested for attempting to sell crack cocaine to an undercover police officer in the school's parking lot. The next day, several reporters received anonymous telephone messages linking the arrests to the in-school suspension program. What otherwise would have been a routine matter in the eyes of the media exploded into a front-page story. Within days, parents who opposed the in-school suspension program were identified and interviewed by reporters. Even several teachers told media representatives that the in-school suspension program was a bad idea.

One of the local television stations aired a five-minute report on drugs at Western Valley High School. The commentator began by saying:

> In-school suspension at Western Valley. A solution to drug use or an idea that is making the problem worse? Parents and teachers at Western Valley are up in arms because students found guilty of possessing or using illegal drugs are given an in-school suspension instead of being expelled as they were in past years. Principal Patricia Tatum changed the school's regulation after being appointed a little over a year ago. Critics charge that the principal's in-school suspension program has contributed to a rise in drug use at the school. Such concerns were heightened by the recent arrests of two students serving in-school suspensions for possessing marijuana. Only five days after they were given this penalty, they were arrested for trying to sell crack cocaine to an undercover police officer in the school's parking lot. School district officials did not want to comment on the matter beyond saying that they were investigating the matter and the effectiveness of the in-school suspension program.

The day after the arrests, Dr. Tatum met with the district's superintendent, Dr. Nicolas Constantine, at his request. He asked her several questions. The first was whether students who had been arrested were receiving counseling as prescribed by the school's new rule. She answered that they were required to see a school counselor at least one hour each week and each had done so during the first week of their suspensions. She added that the counselor could require placement in a drug education program but because the students had met only once with the counselor, such a judgment had not been made.

Superintendent Constantine also asked her if she had considered possible alternatives to in-school suspension. The district operated both an alternative high school and an adult evening school, for example, and students excluded from regular programs were usually permitted to enroll in these programs.

"Do you think in-school suspension is better than having these students at an alternative school?" he asked.

"Our records show that many students over age 16 quit school instead of enrolling in an alternative school. This option was examined by the committee that recommended the in-school suspension program," Dr. Tatum explained.

As the meeting ended, Dr. Constantine said that the in-school suspension program could continue provided students suspended for drug-related offenses were required to enroll in a drug education program in addition to receiving counseling at school.

Two days later, Dr. Tatum received an anonymous letter accusing her of being incompetent. The author contended that the superintendent was protecting her because she is an African American female. The letter was written on Western Valley High School stationery.

For the first time since becoming a principal, Dr. Tatum doubted her ability to be an effective principal. She telephoned Dr. Javier and shared her lack of self-confidence.

"If you are uncomfortable, I am partly to blame. I encouraged you to become a principal. If you leave your current position just because of the current turmoil, you would be making a mistake. You are doing a great job in many ways, and many of the teachers support you. If you decide that you do not want to continue as principal at Western Valley, I'll try to find another position for you on my staff."

PROBLEM FRAMING

1. Assume you are Dr. Tatum. Describe what you would want to accomplish in dealing with the situation described in this case.

2. Based on the evidence of contextual variables, describe the difficulty associated with achieving your objective.

QUESTIONS AND SUGGESTED ACTIVITIES

1. Was Dr. Tatum adequately prepared to become principal of a large high school? Why or why not?

2. Evaluate the behavior of the three assistant principals. If you were the principal, how would you deal with their opposition to the in-school suspension program?

3. Both the superintendent and the associate superintendent for instruction set goals for Dr. Tatum. These goals included reducing the expulsion and dropout rates. In light of this fact, evaluate their reactions to the student arrests and subsequent conflict.

4. What are the arguments for and against zero-tolerance policies?

5. In the school district in which you are employed or reside, how are drug possession, use, and sale offenses handled? Do laws in your state address these issues? If so, in what manner?

6. What are the advantages and disadvantages of an in-school suspension program?

7. Evaluate Principal Tatum's decision to appoint an ad hoc committee to address illegal drug infractions.

8. Politically, should Dr. Tatum have been appointed principal in a school where two older and more experienced assistant principals wanted to become principal? Why or why not?

9. Was it a good idea for Dr. Tatum to incur the risk associated with an in-school suspension program? Why or why not?

SUGGESTED READINGS

Blair, F. E. (1999). Does zero tolerance work? *Principal 79*(1), 36–37.

Bunch, E. A. (1998). School discipline under the Individuals with Disabilities Education Act: How the stay-put provision limits schools in providing a safe learning environment. *Journal of Law and Education, 27*(2), 315–321.

Casella, R. (2003). Zero tolerance policy in schools: Rationale, consequences, and alternatives. *Teachers College Record, 105*(5), 872–892.

Costenbader, V., & Markson, S. (1998). School suspension: A study with secondary school students. *Journal of School Psychology, 36*(1), 59–82.

Eckman, E. W. (2002). Woman high school principals: Perspectives on role conflict, role commitment, and job satisfaction. *Journal of School Leadership, 12*(1), 57–77.

Henault, C. (2001). Zero tolerance in schools. *Journal of Law and Education, 30*(3), 547–553.

Holtkamp, L. A. (2002). Crossing borders: An analysis of the characteristics and attributes of female public school principals. *Advancing Women in Leadership Journal, 10*(1), 2–6.

Johnston, J. (1989). High school completion of in-school suspension students. *NASSP Bulletin, 73*(521), 89–95.

Jones, R. (1997). Absolute zero. *American School Board Journal, 184*(10), 29–31.

Lohrmann, D., & Fors, S. (1988). Can school-based educational programs really be expected to solve the adolescent drug abuse problem? *Journal of Drug Education, 16*(4), 327–339.

Morris, R. C., & Howard, A. C. (2003). Designing an effective in-school suspension program. *Clearing House, 76*(3), 156–159.

Sheets, J. (1996). Designing an effective in-school suspension program to change student behavior. *NASSP Bulletin, 80*(579), 86–90.

Skiba, R., & Peterson, R. (1999). The dark side of zero tolerance: Can punishment lead to safe schools? *Phi Delta Kappan, 80*(5), 372–376, 381–382.

Stader, D. L. (2004). Zero tolerance as public policy: The good, the bad, and the ugly. *Clearing House, 78*(2), 62–66.

Sullivan, J. (1989). Elements of a successful in-school suspension program. *NASSP Bulletin, 73*(516), 32–38.

Watson, D., & Bright, A. (1988). So you caught them using drugs: Now what? *Thrust, 17*(3), 34–36.

Whitfield, D., & Bulach, C. (1996). A study of the effectiveness of in-school suspension. (ERIC Document Reproduction Service No. ED 396 372)

Zirkel, P. A. (1996). Discipline and the law. *Executive Educator, 18*(7), 21–23.

Zorn, R. (1988). New alternatives to student suspensions for substance abuse. *American Secondary Education, 17*(2), 30–32.

REFERENCES

Henault, C. (2001). Zero tolerance in schools. *Journal of Law and Education, 30*(3), 547–553.

Sheets, J. (1996). Designing an effective in-school suspension program to change student behavior. *NASSP Bulletin, 80*(579), 86–90.

Zirkel, P. A. (1999). Zero tolerance expulsions. *NASSP Bulletin, 83*(605), 101–105.

CASE
21

Let's Not Rap

Background Information

Being principal in a school serving diverse ethnic and racial publics can be demanding, especially for administrators unfamiliar with the social and political dynamics common in this type of environment. In the past, diversity was a characteristic associated primarily with urban schools, but that is no longer true. Over the last twenty-five years, a growing presence of racial and ethnic minorities in the United States has prompted scholars to pay increased attention to diversity and its effects on public institutions (Pitts, 2005). In the case of public education, diversity has become a focal point in school reform; a growing number of authors (e.g., Miron, St. John, & Davidson, 1998) point out that resolving racial discord and improving education have become interrelated objectives in many schools—including those small rural and affluent suburban schools.

Initiatives intended to reduce tensions spawned by diversity have not been uniformly supported across local communities. Multicultural education and bilingual education, for example, remain controversial programs (Kowalski, 2003) primarily because opponents see them as attempts to foster social values (e.g., equality and social justice) and political philosophy (e.g., liberalism) that they find objectionable (Reich, 2002). In more than a few districts and schools, the courts have had to intervene to address diversity-related conflict (Zirkel, 2001).

This case describes a situation in which school officials have scheduled a "rap" group to perform at a student assembly. The program's intent is to dissuade students from using illegal drugs; however, the performers prove to be controversial, accused of promoting anti-Semitism. Once the accusation is made public, a small but politically influential group of Jewish residents demands that the principal cancel the assembly. This demand is countered by a much larger but supposedly less influential group of African American residents. As you read this case, pay particular attention to how race, ethnicity, and power intertwine.

Key Areas for Reflection

1. Community diversity
2. School and community relationships
3. Race, politics, and public education
4. Conflict resolution

5. Student assemblies
6. Free speech and public schools

The Case

Principal Doran

Barb Doran is principal of Roosevelt High School, a highly respected institution enrolling 2,340 students and located in a suburb of a major mid-Atlantic city. She has held this position for less than two years, but she has already established herself as an effective administrator. After teaching English for twelve years, she has had three progressively challenging administrative positions: assistant principal of a 350-student middle school, principal of a 500-student rural high school, and principal at Roosevelt High School.

A Controversial Assembly

Principal Doran had just returned from a conference in Orlando, Florida, and was driving from the airport to her office at approximately 7:30 in the evening. The car radio was tuned to a station broadcasting a local talk program, and the primary topic that evening was Roosevelt High School.

"I think the principal should have the courage to cancel this program," a caller proclaimed. "What good is an anti-drug message if the people delivering it are anti-Semites? There are other more acceptable ways to teach students not to use drugs than having the message delivered by negative role models who preach hatred toward others."

The next caller stated an opposing position. "We all know about racial tensions at Roosevelt High. African American students don't get equal or fair treatment and that's a fact. Let me give you an example. Someone told me that a white kid caught smoking in the restroom ended up getting one hour of detention. But the next day, a black kid caught smoking and got a three-day suspension. Now, any reasonable person would see that the penalties are uneven. I predict the principal will cancel the scheduled assembly because she has a record of bowing to the Jewish community. But black folks are not going to roll over on this one."

Without responding to either caller, the show's host prepared for a commercial break, "For those of you just joining us, tonight's topic deals with controversy at Roosevelt High. Should the school principal allow a supposedly anti-Semitic rap group to present a program at the school? Some district residents are saying no, claiming that group members are anti-Semites. Others are saying yes, arguing the assembly has nothing to do with Jews or Judaism. Our last caller, for example, claimed that school officials at Roosevelt High have not treated black students fairly. What do you think? Let us know which side in this dispute is correct. Call me at 555-1500. I'll be back in a moment to answer your calls."

Barb Doran stared at the road ahead as she continued toward her office. Mentally, she asked herself how all of this could have happened in just three days while she was out of town. Though she knew about the scheduled assembly, she never imagined that it would spark a firestorm. She whispered to herself, "Why me, Lord?"

Roosevelt High School

Most Roosevelt students come from middle- or upper-middle class families; however, the student population is diverse racially, ethnically, and religiously. For instance, official school records show the following distribution of students by race and ethnicity:

- Caucasian (non-Hispanic): 61 percent
- African American: 31 percent
- Asian: 4 percent
- Hispanic: 3 percent
- Other: 1 percent

Though the school does not maintain records for student religious affiliation, estimates indicate that 10 percent of the students are practicing Jews and another 5 percent are practicing Muslims.

For much of the school's existence, Roosevelt High School has been considered a model of excellence in a context of diversity. The school has consistently ranked among the top five high schools in the state. In 1995, for example, 81 percent of the seniors entered either a four-year or two-year institution of higher education within a year of graduating. In addition, Roosevelt consistently has had the lowest dropout rate in the state among high schools with more than 700 students.

PARA

In a recent interview conducted by a newspaper reporter, Principal Doran said that her greatest concern about Roosevelt High was the perception among some African American students that they were not treated fairly by teachers and administrators. Though she vigorously denied the accusation, leading members in the African American community did not believe her. A year ago, a small group of parents (between twenty-five to thirty individuals) formed a political organization they called PARA (Parents Advocating Racial Awareness). At their first press conference, PARA leaders identified their purpose as ensuring fair and equal treatment for all students, but especially for African American students at Roosevelt High School. They referred to "unresolved concerns" in explaining why the organization was necessary. When asked to identify the nature of these concerns, a spokesperson cited three issues:

1. The curriculum did not offer African American students ample opportunity to study their cultural heritage.
2. Teachers and administrators often disciplined African American students more harshly than other students.

3. School officials had done little to ensure that the African American community would have a representative voice in critical decisions affecting the school and its students.

Though Principal Doran believed that claims of unfair treatment were exaggerated, she was sensitive to PARA's concerns and offered to cooperate with its members. She attended several PARA meetings and attempted to engage the members in constructive dialogue. She also appointed a PARA member to the principal's advisory council, a group consisting of six teachers, six parents, and six students. After the appointment of the PARA representative, six of the eighteen members were African Americans.

Scheduling the Assembly

Reggie Colter, a senior, was the person who first recommended a rap group to conduct a student assembly. The only African American member of Roosevelt's Student Council, he had become a spokesperson for the school's black students. His father, an attorney, is one of PARA's founding members.

Initiating the effort to schedule the assembly, Reggie told Principal Doran, "I have a great idea for a school program. My cousin is a sound technician for a rap group called the Inner City. They're going to be in town for a concert two months from now. The members often do free shows at local schools while they are on a concert tour. The school programs provide a mix of entertainment and anti-drug messages. My cousin said he could arrange for them to do a program at Roosevelt. If you approve, I can contact my cousin and start making arrangements."

Principal Doran knew nothing about the performers or about the messages they delivered to students; she was understandably hesitant. "Could you be more specific about the show they present to high school students?"

"They are rap music artists. The program can be one to two hours long; you could decide the length. The group performs several of its hit songs and in between, members discourage kids from using drugs. They also talk about mistakes they made with drugs in the past and why they don't want young people to make the same mistakes. My cousin said they don't do things that would create problems in schools—you know, like using foul language and doing dirty dancing. Here's a promotional brochure that provides more information. There is no cost for the school program. Their concert tickets cost $35 or more, and many of our students would not be able to see them perform if we didn't have this program. I have to let my cousin know if you approve of the program as soon as possible."

Wanting to improve relations with African American students, Principal Doran was attracted to the idea. She estimated that PARA members would react positively if the assembly were approved. She told Reggie that Mr. Wallace Slater, one of the assistant principals, was in charge of extracurricular activities. She said she would ask him to look into the prospect of having the assembly and a decision would be made within a week. Mr. Wallace was the school's only African American administrator and Reggie was pleased that he would probably make the final decision.

After being briefed by the principal, Assistant Principal Slater asked Reggie to get a list of the schools that had hosted the group so that he could contact their principals. Two days later, Reggie gave him a list containing the names of thirteen high schools. All the schools were located in other states, and all were in large urban districts. Assistant Principal Slater picked two of them randomly and then contacted the principals via telephone. Both schools had predominately African American students and the principals were African American. The feedback about the Inner City was positive. Both principals indicated that the assemblies were successful and that they had no reservations about recommending the program. Based on this feedback, Assistant Principal Slater told Reggie to have his cousin or the person responsible for booking school programs to contact him so a date and time for an assembly could be set.

At that point, Assistant Principal Slater sent the following email message to Principal Doran.

Barb,

After getting a list of thirteen schools that held student assemblies with the Inner City, I contacted principals at two of these schools. The feedback was very positive. I've asked Reggie to have the group's agent contact me so we can try to set a date and time. Based on what I have learned, I think we should arrange this assembly. Let me know as soon as possible if you do want me to move forward with this matter.

Wallace

Principal Doran felt somewhat uneasy about scheduling an assembly with a rap group. However, attendance at most assemblies was voluntary. Students opting not to attend were required to go to study areas during the period in which the assembly was held. She sent the following email reply to Mr. Slater:

Wallace,

Good work. Move forward but make sure that student attendance at the assembly is voluntary. I don't want parents or students accusing us of promoting rap music.

Barb

Within a week, arrangements for the assembly were complete. The program was announced in the student paper shortly after. Two days later, Principal Doran left to attend a conference in Orlando. On the day she departed, several parents called the school stating opposition to the assembly. Since Principal Doran was gone, their calls were directed to Assistant Principal Slater. The displeased parents claimed the Inner City had made a recording several months ago that had anti-Semitic lyrics. Moreover, several members made anti-Semitic remarks in defending the record, and their comments later appeared in a national tabloid story about a month ago. Assistant Principal Slater told the parents that he would look into the matter and brief Principal Doran when she returned in several days. He also emphasized that attendance at the assembly was voluntary.

Later that day, the rabbi from the local synagogue and several other Jewish community leaders held a press conference objecting to the student assembly. They distributed copies of the lyrics from the song they found objectionable and comments defending the song that appeared in the tabloid story. The next morning, the controversy was detailed in a front page story. At 4:00 P.M. the same day, PARA officials held their own press conference demanding that the assembly not be cancelled and promising to stage a major protest if it were.

Assistant Principal Slater and the two other assistant principals met to discuss the evolving conflict. They agreed that Principal Doran needed to be briefed about the situation immediately and that a decision about the assembly should be delayed until she returned from Florida. Mr. Slater contacted the principal via telephone and told her about the news conferences and subsequent media reports. Principal Doran would return the following day, and she agreed that no decision should be made until she was back at school. She instructed Mr. Slater to inform the superintendent and the press that the accusations would be fully investigated and that a decision would be made as soon as possible.

Reaching a Decision

As Principal Doran drove into the school's parking lot, she was still listening to the local radio broadcast. She parked her car and made her way toward her office. Immediately she saw a stack of mail sitting on her desk and at the top was a folder containing information about the assembly controversy. It included a copy of the article that had been published that morning:

> Controversy "Rocks" Roosevelt High
> Some parents of Roosevelt High School students object to a scheduled student assembly that features a rap group called "The Inner City." Parents and other district residents objecting to the assembly say that the group has a history of anti-Semitism. They believe that the group's appearance at Roosevelt High School would damage rather than promote racial harmony. Principal Barb Doran is out of town and was not available for comment. Assistant Principal Wallace Slater said the assembly was not just designed for entertainment purposes. He emphasized that the primary purpose was to discourage students from using illegal drugs. He added that the assembly had no political objectives and, despite concerns and accusations, administrators at other schools that have had this same assembly indicate that the experience for students has been positive. Principal Doran is scheduled to return this evening, and she is meeting with school officials tomorrow morning to investigate charges made against the group and to decide whether the assembly should be cancelled. Superintendent Paul Tolliver said that student assemblies are part of the high school's co-curricular activities, and he preferred not to comment on the matter until discussing the issue with Principal Doran.

Over two dozen phone messages from persons opposing or supporting the assembly were also in the folder.

Before going home, Principal Doran placed a telephone call to Dr. Tolliver.

"Barb, isn't it great to be back?" the superintendent asked facetiously. "How did you get tangled up with a rap group?"

"Neither Wallace nor I knew about the anti-Semitism charges until after we gave our approval for the assembly. Before leaving for Florida, Wallace told me that he checked out the group and everything he learned was positive. Quite frankly, there was no reason to deny the request for the assembly. Had I done so, PARA would have been all over me."

"You have to make a decision about the assembly as soon as possible. The Jewish community is upset, and two of the board members who are part of that community are extremely upset. PARA members, on the other hand, have promised to stage a major protest if the assembly is canceled. This situation is only going to get worse with time. Therefore, the sooner we act, the better."

"As you know, I've been working with PARA to improve relationships and maybe I was too anxious to score positive points with this assembly. I'm meeting with my assistants in the morning before school starts. I'll call you before 10 A.M., and my intent is to have a decision by then."

"Barb, let's say this situation were reversed. Would we allow a Jewish group that made derogatory comments about African Americans to appear at school—regardless of their message to students?"

"Are you implying that the assembly should be cancelled?"

"No. You know I don't interfere unless it's essential for me do so. I have confidence that you will make the correct decision."

Ms. Doran sat at her desk and considered the options to resolve the controversy. How would she react to this situation if she were African American? How would she react if she were Jewish? She believed that public schools should encourage the exchange of ideas, even controversial ideas, provided that the exchanges did not violate community standards.

During the meeting with the three assistant principals the following morning, Principal Doran said that she intended to make a decision about the assembly that morning. However, she wanted input from her assistants before doing that. To her disappointment, her colleagues did not agree about a solution:

- Assistant Principal Slater opposed cancelling the assembly, arguing that allowing a community group to censor school programs sets a bad precedent. He added that persons finding the assembly objectionable did not have to attend.
- The second assistant principal disagreed with Wallace's proposal. He suggested scheduling a second assembly to be held at the same time as the first. The second assembly would focus on diversity and would examine ways to foster racial and ethnic harmony. This option would give students three choices.
- The third assistant principal disagreed with both previous suggestions. He favored cancelling the assembly, arguing that they had a responsibility to protect the rights of all minorities.

Principal Doran had hoped for consensus but after hearing these suggestions, she knew that would not be possible—at least not before 10:00 A.M. Even though a decision had not been made, she adjourned the meeting with her assistants because students were arriving. She closed her office door and considered her options once more.

PROBLEM FRAMING

1. Assume you are Principal Doran. Describe what you would want to accomplish in dealing with the situation described in this case.

2. Based on the evidence of contextual variables, describe the difficulty associated with achieving your objective.

QUESTIONS SUGGESTED ACTIVITIES

1. Share and critique the problem statements prepared by students in your class.

2. Did Assistant Principal Slater do an adequate job of determining whether the rap group presented a program appropriate for Roosevelt High School? Why or why not?

3. Three different recommendations were made by the assistant principals. Evaluate each of them. What other alternatives could be considered to address the conflict?

4. Attendance at the controversial assembly is voluntary. Is this a relevant issue? Why or why not?

5. Some individuals see diversity as an asset and others see it as a liability. Discuss the nature of these differing views and possible causes of these opposing perspectives.

6. The superintendent in this case tells the principal that she must make the decision regarding the assembly. Did he act appropri-

ately in delegating this responsibility entirely to the principal? Why or why not?

7. Principal Doran believes that public schools should provide a forum for exchanging ideas provided that the dialogue conforms to community standards. Do you agree with this belief? Why or why not?

8. If Principal Doran makes an ethical decision about the assembly, what factors are likely to influence the outcome?

9. If Principal Doran makes a political decision about the assembly, what factors are likely to influence the outcome?

10. Did Principal Doran act responsibly in making this initial decision to schedule the assembly? Why or why not?

11. Is it possible to use the conflict sparked by the assembly as a catalyst for improving racial and ethnic relations at the high school? If so, how might the administrators do this?

SUGGESTED READINGS

Banister, J., & Maher, M. (1998). Recentering multiculturalism: Moving toward community. *Urban Education, 33*(2), 182–217.

Harrington-Lueker, D. (1993). Practicing tolerance. *Executive Educator, 15*(5), 14–19.

Margolis, H., & Tewel, K. (1988). Resolving conflict with parents: A guide for administrators. *NASSP Bulletin, 72*(506), 26–28.

Martinson, D. L. (1998). Vulgar, indecent, and offensive student speech: How should public school administrators respond? *Clearing House, 71*(6), 345–349.

Newsome, Y. D. (2001). Transnationalism in Black-Jewish conflict: A study of global identification among established Americans. *Race and Society, 4*(1), 89–107.

Noguera, P. A. (1999). Confronting the challenge of diversity. *School Administrator, 56*(5), 16–19.

Ogbonna, E., & Harris, L. C. (2006). The dynamics of employee relationships in an ethnically diverse workforce. *Human Relations, 59*(3), 379–407.

Sherman, R. (1990). Intergroup conflict on high school campuses. *Journal of Multicultural Counseling and Development, 18*(1), 11–18.

Stover, D. (1990). The new racism. *American School Board Journal, 177*(6), 14–18.

Stover, D. (1991). Racism redux. *Executive Educator, 13*(12), 35–36.

Tam, M. S., & Bassett, G. W. (2004). Does diversity matter? Measuring the impact of high school diversity on freshman GPA. *Policy Studies Journal*, *32*(1), 129–143.

Zirkel, P. (1998). Boring or bunkum? *Phi Delta Kappan*, *79*(10), 791–792.

Zirkel, P., & Gluckman, I. (1983). Stop, don't raise that curtain. *Principal*, *62*, 45–46.

REFERENCES

Kowalski, T. J. (2003). *Contemporary school administration: An introduction* (2nd ed.). Boston: Allyn and Bacon.

Miron, L. F., St. John, E. P, & Davidson, B. (1998). Implementing school restructuring in the inner city. *Urban Review*, *30*(2), 137–166.

Pitts, D. W. (2005). Diversity, representation, and performance: Evidence about race and ethnicity in public organizations. *Journal of Public Administration Research and Theory*, *15*(4), 615–631.

Reich, R. (2002). *Bridging liberalism and multiculturalism in American education*. Chicago: University of Chicago Press.

Zirkel, P. A. (2001). A gross over-order? *Phi Delta Kappan*, *83*(3), 273–274.

CASE
22

Is the Devil Teaching Spelling?

Background Information

Educational reform efforts have highlighted perennial tensions between teacher professionalism and citizen control of public schools. Both teacher empowerment and community involvement have been widely touted as effective strategies even though the two concepts are difficult to implement simultaneously. The primary intention of empowerment is giving teachers authority to make decisions based on the real needs of their students. In schools, this means teachers are granted discretion over curricular and instructional decisions (Barth, 2001). Community involvement, on the other hand, is nested in an intricate mix of philosophical, political, and economic objectives. School councils, a popular initiative over the past few decades, provide a quintessential example. Proponents argue that these groups are appropriate because they (a) enhance liberty and democracy, (b) provide a mechanism for achieving community support, and (c) ensure fiscal accountability (Kowalski, 2003).

Teachers and parents, however, often disagree over educational priorities and definitions of effective teaching (Davis, 1997). These disparate convictions, arguably relevant even under the best of conditions, become particularly problematic in situations where the rights of educators to function as professionals are challenged by the rights of citizens to control public education. When this conflict emerges, principals and other administrators are expected to manage it adroitly. In essence, they are expected to broaden participation and share authority and to maintain a reasonable level of control over schools. Commenting on these two seemingly contradictory expectations, Corwin and Borman (1988) wrote:

> . . . district administrators are held accountable for things they cannot always control. This condition is a product of decentralization processes within formally centralized school districts. School districts are organized officially as hierarchies. Implementing educational policy is legally and politically the responsibility of high-level district administrators. However, in practice only certain decisions are centralized. Many others have been decentralized, and administrators can never fully control such responsibilities. (p. 212)

In the real world of practice, school administrators must cope with the political norm that they be accountable to the community and the professional norm that they provide expert knowledge to make critical decisions about curriculum and instruction (Shedd & Bacharach, 1991).

Several authors (e.g., Bauch & Goldring, 1998; Darling-Hammond, 1987; Strike, 1993) have explained the dynamics associated with the inherent conflict between participatory democracy and pedagogic professionalism, including the relevance of these tensions to modern-day reforms (e.g., Sykes, 1991; Zeichner, 1991). Examining power and authority in the education profession, Sykes (1991) wrote:

> Democracy institutionalizes distrust. Professionalism relies on trust. Because we distrust our rulers, we have instituted a system of checks and balances to prevent any interest of office from amassing too much power. Because certain practices rest on expertise and knowledge not widely distributed in the populace, we trust professionals on their pledge to use such knowledge in the best interests of their clients. These two systems of preference formation, service delivery, and authority allocation appear fundamentally at odds with one another, and the great historical puzzle is how a strong form of professionalism flourished just in the world's greatest democracy. (p. 137)

Democratic administration certainly is not a new idea; it emerged as a major philosophical movement as far back as 1930. Detractors argued that the concept was overly idealistic and insufficiently attentive to realities of practice (Kowalski, 2006). When confronted with conflicting values, however, the American public, legally and politically, has exhibited a proclivity to forge compromises instead of choosing one value over the other (Kowalski, Petersen, & Fusarelli, 2007). In the case of professionalism versus democracy, neither the quest for citizen involvement nor the expectation of administrative control has been eradicated (Kowalski & Keedy, 2005). As a result, scholars (e.g., Wirt & Kirst, 2001) have concluded that public sector administrators, unlike their counterparts in the private sector, are consistently required to apply their professional knowledge in highly political contexts.

In this case, parents object to the use of instructional materials selected by teachers for use in a gifted education enrichment program. In addition to demonstrating the tensions between professionalism and parental power, the case reveals the difficulty inherent in empowering teachers and promoting parental involvement simultaneously.

Key Areas for Reflection

1. Democratic school administration
2. Parental rights and power to censor instructional materials
3. Teacher professionalism and empowerment
4. Delegation of authority and corresponding accountability

The Case

"I really like this software program. It fits nicely with what we are trying to accomplish in enrichment activities. And besides, students will like this program."

The evaluation came from Sandy Oberfeld, a second-grade teacher who was demonstrating a product to seventeen colleagues in a meeting being held at Samuels Elementary School. The meeting's purpose was to review and then select instructional materials that would be deployed in the district's gifted and talented enrichment program.

"I agree with Sandy," said Beatrice Sachs. "My students like computer games. They have so many toys and gadgets at home, it's become increasingly difficult to motivate them. I think Sorcerer will attract their attention, and the program appears to be well suited to having them work independently on spelling. Given the fact that our students have learned to process information by watching television and playing video games, they should respond positively to Sorcerer."

The elementary school's gifted and talented program in the Maple Creek School District is clustered in three of the system's ten elementary schools. Serving two affluent suburban communities in the Midwest, the district ranks in the top 2 percent in the state in per-pupil expenditures for instruction and in the top 5 percent in student performance on the state achievement tests.

The teachers who participate in the gifted and talented program meet once every two months after school to discuss materials, share ideas, and coordinate curriculum. Sandy Oberfeld, who was demonstrating the products, was the group's coordinator. She had learned about Sorcerer while attending a gifted education conference.

After listening to several positive comments about Sorcerer, Lucy McNeil, also a teacher, suggested that some parents would probably object to the nature of this software program. She cautioned, "Today parental standards for determining what is offensive are neither crisp nor clean. As you know, similar computer games have been intensely criticized by religious fundamentalists. They object to any instructional material that involves magic or witchcraft."

Mrs. McNeil's words of caution drew no immediate response. Concluding there would be no rebuttal, Mrs. Oberfeld said, "If we only purchased materials philosophically acceptable to everyone, we would never purchase any materials." Three teachers who had not spoken previously said they agreed with this statement. After determining that none of those present had additional comments to make about the product, the group by virtue of voice vote decided to purchase thirty copies of Sorcerer, ten for each of the three schools.

Since the early 1990s, teachers in the Maple Creek School District have had considerable autonomy to select supplemental instructional materials. Typically, requisitions were approved by principals and forwarded to the district's business office. The elementary school's gifted and talented program, however, operated differently. Located at three different sites, this program was given its own budget for supplies, equipment, and materials. The assistant superintendent for instruction had supervisory responsibility for the program and its budget. Until four years ago, the principals in the three participating schools attended the bimonthly staff meetings, but since the program was deemed to be operating smoothly, the principals stopped attending the meetings.

As per established practice, the requisition to purchase thirty copies of Sorcerer was sent directly from Mrs. Oberfeld to Dr. Wilbur Youngman, the assistant superintendent for instruction. When he received the form, he neither challenged the recommendation nor contacted any of the three principals to determine their opinion about purchasing the product. He merely verified that funds were available to transact the purchase, signed the requisition form, and forwarded it to the district's business manager.

After the copies of Sorcerer were delivered, all eighteen teachers involved with the program made them available to their students. They could be used in school, or students could take them home for a period not to exceed seven days. The software program is constructed around a system of rewards and punishments that are distributed on the basis of spelling performance. As predicted by the teachers, students responded positively to the software, and Sorcerer became a very popular choice with them.

About one month after Sorcerer was made available to students, the first parental complaint about the product was registered. Elizabeth Baker, the mother of a second-grade student at Lakeside Elementary School, called Principal Nancy Tannin.

"Miss Tannin, I'm concerned about a computer game a teacher gave to my daughter, Sally. She is in the gifted and talented enrichment program, and as you know, students involved regularly bring home books and other supplementary materials. I became inquisitive about this particular game, because Sally just couldn't leave it alone. And she was so intense when she was playing it. She told me the game was called Sorcerer. I had never heard of it. Do you know what I'm talking about?"

The principal had never heard of Sorcerer, and she admitted that fact to Mrs. Baker. She told her that it was not unusual for teachers affiliated with the program to select instructional materials independently. Then she said that she had a great deal of confidence in the teachers to make appropriate decisions on such matters.

"Well, don't you have to approve the purchase of instructional materials?" the mother asked.

"Normally, I do. But the gifted and talented program is not an individual school program. Therefore, responsibility for coordinating the enrichment program rests with the assistant superintendent for instruction. Why are you concerned about this particular product? Do you think your daughter is spending too much time with it? Or do you think that it is ineffective?"

"My concern is about the nature of Sorcerer. The game involves witchcraft and black magic," Mrs. Baker responded. "Surely there are less controversial materials available to help with spelling. Given the moral decay in our society, parents have to be especially sensitive to their children's exposure to destructive materials that undermine family values and beliefs."

Though Miss Tannin said she would look into the matter and respond more completely to the concern, she initially thought that Mrs. Baker was overreacting. Thus, she did not treat the concern as being urgent. Two days passed before Miss Tannin discussed Mrs. Baker's concern with a teacher involved with the gifted and talented program. She was told that Sorcerer was purchased very recently and had already become popular with students. She also learned that the teachers discussed the product before recommending its purchase.

Based on this conversation with one teacher, Miss Tannin telephoned Mrs. Baker to respond more fully as she had promised. She told the parent that the product had been approved by the teachers involved with the enrichment program and that there had been no other parents voicing concerns.

Mrs. Baker asked, "Did you look at the product? Did you actually sit at a computer and play the game?"

"Well, no. I didn't think that was necessary," Miss Tannin answered. "Our teachers are competent professionals. I trust them to make effective decisions about instructional materials."

At this point, Mrs. Baker became angry. "Maybe this time the teachers are wrong. Are you not responsible for what they do? If you are not accountable for the instructional materials used in your school, who is? Telling me that the teachers think Sorcerer is suitable for young children does not alleviate my concerns. Therefore, I'm going to pursue this matter further."

After the conversation ended, Miss Tannin telephoned Deloris Gragolis and Mitch Sancheck, principals in the other two schools participating in the enrichment programs. She learned that they also had received complaints about Sorcerer. She was surprised that neither of her colleagues had shared this information previously. The three principals, while agreeing that the teachers had the authority to select the materials, recognized that concerns over Sorcerer could evolve into a major problem. They met the next day and formulated the following strategy:

- They would co-sign a memorandum to Dr. Youngman informing him that they had received complaints about the software program.
- Copies of this memorandum would be sent to teachers participating in the enrichment program.
- They would contact the parents who had voiced concerns and inform them that they should direct their comments to Dr. Youngman since he was responsible for coordinating the program.

Less than two weeks after Mrs. Baker first complained to Miss Tannin, a letter to the editor, signed by sixteen parents, appeared in the local newspaper condemning the use of Sorcerer:

> We are parents of elementary school children who participate in the gifted and talented program in the Maple Creek School District. Recently, our children have been exposed to a distasteful and evil computer game called Sorcerer. This game is supposed to assist our children with their spelling skills, but in reality, it exposes them to witchcraft and other evil concepts.
>
> Sorcerer is yet another example that our public schools have become a pawn for those who wish to lower the standards and moral fiber of our society. Parents who financially support our public schools have every right to be concerned if they think the positive values taught at home are being eroded by school activities.
>
> The fact that the principals appear unwilling to deal with this matter is especially disconcerting. Our concerns have basically been ignored. As taxpayers and parents, we urge others to join us in a fight to keep control of our public schools. Let's keep our schools free of materials that promote witchcraft, devil worship, and other evil ideas. Call your school board member now and voice your objection!

The district's superintendent, Dr. Philip Montgomery, first learned about the objections to Sorcerer after reading the letter to the editor. He immediately called Dr. Youngman and asked why he had not been briefed on this matter. Anticipating that school board members would be inquiring about the letter, he wanted information immediately. Dr. Youngman told the superintendent that the principals had met with the teachers and neither the teachers nor the principals felt that the parents' objections were valid. He also pointed out that collectively, the principals had only received calls from five families.

Dr. Montgomery instructed Dr. Youngman to set a meeting with the three principals and Mrs. Oberfeld that afternoon. He said he also would attend. The meeting was held in the superintendent's conference room at 4 P.M. Dr. Montgomery indicated that since the letter to the editor was published that morning, he had already been contacted by four of the seven school board members. In pursuing the issue, the superintendent wanted answers to four questions:

1. What are the parents' specific objections?
2. Why are these materials still being used if they are objectionable to some families?
3. Who made the decision to buy the materials?
4. What was the rationale for purchasing the materials?

"Sorcerer is similar to a popular video game that received negative publicity recently," explained Mrs. Oberfeld. "At the time we decided to purchase it, we did not anticipate that parents would object. And even if we knew that they would, we probably would have made the same decision. If right-wing religious groups are allowed to dictate what we use, then we are reduced to being the instruments used to implement their agenda. Now that they no longer are looking for communists under every desk, they've turned their attention to the devil. The fact of the matter is that this software program motivates children. Students are not required or even encouraged to use it. If some parents find it objectionable, they should simply tell their children they cannot use it. Why should they decide what other students can or cannot use?"

Dr. Montgomery asked the principals to comment. Miss Tannin spoke first.

"We have a great deal of confidence in Mrs. Oberfeld and the other teachers involved in this program. They all supported the recommendation to purchase Sorcerer. When I received a complaint, I shared the information with a teacher in my building. She confirmed that students were not required to use the program and disagreed with the negative assessment of the product."

"But did any of you actually test the material to determine the nature of the program?" the superintendent asked.

All four administrators responded that they had not done so. Mrs. Oberfeld, however, said that she had tested the product and confirmed that the other teachers involved in the enrichment program had either tested the product personally or observed other teachers doing so.

"Who authorized this purchase?" the superintendent asked.

Miss Tannin answered, "The teachers involved in the program recommended buying Sorcerer, and the requisition was approved by Dr. Youngman."

"Yes, I approved the purchase," Dr. Youngman said. "But I did so based on my faith in Mrs. Oberfeld and the other teachers. I believe my responsibility is to ensure that the requisition has been processed properly and that sufficient funds are available. I don't think it's my job to second-guess competent teachers."

Mrs. Oberfeld became concerned with Dr. Youngman's apparent defensiveness. "Before we start pointing the finger of blame at each other, let's step back and think about the real issue. Are we going to allow a small group of parents to dictate instructional materials? The parents complaining about Sorcerer would like to control every decision we make. If they win on this matter, they'll be back with more ridiculous demands. These people want to control what we read and how we think."

Miss Tannin spoke next. "Assume that Dr. Youngman refused to approve the purchase order. Wouldn't his refusal have created a major political problem? How would teachers respond if they learned that instructional materials they requisitioned had to meet with the approval of all parents? I think we have to face up to what is at stake here. This is censorship, plain and simple."

Mitch Sancheck then spoke. "We trust and believe in our teachers. Quite frankly, I prefer to have them rather than radical parents deciding what we should use in the schools."

Dr. Montgomery made it clear that he did not want to restrict decisions about instructional materials; nevertheless, he was uncomfortable with a purchase order process that bypassed principals. "When I was a principal, I had to sign every purchase order originated in my building," he told the others. "School district policy required me to do so. Our policy obviously allows some purchases to be made without principal approval. For me, this is a problem. Therefore, we actually have to make two decisions. First, we must decide how to handle the present situation; second, we need to decide what policy changes are needed to prevent this type of problem from recurring."

Miss Tannin commented, "You may be in a better position than we are to answer both questions."

After hearing that suggestion, Dr. Montgomery got up from his chair and stared directly at the others in the room, "That is one option, but being a dictator is not my style. I'm going to leave you alone for a while; I'll be back in two hours. When I return, I expect you to provide recommendations both on how we handle this matter and on what we should do to change existing policy."

PROBLEM FRAMING

1. Assume you are the superintendent. Describe what you would want to accomplish in dealing with the situation described in this case.

2. Based on the evidence of contextual variables, describe the difficulty associated with achieving your objective.

QUESTIONS AND SUGGESTED ACTIVITIES

1. Share and critique the problem statements prepared by students in your class.

2. Should teachers have the freedom to select the instructional materials they use? Why or why not?

3. Assume that Sorcerer is removed from the schools as demanded by the complaining parents. What are the advantages and disadvantages of this decision?

4. In your opinion, was the absence of the principals from the meeting at which the decision was made to purchase Sorcerer a relevant fact in this case? Why or why not?

5. Are liberty (expressed through democratic control of schools) and teacher professionalism (expressed through teacher/administrator control of instructional decisions) basically incompatible concepts? Why or why not?

6. Is it possible for principals to maintain control while allowing both teachers and parents to be involved in decision about instructional materials? Explain your answer.

7. Evaluate the process used to purchase materials for the gifted and talented program and make suggestions for improving the process.

8. Critique the argument that Sorcerer should not be removed because student usage is voluntary.

9. Evaluate the roles of the three elementary principals and the assistant superintendent for instruction in this case. Did they act ethically and responsibly?

10. Evaluate the behavior of the teachers in this case. Did they act ethically and responsibly?

11. What rights do parents have to object to instructional materials?

SUGGESTED READINGS

Browder, L. H. (1998). The religious right, the secular left, and their shared dilemma: The public school. *International Journal of Educational Reform*, 7(4), 309–318.

Donelson, K. (1987a). Censorship: Heading off the attack. *Educational Horizons*, 65(4), 167–170.

Donelson, K. (1987b). Six statements/questions from the censors. *Phi Delta Kappan*, 69(3) 208–214.

Fege, A. F. (1993). The tug of war over tolerance. *Educational Leadership*, 51(4), 22–24.

Georgiady, N., & Romano, L. (1987). Censorship—Back to the front burner. *Middle School Journal*, 18, 12–13.

Jones, J. L. (1993). Targets of the right. *American School Board Journal*, 180(4), 22–29.

Kowalski, T. J. (2003). *Contemporary school administration: An introduction* (2nd ed.). Boston: Allyn and Bacon. (see Chapter 10).

Leahy, M. (1998). The religious right: Would-be censors of the state school curriculum. *Educational Philosophy & Theory*, 30(1), 18, 51.

Meadows, B. J. (1990). The rewards and risks of shared leadership. *Phi Delta Kappan*, 71(7), 545–548.

Petress, K. (2005). The role of censorship in school. *Journal of Instructional Psychology*, 32(3), 248–252.

Pierard, R. (1987). The new religious right and censorship. *Contemporary Education*, 58(3), 131–137.

Rowell, C. (1986). Allowing parents to screen textbooks would lead to anarchy in the schools. *Chronicle of Higher Education*, 33(26), 34.

Smith, S. (1998). School by school. *American School Board Journal*, 185(6), 22–25.

Sullivan, P. (1998). Parent involvement. *Our Children*, 24(1), 23.

Weil, J. (1988). Dealing with censorship: Policy and procedures. *Education Digest*, 53(5), 23–25.

Zirkel, P., & Gluckman, I. (1986). Objections to curricular material on religious grounds. *NASSP Bulletin*, 70(488), 99–100.

REFERENCES

Barth, R. S. (2001). Teacher leader. *Phi Delta Kappan*, *82*(6), 443–449.

Bauch, P., & Goldring, E. B. (1998). Parent-teacher participation in the context of school governance. *Peabody Journal of Education*, *73*(1), 15–35.

Corwin, R. G., & Borman, K. M. (1988). School as workplace: Structural constraints on administration. In N. J. Boyan (Ed.), *Handbook of research on educational administration* (pp. 209–238). New York: Longman.

Darling-Hammond, L. (1987). The over-regulated curriculum and the press for teacher professionalism. *NASSP Bulletin*, *71*(498), 22, 24–26, 28–29.

Davis, O. L. (1997). Notes on the nature of power. *Journal of Curriculum and Supervision*, *12*(3), 189–192.

Kowalski, T. J. (2003). *Contemporary school administration: An introduction*. Boston: Allyn and Bacon.

Kowalski, T. J. (2006). *The school superintendent: Theory, practice, and cases* (2nd ed.). Thousand Oaks, CA: Sage.

Kowalski, T. J., & Keedy, J. (2005). Preparing superintendents to be effective communicators. In L. G. Björk & T. J. Kowalski (Eds.), *The contemporary superintendent: Preparation, practice, and development* (pp. 207–226). Thousand Oaks, CA: Corwin Press.

Kowalski, T. J., Petersen, G. J., & Fusarelli, L. D. (2007). *Effective communication for school administrators: An imperative in an information age*. Lanham, MD: Rowman & Littlefield Education.

Shedd, J. B., & Bacharach, S. B. (1991). *Tangled hierarchies: Teachers as professionals and the management of schools*. San Francisco: Jossey-Bass.

Strike, K. A. (1993). Professionalism, democracy, and discursive communities: Normative reflections on restructuring. *American Educational Research Journal*, *30*(2), 255–275.

Sykes, G. (1991). In defense of teacher professionalism as a policy of choice. *Educational Policy*, *5*(2), 137–149.

Wirt, F. M., & Kirst, M. W. (2001). *The political dynamics of American education* (2nd ed.). Berkeley, CA: McCutchan.

Zeichner, K. M. (1991). Contradictions and tensions in the professionalization of teaching and the democractization of schools. *Teachers College Record*, *92*(3), 363–379.

Background Information

After approximately 1900, the governance structure of public education in the United States became increasingly centralized as policymakers emphasized select values, state control, and uniformity of practice. The following factors were especially influential in the trend toward having fewer but larger local districts:

- *The value of efficiency*. Efficiency is based on a favorable relationship between inputs and outputs; eliminating small school districts was accepted as a way to make education more economical (King, Swanson, & Sweetland, 2003).
- *The value of adequacy*. Adequacy attempts to answer the difficult question: How much education is enough? If local communities were allowed to answer this question without interventions from state government, minimum standards for education (e.g., attendance days, graduation requirements) would likely vary depending on the emphasis a community placed on education (Kowalski, 2003).
- *The value of equality*. Equality has been defined as ensuring that all students in a given state have reasonably equal educational opportunities. Since school districts depended heavily on local tax revenues and since taxable wealth varied considerably from one district to another, having fewer but larger districts was viewed as a means for reducing wealth discrepancies that contributed to unequal educational opportunities (King et al., 2003).
- *Growing number of state standards*. State officials began recognizing that they were ultimately responsible for public education and as a consequence, they developed a common state curriculum for public schools (Spring, 2001). Centralization in local districts was a by-product of increased state control because district administrators had to ensure that individual schools were compliant (Kowalski, 2006).
- *Legislation and litigation*. Legislation and subsequent litigation also played a major role in moving public education toward more centralized authority. Lawsuits in areas such as civil rights, school finance, and special education made local school systems vulnerable to prolonged legal battles and unfavorable judgments. This legal exposure produced a compliance mentality among school board members and administrators—a state of mind that operating procedures needed to be uniform and controlled across a district (Tyack, 1990).

After 1950, centralized authority became more common, both among and within local school districts. Many states enacted consolidation laws requiring small schools and districts to merge. In 1937, there were approximately 119,000 school districts in this country; by 1963, that number dropped to 35,676; today, there are just over 14,000 districts remaining (Kowalski, 2006).

Critics of centralization argue that the organizational preference has diminished liberty. That is, larger school districts have diluted citizen control over public education. As the modern school reform movement gained momentum during the 1980s, this argument was augmented by the contention that highly centralized policies were unresponsive to real student needs. That is, the value of generic improvement goals, set either by the state or by the school board in larger districts, was attenuated because needs varied markedly across a state and even across schools in larger districts (Kowalski, 2006).

Circa 1990, policymakers and education leaders began agreeing that effective reform was more likely if it were pursued locally (Kowalski, Petersen, & Fusarelli, 2007). Both deregulation (easing or even eliminating state standards) and decentralization (reducing district control over individual schools) became popular school reform initiatives. The revamped strategy of making schools the locus of school improvement is nested in two widely accepted motives: increasing the likelihood that school improvement efforts address real student needs and increasing local support for needed change by virtue of citizen participation (Bauman, 1996). Despite its purported advantages and wide political support, decentralization has proven to be a less than perfect strategy. Merely involving teachers and citizens in decision making and forcing administrators to share power do not ensure that meaningful improvement will result (Walberg & Niemiec, 1994). In addition, decentralization that extends to funding and spending authority raises serious questions about the extent to which school districts offer reasonably equal educational opportunities to all students (Nir & Miran, 2006).

Tensions between decentralization and centralization, however, have proven to be persistent. Scholars studying school change (e.g., Fullan, 2001) remind us that neither approach is ideal or problem-free when it comes to organizational development. Whereas centralization tends to err in the direction of overcontrol, decentralization tends to err in the direction of chaos. This reality has been confronted by many superintendents and principals who have engaged in site-based management (SBM). Fullan (2001) advises practitioners that they should not choose entirely between centralization and decentralization but rather they should determine which functions should be centralized and which functions should be decentralized.

In this case study, a superintendent decentralizes budgets and requires schools to establish governance councils. In less than two years, several parents charge that the action has produced resource and program disparities among the district's elementary schools. A parent who is an attorney questions the legality of the district's approach to decentralization, claiming that the process has resulted in unequal educational opportunities for elementary school students. His accusation raises philosophical and legal questions, and school officials must determine if they want to modify the decentralization program or defend it politically and possibly legally.

Key Areas for Reflection

1. Centralized and decentralized governance
2. Conflict between liberty and equality
3. Relationship between district and school administration under school-based management
4. Managing change in school districts
5. Role and responsibilities of school councils
6. Decentralization and possible effects on fiscal equity

The Case

Haver Ridge

Haver Ridge is the seat of government for Marvin County, located in central Illinois. With a population of just over 16,000, the community has grown about 15 percent since the mid-1950s. Much of the increase occurred after a new industrial park was constructed on the edge of town in 1973. The four new businesses that located in the industrial park generated slightly more than 400 new jobs.

Marvin County is predominately rural, with grain farms accounting for about 80 percent of all the acreage. Haver Ridge and Fellington (population, 10,350) are the only two cities in the county with more than 1,000 residents. About fifteen years ago, a new hospital and a municipal airport were built midway between Haver Ridge and Fellington, and the corridor connecting the two towns now is dotted with commercial developments.

River Valley Community College and the East Marvin Community School District are two of the largest employers in Haver Ridge. Collectively, they employ 958 individuals. The college's primary service area is Marvin and two adjoining counties.

School District

In 1962, six public school districts in Marvin County were reorganized into just two districts. Their boundaries were established essentially by a north-to-west state road that runs through the county's center. Consequently, the two districts, East Marvin County School District and West Marvin County School District, are equal in terms of land. The former, however, is about 20 percent larger in population and in student enrollment. The school district's administrative office, its high school, its middle school, and three of its five elementary schools are located in Haver Rige.

The three elementary schools in Haver Ridge are Adams, Clark, and Lincoln. Clark is the oldest facility, having been constructed originally in 1937. It is located in the downtown business district, and although the site and the size of the classroom are arguably inadequate, referenda in 1999 and 2003 to replace the building were soundly defeated. Many residents consider the school building to be a landmark and do not want the structure destroyed. Clark, however, has the oldest and most experienced faculty; the average age among the teachers is eight years higher than the average age at any of the district's other elementary schools. Among the five elementary schools in the district, it also has the highest percentage of students qualifying for free and reduced lunch; 47 percent of the students meet this criterion.

The other two elementary schools in Haver Ridge, Adams and Lincoln, are situated in residential neighborhoods. Both are relatively modern and spacious buildings. Adams was first occupied in 1983 and Lincoln in 1996.

School Board

Until approximately 1980, farmers comprised a majority on the seven-member school board in the East Marvin County School District. After that point, the composition of the board became more diverse. Current board members are a loan officer at local bank, a restaurant owner, a housewife, a community college English instructor, the plant manager at local factory, a retired school principal, and a farmer.

Though they do not always agree on every issue, the board is not divided into political factions. The members exhibit mutual respect and work well with one another and with the superintendent. The school board's relationship with the teachers' union has also been positive.

Administration

When a long-term superintendent retired three years ago, the board employed Burton Packard to replace him. Dr. Packard had been an assistant superintendent for instruction in a Chicago suburb. A mid-career administrator with a reputation as an effective instructional leader, he has promoted decentralization, shared decision making, and teacher involvement in school governance. During his employment interview, he defended these convictions by telling the school board members, "I think teachers and parents should be our partners, and that includes collaborating with us when we make important decisions about how we organize our school and how we spend our resources. I'm not an autocratic administrator."

Ryan Fulton, the district's assistant superintendent for instruction, moved to his present position six years ago after having been the principal of Haver Ridge High School for eight years. Jane Westerman, the assistant for business, moved to her present position four years ago after having been principal at Lincoln Elementary for five years. Only two of the district's seven principals have been employed by Dr. Packard. They are Dr. Elaine Byers at the middle school and Mrs. Norene Vidduci at Adams Elementary School.

Implementing SBM

Shortly after arriving in Haver Ridge, Dr. Packard presented a plan to decentralize authority in the school district the following year. After gaining support from the school board, he announced that the changes would begin in the elementary schools and then would be followed by changes at the secondary schools. Three objectives were included in his plan:

1. *Increasing flexibility and accountability at each school.* School personnel would be responsible for identifying instructional priorities. Variance in curriculum and instructional materials would be allowed if necessary to pursue these priorities, provided that state laws and policies would not be violated.
2. *Involving teachers and parents in school governance.* Every school would have to establish a governance council that must include administrators, teachers, and parents. School council authority would include approving instructional priorities, school budgets, and implementation strategies.
3. *Giving schools greater fiscal autonomy.* The district's budgeting and fiscal management practices would be changed to allow individual schools to have autonomy over funds earmarked for supplies and equipment. Under the decentralization plan, these funds were referred to as "school discretionary allocations."

The board members publicly praised Dr. Packard's plan and pledged to support it. Reactions among the district's principals, however, were mixed. Among the five elementary school principals, those assigned to the district's rural elementary schools, Milltown and Wild Creek, were moderately supportive but nonvocal. Their primary apprehension rested with the third objective involving fiscal autonomy. The principals at Adams and Lincoln were highly supportive and very vocal in touting the merits of the superintendent's initiative. Mrs. Simpson, principal at Clark Elementary School, was the only one to openly oppose the plan. She and most of her staff did not think a school council would be beneficial. Moreover, they feared that the size of school budgets would be determined solely by enrollment, a criterion that they considered disadvantageous because of the nature of their student population.

The superintendent's decentralization plan was officially adopted in January, giving the elementary principals about six months to determine how they would meet the three objectives. By August 1, three weeks before school was scheduled to open the following year, they had to submit an implementation plan to Dr. Packard that included the following information:

- The composition of the school's council
- Methods for selecting council members
- A school budget

Between August 1 and the opening of school year, Dr. Packard met with each principal to discuss implementation plans. Though he raised many questions with the principals, he did not require modifications to the plans.

SBM—The First Two Years

Differences embedded in the plans for the three elementary schools located in Haver Ridge gradually became apparent to the school board and public. At the same time, differences surfaced with respect to spending discretionary funds. As examples, cooperative learning was one of the instructional priorities at Adams Elementary School, and most of this school's discretionary funds were used to implement the paradigm (e.g., staff development and putting more computers in classrooms). At Lincoln, computer-assisted instruction was a priority, and a high percentage of discretionary funds was used to purchase additional computer hardware and software. At Clark, however, improving learning outcomes for students scoring below acceptable levels on the state's achievement tests was identified as the top priority. Most of the school's discretionary funds were used to purchase materials related to remedial instruction.

The school councils in the three elementary schools also exhibited differences. At Adams and Lincoln, the councils consisted of thirteen members with teacher and parent members being active and in leadership roles. At Clark, the council had only nine members and teacher and parent members were passive and reluctant to assume leadership roles. The monthly council meetings at Clark were highly predictable. Mrs. Simpson, the principal, would construct the agenda, do most of the talking, and the members supported every one of her recommendations. The four teachers, all loyal to the principal, saw the council as a politically correct body that would have little or no positive impact on the school. The four parent members seemed insecure about their role and tended to accept whatever was said by the educators. Only two of them attended the meetings regularly.

Problem

Each year, students in grades 2, 4, and 6 are required by the state to take standardized achievement tests. Students receive individual results and schools receive an average score for each grade level. For the last seven years, Lincoln has had the highest average test scores in the district; Clark has had the lowest. Listed below are the results for sixth-grade students for the past three years. Years two and three are years under the decentralization plan.

School	Average test scores	Rank in district
Adams	57.3, 58.2, 58.3	2, 2, 2
Clark	48.7, 48.3, 48.1	5, 5, 5
Lincoln	59.2, 60.1, 61.2	1, 1, 1
Milltown	55.2, 55.3, 55.3	3, 4, 4
Wild Creek	54.6, 55.4, 55.7	4, 3, 3

In the past, the local newspaper paid little attention to differences among school scores, but after decentralization, the reporter covering education, Janice Bell, showed interest in the topic. She wrote a series of articles in which she tried to connect test scores with instructional priorities and discretionary spending. She suggested that increases in student test scores at Lincoln were the result of the school's investment in technology. Conversely, she questioned whether a continued emphasis on remediation at Clark was a factor in student test performance at that school. At the least, the series of articles created a public perception that council decisions and spending could be associated with student test performance.

Dr. Packard was not pleased that Ms. Bell implied that differences in school performance were connected to his decentralization plan. He told her that the nexus implied in her articles could not be substantiated—at least not yet. He expressed confidence that Principal Simpson and the Clark school council were making good decisions based on the real needs of students and on the school's instructional priorities. He explained that many factors affected student performance on standardized tests, including some beyond the school's control. He cited the social and economic conditions of a student's home life as examples.

During her meeting with Superintendent Packard, Ms. Bell took many notes but did not dispute any of his statements. Later, she had telephone conversations with three board members. She discovered that Dr. Packard had already expressed the same concerns about the articles with the entire school board and that the board members supported the superintendent's views on this matter. The board president, however, added that the board expected test scores to improve incrementally as the effects of decentralization became more pronounced.

Several parents of Clark students agreed with the associations suggested by Ms. Bell in her articles. The most vocal of them was Anthony Bacon, an attorney and director of employee relations at the local community college. He wrote a letter to the editor of the newspaper objecting to the idea that the district's elementary schools should have considerable autonomy. He also voiced his misgivings about the superintendent's initiative at a school board meeting. His statement read as follows:

> Ladies and gentlemen, Dr. Packard, and members of the school staff, I appear here today as a concerned parent of two children attending Clark Elementary School. When we moved to Haver Ridge four years ago, my wife and I bought an older house in the downtown area because we enjoy remodeling. We were concerned initially about our children attending Clark Elementary School, largely because the other elementary schools in Haver Ridge are newer and have more positive reputations. Before purchasing our house, I talked with the former superintendent and he assured me that programmatically, all the elementary schools in this district offered the same curriculum and equal instructional opportunities. His assurance influenced our decision to purchase a house in the downtown area.
>
> I realize that conditions change. When Dr. Packard arrived three years ago, he made it clear to the public that he would initiate changes in an effort to improve the schools. My wife and I applauded his intentions. Until recently, however, we did not pay close attention to what was being done across the district's elementary schools. The recently published articles enlightened us and that is why I am here today. Working in the realm of public education, I know that decentralizing governance is a popular idea; but as an attorney, I also recognize that giving schools considerable independence produces a political environment that breeds inequities.
>
> I wish to relate several specific concerns to you this evening. First, it is obvious that the school councils do not operate uniformly. A parent on the Clark council told me that her role essentially involved rubber stamping decisions already made by the principal. But at Lincoln, parents and teachers regularly introduce agenda items and assume leadership roles. For example, Mary Burgess, the director of instructional technology at the community college and a parent of two Lincoln students, influenced the decision to invest so heavily in technology at that school.

Second and more importantly, I believe that the superintendent's decentralization plan will actually widen student test performance across the elementary schools.
Discretionary budgets at each school are based on an equal per pupil allotment. This
process is hardly defensible in light of the fact that student needs are not the same across
the schools; for example, Clark enrolls a higher percentage of special needs students
than the other elementary schools. The principal at Clark, Mrs. Simpson, told me that
she devoted more resources to remedial activities because so many students at the
school needed the extra help. As a result, Mrs. Simpson said that she had limited resources for other needs, such as purchasing technology.

Given what has occurred under the superintendent's plan over the last two years,
I ask you: At what point do board members intervene to ensure that educational opportunities remain reasonably equal across the five elementary schools? I respectfully
request that you reexamine the superintendent's decentralization plan and take necessary measures to restore and maintain equal educational opportunities for all of our
students.

Copies of his statement were distributed to all attendees. The board president
thanked him for his comments and then asked the superintendent if he wanted to respond to Mr. Bacon. The superintendent indicated that he would look into the matter
and reply in the next two weeks.

Mr. Bacon knew only two of the school board members personally, the English
instructor at the community college, and the owner of a local business. Prior to attending the school board meeting, he had never met Dr. Packard.

In the days following the board meeting, three of the board members telephoned
Dr. Packard suggesting that he not take Mr. Bacon lightly. He was highly respected by
his colleagues at the community college, and the two board members who knew him
personally did not consider him a malcontent.

A week after Mr. Bacon made his statement to the school board, the board president, at the urging of Superintendent Packard, convened an executive session. The
purpose was to discuss the concerns and to prepare a formal response to them. The
board's attorney also attended the executive meeting. At the closed meeting, Dr.
Packard made the following points:

- Mr. Bacon's claims about the behavior of school council members were only
  partially correct. While it was true that the councils did not function uniformly,
  differences were not by design, and they certainly were not the fault of school administrators. Mrs. Simpson, for example, had tried repeatedly to have parents
  place items on the agenda and to be more vocal at the meetings.
- Members of the Clark Elementary School council were appointed—a decision
  made by the school's PTA and not by the principal. When the council was
  formed, Mrs. Simpson asked Mr. Bacon to be a council member; he declined,
  stating that his position at the community college and his need to remodel his
  residence did not allow him to devote the time necessary for this assignment.
- Budget allocations to the schools were made on a per-pupil basis as claimed by
  Mr. Bacon. No exceptions, such as providing additional funding for special needs
  students, were made because doing so would have been difficult and controver-

sial. For example, the Lincoln principal could have requested additional funds to support a gifted and talented program.

- While it was true that the decision to invest heavily in remedial materials at Clark was recommended by the principal, it was approved unanimously by the school's faculty and council.

- The number of students from low-income families enrolled at Clark was increasing. For example, the percentage of students qualifying for free and reduced lunches increased from 40 percent to 47 percent in just the last three years. This socioeconomic factor is a major consideration that should be weighed in evaluating student performance at the school.

- Programs at all the district's schools meet or exceed state standards. If Mr. Bacon's argument about inequities were taken at face value, virtually every school district with more than one elementary school could be found not to provide equal educational opportunities.

In the summary section of his report, Dr. Packard recommended that the board not alter its decentralization policy, including provisions regarding discretionary budget allocations. He added, however, that Mrs. Simpson would have to allocate at least 25 percent of the discretionary funds given to Clark Elementary School to purchase additional computer hardware or software.

After reading Dr. Packard's report, the board's attorney advised them that the superintendent's response to Mr. Bacon was appropriate and sufficient. He urged the board to have Dr. Packard send his report, as written, to Mr. Bacon. The board followed his advice.

After receiving the superintendent's report, Mr. Bacon called the board member who was a fellow employee at the community college. He told her, "I don't think the superintendent's perception of equal opportunity is legally correct. Providing the prescribed state curriculum is a matter of adequacy and not equity."

The board member informed Mr. Bacon that the superintendent's response was approved by the board's attorney and subsequently endorsed by the board. She also pointed out that a first step was being taken to ensure that discretionary funds at Clark would be used for computers or software. She then urged him to meet privately with the superintendent to discuss other possible changes to diminish his concerns without destroying the decentralization initiative. He said he would follow her advice.

Two day later, Mr. Bacon met with Dr. Packard, but instead of exploring ways to modify the decentralization program, he continued to argue that the superintendent's perception of reasonably equal educational opportunities was invalid.

Dr. Packard responded by telling Mr. Bacon, "Differences among our schools are not great. For example, both Milltown and Clark have the same number of computers. There are many ways to define educational opportunities and different perspectives on equality. Computers are not the only instructional tool that matter. I believe schools are most effective when they respond to the real needs of their clients."

The conversation lasted about an hour and at the end, Mr. Bacon remained convinced that the superintendent's decentralization program has created greater inequities among the elementary schools. Following the meeting, Mr. Bacon enlisted the support of five other Clark Elementary School families. In mid-May, the six families retained an attorney who notified the superintendent that a lawsuit would be filed if the school board did not rescind or sufficiently alter the decentralization plan.

The board members were concerned about the possibility of a lawsuit, and they held another executive session to discuss the matter. The board's attorney was asked to comment about the merits of the threatened lawsuit.

"As I told you previously, Dr. Packard's response in this matter is reasonable. I cannot predict the outcome of a lawsuit, especially prior to reading the legal issues on which it is filed. Litigation is expensive, time consuming, and there is never a guaranteed outcome. At the same time, however, the families pressing this matter will incur legal costs—and they could be substantial. They have retained a competent attorney, and his fees tend to be above average."

The board members were hoping for more specific direction from their attorney. At least three of the board members appeared to be changing their position on the decentralization plan. They urged Dr. Packard to eliminate the discretionary funding portion of the plan, indicating that Mr. Bacon would drop the matter if this were done.

Before adjourning the meeting, the board president again asked Dr. Packard if he had changed his position on decentralization. The superintendent responded, "In light of concerns now being expressed, I would like to think about this matter and confer with staff members. Let's meet again in one week and I'll give you my recommendation at that time."

PROBLEM FRAMING

1. Assume you are Superintendent Packard. Describe what you would want to accomplish in dealing with the situation described in this case.

2. Based on the evidence of contextual variables, describe the difficulty associated with achieving your objective.

QUESTIONS AND SUGGESTED ACTIVITIES

1. What are the advantages and disadvantages of Dr. Packard's deciding not to eliminate the discretionary funding portion of the decentralization program?

2. Discuss the guiding values of adequacy, equity, and liberty. How does each relate to decentralization of authority?

3. In small groups, identify the intended purposes, strengths, and weaknesses associated with decentralizing authority.

4. Evaluate the manner in which Superintendent Packard introduced and then pursued decentralization.

5. Invite a principal from a school with a site-based council to discuss this case with the class.

6. Based on what you read, do you think the administrative staff was prepared adequately to implement the changes required by the superintendent's decentralization plan? Why or why not?

7. Do you agree with the superintendent's contention that making associations between average student test scores and discretionary spending is premature? Provide a rationale for your answer.

8. Ideally, what should the superintendent have done to build political support in the community for decentralization?

9. Do you believe that Mrs. Simpson, principal at Clark Elementary School, is responsible for the manner in which the council at that school has operated? Explain your answer.

10. What constitutes reasonably equal educational opportunities?

11. If the discretionary spending portion of the decentralization plan is eliminated, would the remainder of the plan suffer? Why or why not?

SUGGESTED READINGS

Bauer, S. C. (1998). Designing school-based systems: Deriving a theory of practice. *International Journal of Educational Reform, 7*(2), 108–121.

Brick, B. H. (1993). Changing concepts of equal educational opportunity: A comparison of the views of Thomas Jefferson, Horace Mann, and John Dewey. *Thresholds in Education, 19*(1–2), 2–8.

Candoli, I. C. (1995). *School-based management in education: How to make it work in your school.* Lancaster, PA: Technomic (see Chapter 3).

Dempster, N. (2000). Guilty or not: The impact and effects of site-based management on schools. *Journal of Educational Administration, 38*(1), 47–63.

Florestal, K., & Cooper, R. (1997). *Decentralization of education: Legal issues.* (ERIC Document Reproduction Service No. ED 412 616)

Henkin, A. B., Cistone, P. J., & Dee, J. R. (2000). Conflict management strategies of principals in site-based managed schools *Journal of Educational Administration, 38*(2), 142–158.

Holloway, J. H. (2000). The promise and pitfalls of site-based management. *Educational Leadership 57*(7), 81–82.

Hughes, L. W. (1993). School-based management, decentralization, and citizen control—A perspective. *Journal of School Leadership, 3*(1), 40–44.

Kowalski, T. J. (2003). *Contemporary school administration: An introduction* (2nd ed.). Boston: Allyn and Bacon (see Chapter 8).

Kowalski, T. J., Petersen, G. J., & Fusarelli, L. D. (2007). *Effective communication for school administrators: An imperative in an information age.* Lanham, MD: Rowman and Littlefield Education (see Chapter 11).

Leithwood, K., Jantzi, D., & Steinbach, R. (1998). *Do school councils matter?* (ERIC Document Reproduction Service No. ED 424 644)

Leonard, L. J. (1998). Site based management and organizational learning: Conceptualizing their combined potential for meaningful reform. *Planning and Changing 29*(1), 24–46.

Lifton, F. B. (1992). The legal tangle of shared governance. *School Administrator, 49*(1), 16–19.

Mitchell, J. K., & Poston, W. K. (1992). The equity audit in school reform: Three case studies of educational disparity and incongruity. *International Journal of Educational Reform, 1*(3), 242–247.

Myers, J. A. (1997). Schools make the decisions: The impact of school-based management. *School Business Affairs, 63*(10), 3–9.

Nir, A. E., & Miran, M. (2006). The equity consequences of school-based management. *International Journal of Educational Management, 20*(2), 116–126.

Ortiz, F. I., & Ogawa, R. T. (2000). Site-based decision-making leadership in American public schools. *Journal of Educational Administration, 38*(5), 486–500.

Peternick, L., & Sherman, J. (1998). School-based budgeting in Fort Worth, Texas. *Journal of Education Finance, 23*(4), 532–556.

Polansky, H. B. (1998). Equity and SBM: It can be done. *School Business Affairs, 64*(4), 36–37.

Reyes, A. H. (1994). *The legal implication of school-based budgeting.* (ERIC Document Reproduction Service No. ED 379 753)

Sorenson, L. D., & Evans, R. D. (2001). Superintendent use of site-based councils: Role ambiguity and accountability. *Planning & Changing, 32*(3/4), 184–198.

Walberg, H. J., & Niemiec, R. P. (1994). Is Chicago school reform working? *Phi Delta Kappan, 75,* 713–715.

Wilson, S. M., Iverson, R., & Chrastil, J. (2001). School reform that integrates public education and de-

mocratic principles. *Equity and Excellence in Education, 34*(1), 64–70.

REFERENCES

Bauman, P. C. (1996). *Governing education: Public sector reform or privatization.* Boston: Allyn and Bacon.

Fullan, M. (2001). *Leading in a culture of change.* San Francisco: Jossey-Bass.

King, R. A., Swanson, A. D., & Sweetland, S. R. (2003). *School finance: Achieving high standards with equity and efficiency* (3rd ed.). Boston: Allyn and Bacon.

Kowalski, T. J. (2003). *Contemporary school administration: An introduction* (2nd ed.). Boston: Allyn and Bacon.

Kowalski, T. J. (2006). *The school superintendent: Theory, practice, and cases* (2nd ed.). Thousand Oaks, CA: Sage.

Kowalski, T. J., Petersen, G. J., & Fusarelli, L. D. (2007). *Effective communication for school adminis-*

trators: An imperative in an information age. Lanham, MD: Rowman and Littlefield Education.

Nir, A. E., & Miran, M. (2006). The equity consequences of school-based management. *International Journal of Educational Management, 20*(2), 116–126.

Spring, J. (2001). *American education* (10th ed.). New York: McGraw-Hill.

Tyack, D. (1990). Restructuring in historical perspective: Tinkering towards utopia. *Teachers College Record, 92*(2), 170–191.

Walberg, H. J., & Niemiec, R. P. (1994). Is Chicago school reform working? *Phi Delta Kappan, 75,* 713–715.

CASE
24

Who Should Create the School's Vision?

Background Information

Visioning and long-range planning have become increasingly important administrative responsibilities for several reasons. One is that the pace of societal change continues to accelerate, requiring organizations to engage in constant renewal. Another is the belief that meaningful reform is much more likely to be achieved if it is pursued at the district and individual school levels. These and related conditions have prompted superintendents and school board members to find "visionary" principals. But what is the essence of this desired attribute? Consider the following perceptions of visionary leaders that have been applied to public education:

- Administrators who possess knowledge about society and education enhancing their ability to predict the future
- Administrators who are identified with a specific reform agenda that requires substantial change in schools (e.g., site-based management)
- Administrators who understand the dynamics of change and who earned reputations as change agents

Such images reflect a common but misguided belief that a new principal can transform a failing school into a school of excellence, single-handedly and in a relatively brief period of time (Kowalski, 2006).

In the context of school reform, both institutional mission and vision are critical concepts. Unfortunately, they often get confused, misinterpreted, or ignored (Kowalski, Petersen, & Fusarelli, 2007). A school's mission statement focuses on the present and details what the school is expected to accomplish; for public schools, much of the mission is established by state government in the form of laws, policies, and mandates. Local officials can and often do augment state requirements by stating local expectations (e.g., offering a sufficiently broad range of extracurricular activities to ensure student engagement) (Kowalski, 2003). A vision, on the other hand, has a future orientation. It is intended to provide a picture of what the school should look like in meeting its mission at some designated point in the future (Chance & Björk, 2004). Properly construed, it is established using accurate data and reliable societal and educational forecasts (Kowalski, 2006); that is, the vision has a rational basis, making it likely that it can be achieved. In a democratic society, especially one in which liberty is emphasized through local control of schools, the vision should also be developed by melding the collective visions of community members (Chance & Björk, 2004; Fullan, 2003). Public schools in the United States should personify the foundational values of a democratic society.

When visioning is conceived as a collective responsibility between citizens and professional educators, a school principal's role becomes largely facilitative. That is, the administrator collects pertinent data, identifies trends, shares information, encourages dialogue, and guides the process of reaching consensus. This facilitative role, however, does not mean that principals should not be visionaries. As professionals, principals should be expected to have a vision for the future, but they also must be willing to subject that vision to democratic discourse and critique (Kowalski, 2003). In this vein, they walk the fine line between their role as professional leaders and as information managers in a democratic context (Wirt & Kirst, 2001).

This case takes place in a rural community where school officials are preparing to open a new middle school. The founding principal, employed from outside the district, attempts to create a broad-based committee to develop a vision for the new school. Her efforts are opposed by several influential teachers who believe that the principal, a recognized expert on middle school education, should create the vision unilaterally. As you read this case, try to identify factors that contribute to philosophical dissonance between the principal and the teachers.

Key Areas for Reflection

1. Visioning
2. School culture
3. Principal leadership style
4. Professionalism versus democracy
5. Principal role expectations

The Case

Community and School District

The Lightville Community School District serves two predominately rural townships in south central Illinois, and just over 60 percent of its residents live on farms. The system has operated two schools: an elementary school serving grades K–6 and a junior-senior high school serving grades 7–12. Both buildings are located on a 65-acre site two miles from the town of Lightville. The elementary school opened nineteen years ago and was the first building erected on the site. The secondary school was constructed eleven years later.

Despite its rural location, the school district's population has been increasing. Twenty-five years ago, there were only 758 students enrolled in the district; now, the enrollment has exceeded 1,200 pupils. Virtually all of the growth has been attributable to single-family-dwelling subdivisions located on the school district's western boundary. Most residents in this area work in an adjoining county, where land costs and property taxes are higher.

When the junior-senior high school facility opened, most residents thought there would be no need for further school construction—at least not for the next thirty or forty years. They were wrong; the rate of population growth accelerated. As a result, the school board reluctantly approved construction of the district's third school, a middle school for grades 6, 7, and 8. The project was not only intended to expand overall classroom space in the district, it was also intended to alleviate crowded conditions at the other two schools. The middle school was constructed on the same campus where the other two schools were already located.

Middle School and the New Principal

Creating a separate middle school was a controversial issue among district residents. Many of the large land owners opposed the initiative, but they accepted the fact that the need for more classroom space was real. Architects retained by the school board evaluated three possible solutions: enlarging the junior-senior high school and moving the sixth grade out of the elementary school; enlarging both existing schools; and building a separate middle school. Superintendent Joe Rawlings openly favored building a new middle school, even before the architects did their analysis.

Though the architects' analysis supported the superintendent's preference, many residents voiced opposition to building a new school. Opponents were divided between those who wanted no new construction and those who wanted to place an addition on the junior-senior high school so that the sixth grade could be moved to that facility. Virtually all of the residents residing in the subdivisions in the western part of the district, however, wanted a new middle school constructed. After more than four months of public debate, Superintendent Rawlings formally recommended construction of the new middle school; all but two board members, both farmers, voted to approve the recommendation.

The new middle school was to be built on the same site with the existing two schools; it was to accommodate up to 450 pupils and was designed to support both teacher teaming and block scheduling. Edgar Findley, principal of the Lightville junior-senior High School, was given the option of remaining at the high school or becoming the middle school principal; he opted to remain at the high school. His assistant principal, though not given the same option, announced that he too wanted to remain at the high school and would not be an applicant for the new principal's position. Shortly after construction of the new school started, Superintendent Rawlings began searching outside the school system for a middle school principal.

Prior to conducting the search, the superintendent had convinced the school board that the principal should be employed one semester before the school actually opened. His rationale was that the new principal would need the time to select staff, formulate the curriculum, and schedule the school. After reviewing twenty-two applications, the superintendent invited four candidates for interviews.

A selection committee consisting of four teachers, both existing principals, and four parents interviewed the finalists, as did the superintendent and school board members. One candidate became the consensus choice of the interviewers. Susan Potter was an experienced teacher and a middle school assistant principal employed in an affluent suburban Chicago school district. She very much wanted to become a principal and while moving to a rural community was not a preference, having the opportunity to construct a middle school program from the ground floor was extremely appealing to her. Her apprehensions about moving from an affluent suburb to a rural community were tempered by the warm reception she received during the interviews.

Susan Potter's employment with Lightville started officially on January 5—six and one-half months before the school became operational. As directed by the superintendent, she had three primary responsibilities during this period: make final staffing decisions, organize the school's programs, and complete the schedule. Though a decision to use teaming and block scheduling had been made by the superintendent prior to her employment, implementation planning for these concepts had not been completed.

Staffing proved to be the easiest task for Susan. Teachers already employed in the district who requested to be assigned to the new school received the support of both the superintendent and high school principal; after interviewing them, Susan agreed that each was qualified. She then had to employ four new teachers, a task that was time consuming but not especially difficult. Once the school's staff was in place, she created a committee to assist her with the remaining two assignments.

The Advisory Committee

With input from Superintendent Rawlings and the school board members, Susan appointed four teachers (each from a different subject area) and four parents to serve on the advisory committee, a group she called the "visioning and planning committee." At the group's first meeting, Principal Potter outlined her philosophy and objectives regarding the committee's responsibilities:

- The committee should operate democratically.
- Consensus should be the preferred method for making decisions.
- She should be a voting member of the committee but not the committee chair.
- The committee's first task should be to develop a vision statement that would provide parameters for planning program scope and implementation.
- The vision statement should reflect the collective values and beliefs of the committee members.
- The broader community, including the middle school's faculty, should have an opportunity to react to the proposed vision statement before it is adopted formally.

The committee members agreed with these preferences except they wanted Susan to chair the committee. They stated that she was the most qualified individual for this key role. After considerable discussion, however, she convinced them to select another member to chair the committee.

Helen Burke, an English and social studies teacher, became the committee's chair. At the time, she was chairperson of the English department at the junior-senior high school and the sister of one of the school board members. Her brother, a farmer, was influential in the decision to build a new school because he was the only farmer on the board to support the project. Helen surprised her colleagues when she requested to be assigned to the new middle school. Though she did not say so publicly, she felt obligated to move to the school since she had lobbied vigorously for the project's approval.

Conflict

Helen Burke and Susan Potter decided to meet together after the initial committee meeting to develop the agenda for the next meeting. Helen agreed to serve as the committee chair provided that Susan would assist her in performing the task. So two days after the initial committee meeting, Helen and Susan had lunch together to discuss the agenda for the committee's next meeting. As their discussion focused directly on their purpose, Helen said, "Susan, I want you to know that I will do what I can to help you develop a quality school. We are thrilled that you are here because we believe you will provide the leadership we need to accomplish this goal. So don't hesitate to call upon us for help, even if it doesn't relate to the committee's work. We have an excellent committee, and I'm certain the members will support your ideas."

"Thank you, Helen. I am grateful that you accepted the role of committee chair. Obviously, the other members also see you as a leader," Susan responded. "The committee has a great deal of work to do in the next two months, and therefore we need to keep everyone focused."

Susan then told Helen that the committee's first task was to fashion a vision statement. She explained how the school's vision interfaced with its mission. Specifically, she detailed why the vision was essential to good planning.

Helen responded, "After you interviewed with the school board, my brother told me that you were a visionary leader—just the type of person we needed to direct our new school. I think we should spend most of the next meeting listening to your middle school philosophy. This community has always respected school administrators and they expect the superintendent and principals to provide direction. Consequently, the committee members are expecting you to shape the school's vision; we see our role as being largely supportive."

Susan was surprised by Helen's comments. Was she suggesting that the committee preferred to "rubber stamp" the principal's vision?

"Helen, I really appreciate your support and confidence. However, I don't think having me develop the vision alone is appropriate. As I noted in our first committee meeting, a vision statement should reflect the collective thinking of the school and the community. Every committee member should have an opportunity to reflect on what he or she believes the new school should become in the next decade. I'm new in this community and even if I were not, unilaterally constructing the vision makes me uncomfortable."

"But Susan," Helen said, "you're the expert. You're the person we employed to lead us in opening our new school. Why should we pretend that you are not the expert?"

"I don't have a problem with sharing my philosophy or in being a facilitator. For example, I can provide information about the middle school philosophy and answer committee member questions. I can tell you about effective practices and participate in discussions. But I don't want to stifle other opinions. If we begin by having me draft the vision, I'm afraid committee members will fall victim to groupthink."

"What do you mean?" Helen asked.

"Groupthink is a common problem when three or more individuals attempt to make collective decisions. Participants often are reluctant to state their own views or to disagree with the views stated by others because they want to be socially accepted in the group. Simply put, it's going along to get along."

Helen thought for a moment and then said, "I don't think we need to worry about groupthink with this committee. If a member doesn't agree with something you say, he or she will let you know. They are not bashful. But on the other hand, I doubt that the committee members, including the teachers, know what you know about middle schools. If we start by having members state personal visions, we may never complete our task—and as you reminded me earlier, we must keep focused because time is limited."

Sensing that she was not going to convince Helen to accept her position, at least not at this luncheon meeting, Susan suggested that the issue be placed first on the next committee meeting agenda. Helen agreed but commented that the discussion would simply waste time.

At the next meeting, Helen explained that she and Susan had met to discuss how the committee would proceed with developing the vision statement. She explained her position and asked Susan to state her opposing position. As she had done previously in the luncheon meeting with Helen, Susan explained that vision statements should reflect the collective thoughts of the school's broader community.

"Sure, I can give you a boilerplate vision statement reflecting common elements of the middle school philosophy. But some of those elements may not be acceptable to this community. Let me give you an example. Not all middle schools treat social activities in the same way. Should sixth-grade students be allowed to attend dances? Should the sixth grade be fully integrated academically with other grades? Often community values and beliefs influence the answers to such questions. This is why it is important to identify what the community wants and needs."

Dan Kelby, a physical education teacher, was the first committee member to respond to Susan. "I have several thoughts about the new school, especially related to athletic programs. But if we all start sharing our dreams, we may end up arguing endlessly. I think we should follow Helen's suggestion. We should start by critiquing your vision statement. If we think certain aspects are unacceptable, we'll tell you."

Two other committee members, both parents, quickly agreed with Dan. Susan was not willing to surrender. She told the members, "Several days ago I met with Helen and shared why I was apprehensive about following her proposal. If I provide the initial vision statement, you may not be willing to state your personal values and beliefs. And if that occurs, we may not know if our vision is compatible with community culture."

Helen asked Susan, "Would you be specific about the process you prefer?"

"Certainly. Each member of the committee would share his or her beliefs about what the school should look like ten years from now. Then we would ask questions about the individual visions and identify commonalities and differences among them. Our objective would be consensus. All of us would be required to state a personal vision."

"Susan, we appreciate your sensitivity to community values," Helen said. "And your commitment to collaboration is admirable. However, you are the principal; the principal is supposed to lead. The school board hired you because of your knowledge and experiences. Just because we begin with 'your' vision doesn't mean that we will not end with 'our' vision."

After about 10 minutes of additional discussion, a motion was made to have the principal craft a vision statement as a starting point for the committee's work. Seven members of the committee voted to support the motion, one abstained, and Susan voted against the motion. Helen met with Susan after the others left.

"I hope you don't feel discouraged by this meeting, Susan. You said you didn't know our culture. Well, part of our culture is that we want administrators to lead. We are accustomed to principals having authority. Trust me on this matter. When the committee is finished, we will have a vision statement the community can support."

After Helen left the school, Susan sat in her office and thought about what she could and should do before the next committee meeting scheduled for the following week.

PROBLEM FRAMING

1. Assume you are Susan. Describe what you would want to accomplish in dealing with the situation described in this case.

2. Based on the evidence of contextual variables, describe the difficulty associated with achieving your objective.

QUESTIONS AND SUGGESTED ACTIVITIES

1. Share and critique the problem statements prepared by students in your class.

2. What is your definition of a visionary leader? What is the basis of your definition?

3. In this case, Susan refers to the community's culture. What does this mean?

4. Should Susan agree to follow the committee's preference on developing a vision statement? Why or why not?

5. Do you believe that too much emphasis is being placed on the development of a vision statement prior to the school opening? Why or why not?

6. According to the case, the committee has considered two proposals for developing a vision statement: the one proposed by Helen and the one proposed by Susan. Are there other alternatives? If so, what are they?

7. At several points in the case, Helen alludes to the community's disposition toward administrators. Are her comments important to resolving the conflict?

8. Susan believes that Helen has power in relation to the other committee members. What does this mean? Why is personal power relevant to this case?

9. Discuss the purpose of having a vision statement and distinguish a vision statement from a mission statement.

10. Discuss the meaning of groupthink and evaluate if Susan's concerns regarding this potential problem are warranted.

SUGGESTED READINGS

Brouillette, L. (1997). Who defines "democratic leadership"? Three high school principals respond to site-based reforms. *Journal of School Leadership, 7*(6), 569–591.

Chance, P. L., & Björk, L. G. (2004). The social dimensions of public relations. In T. J. Kowalski (Ed.), *Public relations in schools* (3rd ed., Chapter 6, pp. 125–148). Upper Saddle River, NJ: Merrill, Prentice Hall.

Fullan, M. (2003). *Change forces with a vengeance.* Philadelphia: Taylor and Francis.

Fullan, M., & Hargreaves, A. (1997). 'Tis the season. *Learning, 26*(1), 27–29.

Hallinger, P., & Heck, R. H. (1999). Exploring the principal's contribution to school effectiveness: 1980–1995. *School Effectiveness and School Improvement, 9*(2), 157–191.

Keedy, J. L., & Finch, A. M. (1994). Examining teacher-principal empowerment: An analysis of power. *Journal of Research and Development in Education, 27*(3), 162–175.

Krajewski, B., & Matkin, M. (1996). Community empowerment: Building a shared vision. *Principal, 76*(2), 5–6, 8.

Rideout, G. W., McKay, L. M., & Morton, L. L. (2004). The framework and measure of effective school visioning strategy (MCP-FIV). *Alberta Journal of Educational Research, 50*(1), 68–86.

Smith, S. C., & Stolp, S. (1995). Transforming a school's culture through shared vision. *OSSC Report, 35*(3), 1–6.

Starratt, R. J. (1995). *Leaders with vision: The quest for school renewal.* Thousand Oaks, CA: Corwin.

Yearout, S., Miles, G., & Koonce, R. H. (2001). Multilevel visioning. *Training & Development, 55*(3) 7, 30.

REFERENCES

Chance, P. L., & Björk, L. G. (2004). The social dimensions of public relations. In T. J. Kowalski (Ed.), *Public relations in schools* (3rd ed., pp. 125–148). Upper Saddle River, NJ: Merrill, Prentice Hall.

Fullan, M. (2003). *Change forces with a vengeance.* Philadelphia: Taylor and Francis.

Kowalski, T. J. (2003). *Contemporary school administration: An introduction* (2nd ed.). Boston: Allyn and Bacon.

Kowalski, T. J. (2006). *The school superintendent: Theory, practice, and cases* (2nd ed.). Thousand Oaks, CA: Sage.

Kowalski, T. J., Petersen, G. J., & Fusarelli, L. D. (2007). *Effective communication for school administrators: An imperative in an information age.* Lanham, MD: Rowman and Littlefield Education.

Wirt, F. M., & Kirst, M. W. (2001). *The political dynamics of American education* (2nd ed.). Berkeley, CA: McCutchan.

25 The Maverick School Board Member

Background Information

Relationships between a superintendent and individual school board members can influence the political climate of an entire school system because these associations help shape behavior in relation to critical functions such as problem solving, visioning, and planning. In the typical school district, power is distributed, and therefore various internal and external groups have the ability to initiate new ideas or disrupt current operations. When school board members and the superintendent operate in a spirit of teamwork, they are more likely to respond to these challenges in a positive manner (Carr, 2003). Much like a solid marriage, good relationships weather power struggles, misunderstandings, and competing needs that are manifestations of inevitable conflict found in all organizations (Hanson, 2003).

If personal associations are negative or weak, superintendents and board members usually consume much of their time and energy sniping at each other (Vail, 2001). This not only prevents them from completing their designated duties, it presents a public perception of disharmony. Political strife of this nature has become more disconcerting in a social context that requires local officials to forge a school improvement agenda and to be accountable for the outcomes (Kowalski, 2006).

A superintendent's relationship with a school board is multifaceted; rather than a single association, it is really a set of individual relationships. The following two factors are primarily responsible for this reality:

1. School boards today are often more factional than pluralistic (Shibles, Rallis, & Deck, 2001), and consequently, political behavior among board members tends to be intense. Referring to a single relationship between a superintendent and a school board is impractical if not impossible because in the typical school district board members share neither a single agenda nor the same opinion regarding their superintendent (Kowalski, 1995).
2. The superintendent's reputation and possibly job survival depend on influencing critical policy decisions. Efforts to garner board member support for these decisions usually occur on a one-to-one basis and depend on the superintendent's credibility and trust with individual board members (Blumberg, 1985).

Superintendents build and maintain positive rapport with board members by being honest, providing knowledge and assistance, using two-way communication, establishing mutual respect, being cooperative, and earning trust (Kowalski, 2006). Though the superintendent, as a professional leader, has the primary responsibility for positive relationships, they clearly require the good intentions of both parties. When board members use their office to pursue personal interests or when they intrude into day-to-day administrative activities, they actually deter positive relationships from evolving (Amundson, 2000). In large measure, this is because board members have no legal authority when acting alone or in areas beyond the jurisdiction of the school board (Kowalski, 2006).

This case is about a school board member who is angered by a high school football coach's decision concerning a star athlete. The choice the coach makes is detrimental to the board member's grandson. Seeking revenge, the board member, acting alone and surreptitiously, attempts to have the coach and the school penalized by the state high school athletic association. Despite recognizing that this board member's action is inappropriate, other board members are reluctant to confront their colleague. Instead, they ask the superintendent to issue a reprimand on their behalf. The situation raises several critical questions about the relationship between a superintendent and school board members.

Key Areas for Reflection

1. Superintendent and school board member relationships
2. School board member ethical behavior
3. Conflict resolution
4. Scope of superintendent's legitimate authority
5. Superintendent's responsibility to adjudicate intrusions into administration

The Case

The School District and The School Board

The Richmond County School District, covering 420 square miles of predominantly rural land and including two high schools, five middle schools, and eleven elementary schools, enrolls approximately 8,000 students. The seven school board members are elected to office, each from a designated geographic area in the county. By occupation, the board members include an accountant, an attorney, a farmer, a nurse, a pharmacist, a real estate broker, and a retired business executive. Elmer Hobson, the farmer, is the longest serving board member, having been in office for eleven years.

In the last two years, Mr. Hobson has voted against approximately 50 percent of the superintendent's recommendations—over three times more often than other board members. Representing two rural townships, he has consistently opposed efforts to raise local taxes, regardless of the intended purposes. He has also opposed efforts to improve school facilities outside the two townships he represents. Though fiercely independent and outspoken, he believes that his relationships with other board members and with the superintendent are "congenial."

The Superintendent

Matthew Karman replaced Elton Simcox as superintendent three years ago. Previously, he was superintendent of a smaller district for eight years. Mr. Simcox had been superintendent for five years before being given an ultimatum: resign or be dismissed. He picked the former alternative but then openly criticized the school board after leaving office. A former elementary school principal in the district, Mr. Simcox had been aligned with a coalition of four farmers who were on the school board when he was promoted. Over the next four years, three of them were voted out of office. Mr. Hobson is the only remaining member of the coalition.

Knowing why Mr. Simcox was forced to leave office, Mr. Karman has worked very hard to maintain a good relationship with every board member, including Mr. Hobson. According to his last performance evaluation, he has succeeded; all seven board members rated their relationship with the superintendent as "excellent." Superintendent Karman attributes his success in this area to good communication and mutual respect.

After receiving his second annual performance evaluation, the board voted unanimously to renew his employment contract for another three years, an action that surprised many in the community. Most observers expected that Mr. Hobson would vote against renewal since he was the only board member who voted against his selection as superintendent.

Trouble Emerges

Superintendent Karman was driving down a lonely country road as the winds swirled across barren cornfields partially covered by snow. He was delivering school board packets for an upcoming meeting. Though it was only mid-November, the chilling temperatures made it feel more like January. The fields were dotted with corn stalks cut about two inches above the ground; they looked like wooden spikes someone had arranged to discourage trespassers.

When the superintendent pulled into the driveway beside a large three-story farmhouse, a German shepherd barking alongside his car greeted him. The dog's barking summoned John Mosure from the house. John, a retired vice president of a marketing research firm, had lived in Richmond County until the time that he graduated from high school. Having returned four years ago, his 12-acre property included a large pond, a fruit tree orchard, and several gardens in which John and his wife grow flowers and vegetables. In Superintendent Karman's mind, John Mosure was the ideal school board member. After being elected to the board two years earlier, he quickly won the respect of the other board members and was elected president after having been on the board for just one year.

The superintendent and board president worked well together and most everyone knew that they were friends. Several times each month, they and their wives had dinner together.

As the two men sat at the kitchen table and enjoyed a cup of warm coffee, Superintendent Karmen handed the board packet to Mr. Mosure and then said, "John, I hope you've got some time to talk to me today. I want to discuss a potentially messy issue, and it may take a while to give you all the details."

John told him to proceed.

"Two days ago," the superintendent began, "Bob Daily [principal of North Richmond County High School] received a telephone call from Joe Sutton, the associate commissioner of the state high school athletic association. Joe also happens to be Bob's friend; the two were principals in the same school district about fifteen years ago. Joe asked Bob if he knew Elmer Hobson."

There was a moment of silence and then John said, "Oh, no!"

John and other board members rarely agreed with Elmer, but they wanted to maintain a good relationship with him. When John was first elected to the school board, Elmer attempted to forge a political alliance with him since both represented rural townships. The two men quickly discovered that their philosophies and priorities were dissimilar and as might be expected, their votes on major recommendations were rarely the same.

The superintendent continued with his story. "Bob of course acknowledges that he knows Elmer and then tells Joe Sutton that Elmer is a school board member. Joe then tells Bob that Elmer is sitting in his outer office waiting to see him. He told the secretary that he wanted to talk to someone because he was filing a complaint against Coach Yates [the head football coach at North Richmond County High School]."

"A complaint about what?" John asked.

"Joe Sutton didn't know at the time he called Bob because he had not talked to Elmer yet. After discovering that Elmer was a school board member, Joe told Bob he felt obliged to meet with him. An hour later, Bob got another telephone call from Joe Sutton. Elmer's complaint alleges that Coach Yates violated state high school athletic association rules by allowing his team's starting quarterback to remain enrolled at the school after his parents established legal residence in another state. The student in question, Jeb Boswell, is now living with the Yates family. Elmer demanded that the athletic association take action against the high school, against Coach Yates, and Bob Daily if he approved the arrangement. He is also insisting that the association rule that Jeb Boswell is ineligible to play football at North Richmond this year."

"Is there any merit to Elmer's charges?" John asked.

"The student's parents agreed to let him live with Coach Yates so that he could graduate from North Richmond High. Jeb and Coach Yates are close and Jeb's parents are paying Coach Yates $200 a month for room and board. The student's family believes this is a good investment since an athletic scholarship to college is likely if he has another successful football season. Therefore, Jeb has been living with the Yates family since last June."

"Is such an arrangement permissible by the athletic association rules? Is it in compliance with our policies?"

"Coach Yates had asked the athletic director at North Richmond to get a ruling from officials at the athletic association before agreeing to this arrangement. The athletic director has a letter from the state commissioner stating that the arrangement was acceptable, provided it was approved by the student's family and by the school principal. Principal Dailey and the parents assured Coach Yates that they had no objections. As to school district policy, I could find nothing that addresses this issue. I don't believe there is precedent."

"So from the association's perspective, Elmer's complaint is invalid?" John asked.

"Yes, but there is more. We are one week away from the state football tournament. North Richmond has a 9 and 1 record and is one of the favorites to win the championship in their division. Jeb Boswell, the student in question, is the star of the team—he may even end up being all-state. You know who his backup is?"

John said he had no idea. "You have to remember, Matt, I don't live in the North Richmond area. I'm a South Richmond High booster [the other high school in the district]."

"The second-string quarterback is a senior named Ron Hobson. He is Elmer Hobson's grandson. Get the picture? Elmer's got an axe to grind because he feels Coach Yates prevented his grandson from being the starting quarterback. Now that the team has been successful and will be in the state championship playoffs, Elmer wants his grandson to move into the spotlight. Principal Dailey told me that the grandson is probably innocent in this matter. He's a good student and the principal thinks he would be embarrassed if he knew what his grandfather did."

John then commented, "I just remembered something. Last summer when we were approving contracts for driver education teachers, Elmer opposed your recommendation to extend a contract to Coach Yates. Elmer claimed that he had received complaints about Coach Yates being a poor driver's education instructor. Do you think that matter was connected to all of this?"

"Who knows," the superintendent answered. "With Elmer, it's hard to tell. He votes against a lot of things. Going to the athletic association without informing the board or the administration, however, is an ethical breach. As a board member, he should have voiced his concerns to either you or me before making a complaint to the state athletic association. Had he talked to me or Bob Daily first, he would have found out that his charge was invalid. Dealing with the athletic association is an administrative responsibility."

"What did Joe Sutton from the athletic association do with Elmer's complaint?"

"Elmer identified himself as a school board member and demanded to know what would be done to adjudicate the matter. Joe Sutton explained that there was no violation, and he then showed him a copy of the letter the commissioner had written to North Richmond's athletic director last May. Elmer then stormed out of the office indicating that keeping this letter from the school board was additional evidence of a conspiracy involving several administrators and coaches."

"Matt, I have a suggestion. Let's forget about this. Elmer is Elmer and he is not going to change his behavior. Few people take him seriously. He'll always be a pain in the neck. Why voters keep electing him is a mystery to me. Sometimes I think they enjoy the conflict he initiates."

The superintendent had a different suggestion. "At the very least, we need to inform the other board members, and Elmer should be reprimanded or censured. What he did was clearly unethical. Maybe it's time to say enough."

John refilled the coffee cups and returned to his chair. "I don't know. I'm not sure a reprimand will do any good. Elmer's pretty stubborn. A reprimand may be just what he desires. He loves getting his name in the paper and relishes conflict. Matt, how about if you talk to him privately? You're experienced in dealing with these matters and you have a pretty good relationship with him. Maybe the best way to handle this is for you to tell him that he made a mistake. We should get the support of the other board members, though, and then you can say you are speaking for all of us. Don't you think this would be the best way to handle this?"

PROBLEM FRAMING

1. Assume you are the superintendent. Describe what you would want to accomplish in dealing with the situation described in this case.

2. Based on the evidence of contextual variables, describe the difficulty associated with achieving your objective.

QUESTIONS AND SUGGESTED ACTIVITIES

1. Do you agree that Elmer Hobson's behavior was unethical? Why or why not?

2. John Mosure, the board president, first suggested that nothing be done because Elmer might actually enjoy being reprimanded. What are the advantages and disadvantages of ignoring this situation?

3. Identify the conflict of interest law in your state that covers school board members. According to that law, did Elmer Hobson act illegally?

4. Who should be responsible for ensuring that board members act ethically?

5. In response to a question from the board president, Superintendent Karman indicated that there was no school district policy or precedent addressing the situation in question. Is this fact relevant to what should be done to resolve the problem?

6. Obtain a copy of the code of ethics for school boards' association in your state. Determine if the code addresses behavior pertinent to this case.

7. If Elmer had not identified himself as a school board member to the associate commissioner, would the circumstances in this case be different? Why or why not?

8. Is Elmer Hodson's voting record as a school board member pertinent to this case? Why or why not?

SUGGESTED READINGS

Bolman, L., & Deal, T. (1992). Images of leadership. *American School Board Journal, 179*(4), 36–39.

Bryant, M., & Grady, M. (1990). Where boards cross the line. *American School Board Journal, 177*(10), 20–21.

Caruso, N. D. (2004). Managing board members with personal agendas. *School Administrator, 61*(10), 6.

Castallo, R. (1992). Clear signals. *American School Board Journal, 179*(2), 32–34.

Dawson, L. J., & Quinn, R. (2004). Why board culture matters. *American School Board Journal, 191*(9), 28–31.

Duffy, F. M. (2002). Courage, passion, and vision: Leading systemic school improvement. *International Journal of Educational Reform, 11*(1), 63–76.

Hamilton, D. (1987). Healing power: How your board can overcome the heartbreak of disharmony. *American School Board Journal, 174*(9), 36–37.

Harrison, P. (2002). Can this marriage be saved? *American School Board Journal, 189*(6), 36–37.

Hayden, J. (1987). Superintendent-board conflict: Working it out. *Education Digest, 52*(8), 11–13.

Herman, J. (1991). Coping with conflict. *American School Board Journal, 178*(8), 39–41.

Irvine, J. (1998). Welcome to the board. *American School Board Journal, 185*(7), 38–40.

Kowalski, T. J. (2006). *The school superintendent: Theory, practice, and cases* (2nd ed.). Thousand Oaks, CA: Sage (see Chapters 5 and 6).

Lister, B. (2006). A pocket guide to board service. *American School Board Journal, 193*(5), 48–49.

Marlowe, J. (1997). Good board, bad board. *American School Board Journal, 184*(6), 22–24.

Myer, R. (1983). How to handle a board member who wants to play his own game. *American School Board Journal, 170*(11), 27–29.

Natale, J. (1990). School board ethics: On thin ice? *American School Board Journal, 177*(10), 16–19.

Ondrovich, P. (1997). Hold them, fold them, or walk away: Twelve cardinal rules for dealing with school board conflict. *School Administrator, 5*(2), 12–15.

Petersen, G., & Williams, B. M. (2005). The board president and superintendent: An examination of influence through the eyes of the decision makers. In G. Petersen & L. Fusarelli (Eds.), *The politics of leadership: Superintendents and school boards in changing times* (pp. 21–36). Greenwich, CT: Information Age Publishing.

Riede, P. (2004). Board ethics: In states and communities, the ongoing struggle to codify appropriate behavior of school board members. *School Administrator, 61*(8), 20.

Rickabaugh, J. R., & Kremer, M. L. (1997). Six habits to make you a hit with your school board. *The School Administrator, 54*(6), 30–32.

REFERENCES

Amundson, K. J. (2000). What I wish I'd known . . . *American School Board Journal, 187*(1), 32–33, 36.

Blumberg, A. (1985). *The school superintendent: Living with conflict.* New York: Teachers College Press.

Carr, N. (2003). Leadership: The toughest job in America. *Education vital signs: A supplement to the American School Board Journal, 14,* 15, 18–20.

Hanson, E. M. (2003). *Educational administration and organizational behavior* (5th ed.). Boston: Allyn and Bacon.

Kowalski, T. J. (1995). *Keepers of the flame: Contemporary urban superintendents.* Thousand Oaks, CA: Corwin Press.

Kowalski, T. J. (2006). *The school superintendent: Theory, practice, and cases* (2nd ed.). Thousand Oaks, CA: Sage.

Shibles, M. R., Rallis, R. F., & Deck, L. L. (2001). A new political balance between superintendent and board: Clarifying purpose and generating knowledge. In C. C. Brunner & L. G. Björk (Eds.), *The new superintendency* (pp. 169–181). New York: JAI.

Vail, K. (2001). Teamwork at the top. *American School Board Journal, 188*(11), 23–25.